THE GREAT BOOK

of

WILDFOWL
DECOYS

GENERAL EDITOR
JOE ENGERS

PHOTOGRAPHY BY BILL BUCKNER

THUNDER BAY

Published by Thunder Bay Press, Inc.
5880 Oberlin Drive, Suite 400
San Diego, CA 92121

ISBN 0–934429–75–8

Created and produced by Cynthia Parzych Publishing, Inc.

General editor: Joe Engers
Project editor: Jay Hyams
Photography by Bill Buckner
Design by Mike Rose
Typesetting by Pagesetters, Inc.
Separations by Oceanic Graphic Printing, Inc.
Printed and bound by Heraclio Fournier, S.A.

Library of Congress Cataloging-in-Publication Data

The Great book of wildfowl decoys / general editor, Joe Engers :
    photography by Bill Buckner.
        p.   cm.
    Includes bibliographical references.
    ISBN 0-934429-75-8 : $75.00
    1. Decoys (Hunting)—United States—Collectors and collecting.
2. Folk art—United States—Collectors and collecting.   I. Engers,
Joe.   II. Buckner, Bill.
NK9712.B74   1990
745.593′6—dc20   89-51748
                                                                      CIP
Printed in Spain

ACKNOWLEDGMENTS

When Cynthia Parzych first offered me the chance to edit a book on decoys, I immediately recognized the excellent opportunity I was being given. Besides the excitement of producing a book on a topic I have come to love, I was enthusiastic about the chance to present these fine examples of American folk art in a full-color format. Indeed, this is the first full-color survey of North American decoys, something of which we can be proud.

Through my association with *Decoy Magazine,* which I have published for the past ten years, I have had the opportunity to meet many expert decoy collectors from around the country. I was confident that through these associations I would be able to elicit the help I needed to produce the caliber of book the subject deserved. After much perseverance and many hours spent on the telephone, I was able to round up a team of authors with a greater wealth of knowledge on the subject than I or any single individual could ever possess.

I would like to thank the authors of this book for sharing their time and knowledge with me. I could never have accomplished this book without them. I would also like to offer my greatest appreciation to the many collectors who allowed us to come into their homes to photograph what are among the most valuable decoys available throughout the country. Many made time to accommodate our hectic schedule, and for this I am grateful.

I would also like to thank Bill Buckner, who not only did a wonderful job photographing the decoys but also cheerfully persevered throughout our whirlwind tour of the country. I'd like to thank Jay Hyams for his excellent job editing the manuscripts, and Mike Rose for a wonderful design. Once again, I'd like to thank Cindy Parzych for having faith in my abilities to produce a quality book.

Most of all I'd like to thank the many collectors, some of whom were not directly involved with the project, who over the years have shared with me their knowledge, their enthusiasm, and their appreciation for one of America's finest folk arts.

PAGE 1: *Close-up of gadwall by Reme Rousseau that reveals his remarkable paint work.*
PAGES 2–3: *Spread-wing Canada goose by A. Elmer Crowell.*

THE GREAT BOOK
of
WILDFOWL DECOYS

CONTENTS

PREFACE

Wildfowl decoys exist in North America because of this continent's abundant waterfowl. Those birds—the flocks of ducks and geese that once darkened skies from Canada to Mexico—are the simple and beautiful reason for the carving of decoys. The decoys themselves are, in a sense, portraits of the birds: black ducks and ruddy ducks, mergansers and blue-winged teal, buffleheads and wigeon. Those birds have long migrated along flyways running north to south: thus, portraits in wood of the various species can be found, with local variations in style, from northern Canada down through several states. All decoys are treasured as folk art, and those local variations make the collecting of decoys a regional, national, and even international passion.

That passion has grown. Over the past fifteen years, decoys have become the most talked about and written about subject in North American folk art. At auctions throughout the continent, decoy prices have soared to incredible heights—in 1986, a preening pintail by Elmer Crowell sold for $319,000, a record for North American folk art at auction. Just what is it that attracts collectors to decoys?

Answering that question is one of the major purposes of this book. Although many seasoned collectors will no doubt add this book to their library, it may be the first introduction to this wonderful and unique folk art for many readers. This book does not pretend to tell the reader everything there is to know about decoys; many of the chapters would warrant a book of their own. We hope, however, that our attempt will whet the appetite of our readers and lead them to further study and investigation.

Painting by A. Elmer Crowell,
I Built the Blind; *oil on*
canvas dated 1908.

This book approaches decoys with a novel method: the subject is divided into states, provinces, and regions, with an expert from each presenting his or her area. We've also included an introduction to give the reader a historical overview of the origin of decoys, the methods of construction, regional differences, and variations in use. Finally, we've included a chapter on collecting so the reader can gain some insight into how a seasoned collector goes about choosing new additions. We believe our joint effort is the most thorough and efficient way of presenting the regional similarities and differences in this North American art.

Each chapter begins with an introduction to the area highlighting the major geographical waterways where the decoys were used. The major carvers, the trendsetters from each region, are identified with basic biographical material on each. Most importantly, choice examples of the finest decoys from each region are illustrated. Various species are presented so readers will be familiar with the ducks hunted in each area.

We hope to leave the reader with a bit of the appreciation we share for decoys. Although few of the makers of these wonderful decoys ever intended them to be more than tools, they have become cherished pieces of folk art. Made as functional tools to decoy ducks, they have become more than simple lures. Their skyrocketing prices sometimes bring envy on the Dow Jones, but to the dedicated collector they are more than simply investments. They are welcomed as a part of our heritage, a piece of our culture, and a captured moment from our varied and colorful past.

THE ART OF DECOYS

by Robert Shaw

Shooting on the Beach, *an undated Currier and Ives lithograph.*

Our forefathers had an entirely different relationship to the land than we do. In the 19th century this continent's natural resources seemed endless. Wild game was abundant and available to anyone able to use a gun. Hunting restrictions, in the form of seasons, bag limits, and specified methods and weaponry, were unheard of. Wildfowl could be easily shipped and sold at market and was in much demand by restaurateurs and city people. Like the supply of game, the opportunities for both sportsmen and professional gunners, hunting birds for pleasure or for profit, appeared to be virtually without limit.

The following account, from Elisha J. Lewis's 1855 *American Sportsman*, captures some of the flavor of that bygone era. To our modern, conservation-minded sensibilities, it seems grim and even foreign, but it presents an important background to the world of American decoys.

> The boat is anchored out on the feeding grounds, surrounded by innumerable Decoys, resembling as much as possible the Canvass-Backs, and so balanced in the water that the most observant eye can hardly distinguish them from the living Fowl, as they ride gently on the surface and appear to be employed in feeding, owing to the constant motion of their heads and body, imparted to them by the quiet rippling of the water.
>
> Decoys made of solid blocks, such as are universally used, can be had of Duckers on the bay, if ordered during the idle season, at a moderate price ranging from twenty to thirty dollars a hundred.
>
> . . . The number of Decoys set out around the Battery is not often less than two hundred, and most generally two hundred and fifty, or even more. Each Decoy has a string several feet long attached to it from a loop in the breast, and to the end of each string is tied a small piece of leaden pipe or other convenient metal, or even a fragment of stone sufficiently heavy to anchor the Decoy, and prevent its floating from its position.
>
> The arranging or putting-out of so great a number of Decoys around the Battery, on a cool, blustering December morning is no child's play, we can assure the uninitiated reader, and is only equalled, or rather excelled, in point of discomfiture, by the process of taking them up again in the evening, when it is necessary to wind the wet and half-frozen strings around each one to prevent entanglement when placed together in the boat.
>
> The construction of this skiff is such that when anchored out, loaded with the Shooter, his ammunition, and the necessary ballast, the water is on a level with the deck of the box, and when reclining, the occupant and all his paraphernalia are entirely concealed from observation, insomuch that it is next to impossible to distinguish any portion of this curious ambush, even when within a hundred feet of it. We have often been amazed when gazing at the surface of the water in the direction of the flats, to see a black figure rise up suddenly, as if from the deep, and blaze forth a destructive volley into a flock of Ducks about to alight, and then immediately sink again from view. The Shooter having delivered his well-directed fire, he quickly reloads his gun or guns, and throwing himself again on his back, awaits another opportunity to repeat the sport, which almost immediately follows, provided the day be favorable for the flying of Wild Fowl. It is better, in fact usual, to have two or more double-barrelled guns in the Sink, as a great many Ducks are only winged at the first discharge, and require reshooting to secure them.
>
> Thus in rapid succession, immense numbers of Canvass-Backs, as well as other Wild Fowl, are killed, and the water for an hundred feet or more is crimsoned with the rich blood, and covered with the mangled bodies of this far-famed Duck. Those engaged in this profitable way of killing Canvass-Backs are always accompanied by a companion in a sail or row boat, who keeps a respectable distance for the purpose of watching over the safety of his associate, as well as running down upon the adjacent feeding-grounds and putting the Ducks to flight, so that they may chance to join the Decoys that are set to allure them as they pass up and down the feeding-shoals. On the flats in the coves near to Havre de Grace and Spesutia Island, where this method of shooting Ducks has been more particularly practiced during the last three seasons, there is but little or no current during calm weather, and therefore is singularly suitable for this kind of sport. The Ducks, after being shot, will remain nearly in the same place where they dropped for a considerable time without drifting away; the Shooter, therefore, pays no heed to them until he has a large number killed, when he makes a signal to his companion to come and pick them up.
>
> The numbers of Ducks killed in this way during the three past seasons have been enormous—almost beyond belief.
>
> We are credibly informed that Mr. W. W. Levy, a Ducker well known on the Chesapeake, for his skill in this particular sport, has killed as many as one hundred and eighty-seven Ducks in one day, and during the seasons of 1846 and 1847, actually bagged seven thousand Canvass-Backs.
>
> This system of killing Ducks, we believe, was introduced on the Chesapeake Bay by some of the experienced Wild Fowl Shooters from the vicinity of New York, and who now reap a rich harvest from their hardihood and ingenuity. It is no unusual thing for one of these men to kill as

many as fifty couples of Canvass-Backs in the course of a day; and if the weather prove favorable for this kind of shooting, they have been known to fill a small vessel with Ducks in two or three days, and which they immediately dispatch for the markets of New York, Baltimore, or Philadelphia.

Better than any other artifact, decoys evoke the story of man's evolving relationship with America's wildfowl. The greatest wildfowl hunt in the history of the world took place on this continent between 1840 and 1918. The unfortunate history of our willing and wanton slaughter of millions upon millions of wild birds during this time is inextricably linked with the development of the decoy as a hunting tool. Yet, like the birds they were made to lure, decoys are often things of remarkable beauty, and they speak to us of their creators' admiration for their quarry. Today, these deceptively simple tools of

gunners are recognized as an important American art form and coveted by collectors as relics of a uniquely American time and way of life, rich with freedoms and opportunities that will never come again. Although decoys were never intended to attract the attention of anything but a living bird or to please anyone but a sportsman or market gunner in search of a functional lure, in recent years the finest surviving examples have found their way into the hands of collectors and museums and can command prices well into five figures. Such master carvers as John Blair, Nathan Cobb, Jr., Elmer Crowell, Bill Bowman, and Albert Laing have come to be renowned as among our country's finest native craftspeople, and their best birds, made only for use as gunning tools, are considered by many to be enduring works of art.

The wildfowl decoy is the only folk art truly indigenous to North America. Unlike quilts, hooked rugs, carved trade signs, carousel figures, weathervanes, and ship carvings—all of

12

Hunting scene with a full rig of decoys spread on the water.

which have European precedents—the roots of the decoy lie deep in the American land and its vast natural resources. The decoy is an Indian invention. White explorers reported a variety of Indian devices used to lure wildfowl from this country's early skies. Among other ingenious methods, Indians roughly simulated resting flocks of birds by shaping mud or piling stones in shallow water, mounted dead birds' heads or bodies on sticks on shore, and floated wildfowl skins stuffed with dried grass in deeper water.

The oldest Indian-made decoys extant were discovered in an archaeological dig at the Lovelock Cave in Nevada in 1924, buried in baskets in the dry earth of the cavern floor. These decoys, which have been established by carbon dating to be at least 1000 years old, are now in the collection of the Museum of the American Indian, Heye Foundation, in New York (soon to become part of the Smithsonian Institution in Washington). Among the decoys found in the Lovelock cave are several float-ing lures made of reeds and clearly recognizable as canvasback ducks, the favored American species of Indian and settler alike. There were also a variety of fairly crude stuffed birds, probably made to be mounted on sticks. The birds made from reeds, however, were very carefully crafted, the reeds tightly bound together and painted to imitate the canvasback's distinctive plumage. As a finishing touch, real feathers were laid along the sides of the decoys. While the Lovelock decoys are by far the oldest decoys extant, the relative sophistication of the canvasbacks suggests that the concept was well established in Indian hunting tradition long before their creation.

These kinds of Indian decoys were later adopted by white settlers. But by white standards, the Indian lures were impractical because they weren't made to last. Our forefathers applied European woodworking traditions to the notion of the wildfowl lure to create the wooden decoys depicted in this book. The first wooden decoys probably were fashioned sometime in the

13

Archaeologist with a basket of canvasback decoys found in Nevada's Lovelock Cave in 1924. The decoys, made of reeds by members of the Tule Eaters tribe, ca. 1000, are the earliest documented.

14

late 1700s. We can only guess what these early lures looked like. The earliest examples may well have been simple flat forms stuck on poles like the bird skins and heads they replaced. Or they may have been rough-hewn floating lures, perhaps no more than sections of logs with heads fashioned from naturally forked roots or branches. Whatever their appearance, these early experimental models must have produced good results, for by the early 1800s the wooden decoy was a firmly established tradition in America, second only to a hunter's gun, powder, and shot in importance as a hunting tool.

Decoys were made in two basic forms: floaters and stickups. Floating lures were made either of a solid piece of wood or from two or more pieces hollowed out and joined with nails. In either case the head was almost invariably a separately carved piece, attached to the body with nails or a screw or wooden dowel. A weight was usually attached to the bottom of the decoy to balance it in the water; another weight tied to a lead line at the bird's breast often served as an anchor. Floating lures were made to represent many species of swimming game birds, including all types of ducks and geese as well as swans and gulls. Stickups, mounted on poles that were pushed into beach sand or marsh muck, were made primarily to represent wading shorebirds, such as the peeps, plovers, yellowlegs, and curlews commonly found feeding at the water's edge. Stickups were also occasionally made of herons, gulls, terns, owls, crows, songbirds, doves, and pigeons as well as geese and ducks. Shorebird stickups were usually solid bodied with head and body carved from a single piece of wood. The birds' thin and fragile bills, made from hardwood, whale baleen, or hand-

forged nails, were often attached separately so they could be easily replaced. Some clever carvers solved this problem by using naturally forked roots or branches to form head and bill. Stickups also were sometimes made with thin flat bodies. These so-called flatties provided a silhouette of the species represented at the same time they lightened the gunner's equipment bag.

North America encompasses a vast range of wildfowl habitats and species. For centuries North American wildfowl have migrated north each spring and south each fall along four major flyways: the Atlantic and Pacific flyways, which follow our continent's eastern and western coastlines, the central flyway, running from Canada to Mexico and crossing the Dakotas and other sparsely populated areas, and the Mississippi flyway, which runs from Ontario to the Gulf of Mexico. The primary gunning seasons have always coincided with migration, when birds travel in large groups and settle together to feed and rest. In 19th-century America, the migration routes became a gauntlet manned by gunners waiting to take advantage of every opportunity to thin the passing flocks. American gunners sought seagoing eider, scoter, and merganser ducks along the rocky coasts of northern New England and the Canadian maritimes, shot shorebirds on the sandy tidal flats of the Atlantic coast from New Brunswick to the Carolinas, sculled after fresh-water puddle ducks, such as mallards and pintails, on the upper Delaware River, and stalked crows and geese in the corn and grain fields of the Midwest. Every gunning area in North America, from the ocean shores of New England and California to the bayous of Louisiana, developed decoy styles partic-

Hand-colored engraving of eider ducks by Robert Howell after J. J. Audubon for Birds of America.

ularly suited to local hunting conditions and methods. These styles were developed over many long seasons of trial and error in the field and brought to perfection by master craftsmen who set regional standards followed by succeeding generations of carvers.

Although decoys were far more often marked by their owners than their makers, a practiced eye can pinpoint with considerable accuracy the region where a particular decoy was used and often identify the carver as well by observing characteristics of the bird's form, carving and construction details, and paint. The various regional styles and characteristics have been carefully studied by many researchers in recent years and are dealt with in depth by the experts who have contributed to this book. Regional styles provide an endlessly fascinating area of study, offering hundreds of subtle variations on the seemingly simple theme of the carved wooden bird. Two examples will suffice to give a sense of the enormous range of hunting conditions and resulting styles in North American decoys. Upper Chesapeake Bay decoys, used for the sinkbox shooting described in the quotation that opens this essay, were made with simply carved, rounded solid bodies. Because so many decoys were required, craftsmen could not lavish time on intricate construction details. In fact, craftsmen from this area were among the first to take advantage of the lathe to fashion decoy bodies from a set pattern. The numbers used also precluded detailed attention to their use and care; the decoys had to be piled in heaps in the boats and boathouses and were frequently damaged in collisions with one another. The decoys were always bottom weighted, often with square lead pads, and were

16

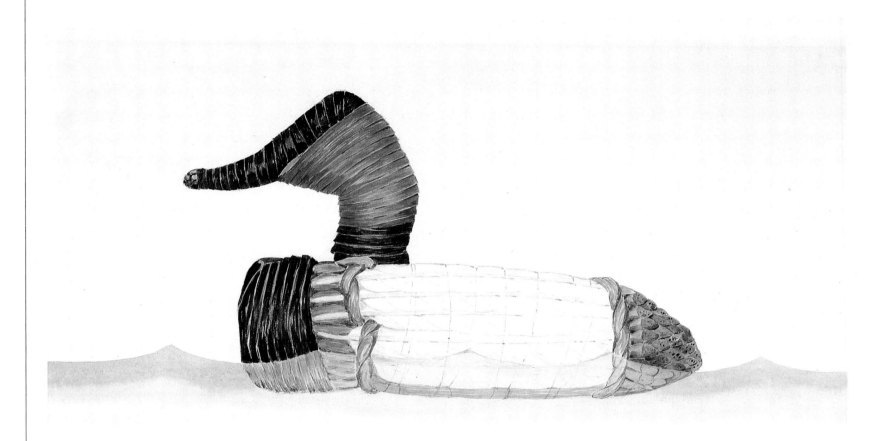

anchored with heavy weights often in a molded pyramid shape. The paint patterns of Chesapeake Bay decoys also were simple and stylized because the birds were used in corrosive salt water and had to be repainted frequently. Eyes were usually painted, as fragile (and expensive) glass eyes would not stand up to the rigors of local use. In marked contrast, decoys from southwest Ontario were used in small groups on calm, fresh water and had to be carried to the gunning grounds in small lightweight punts. The region's decoys also are extremely lightweight, with bodies hollowed out to a thin upper shell (often less than one-half inch thick) attached to an equally thin flat bottom board. The decoys usually did not have bottom weights but were anchored with small teardrop-shaped weights attached to lead lines. The carvings are by and large carefully wrought with great attention paid to anatomical details; many feature intricate paint patterns applied with comb and brush to imitate feathering. Glass eyes were usually used as well. Owners treated these delicate decoys with great care, sometimes even fitting them with individual carrying bags for protection in transit and off-season storage.

For the most part, decoy making was a humble art, practiced by men who made their living from the water they lived near. These men "followed the water" through the seasons by fishing, gunning, guiding, clamming, oystering, or manning gunning camps or lighthouses. More than a few decoy makers, including such notables as Virginia's Ira Hudson and Toronto's George Warin, also were proficient at the closely related trade of boatbuilding. (Indeed, Warin was best known during his lifetime as the maker of racing sculls used by the legendary Canadian oarsman Ned Hanlon.) Other professional decoy makers, such as the masterful Massachusetts carver Joe Lincoln, who was also a shoemaker, upholsterer, and clock repair-

man (as well as a grower of prize-winning dahlias), and Martha's Vineyard's Keyes Chadwick, who lettered diplomas for Harvard with his fine old-fashioned calligraphy, supplemented their income with other handcrafts. Decoy makers usually worked in small shanties or home workshops that were generally equipped with only the most basic of hand tools: hatchet, penknife, saw, rasp, chisel, screwdriver, sandpaper, and paint brushes. Lumber for bodies was often salvaged from ship spars, fence posts, telephone poles, or other readily available sources. One of the finest St. Clair Flats decoys ever made has a bottom board crafted from one side of a discarded orange crate. Most makers used ordinary household oil paint to decorate their creations. White cedar, which cured well and was resistant to rot, was the favored wood for decoy bodies, while pine, a softwood that was easy to carve, was favored for heads. Locally prevalent woods, such as redwood in California and tupelo in Louisiana, were favored by regional carvers. Carvers cut patterns for heads and bodies from paper or thin sheets of wood and traced around them on the solid blocks of wood from which the bird would be carved. Some makers also used cut patterns to aid with their painting. The use of patterns brought precision and speed to the crafting of large numbers of similar decoys, although some makers resisted this uniformity in their work and carved without patterns of any sort.

While museums and collectors tend to focus on the artistry of individual examples, decoys were actually used in groups called rigs. Depending on such locally diverse conditions as the weather, the size and type of water and boat, and the species sought, a gunner's rig could range in number anywhere from a handful of decoys to over 500. Hunters often mixed species in their gunning rigs to present a more natural and appealing scene to passing birds. So-called confidence

OPPOSITE: *Watercolor on paper of one of the Lovelock Cave canvasbacks, by Joel D. Barber; 1929.*

RIGHT: *Sketches of decoys by Joel D. Barber.*

BELOW: *Rig of decoys piled on a waterfront.*

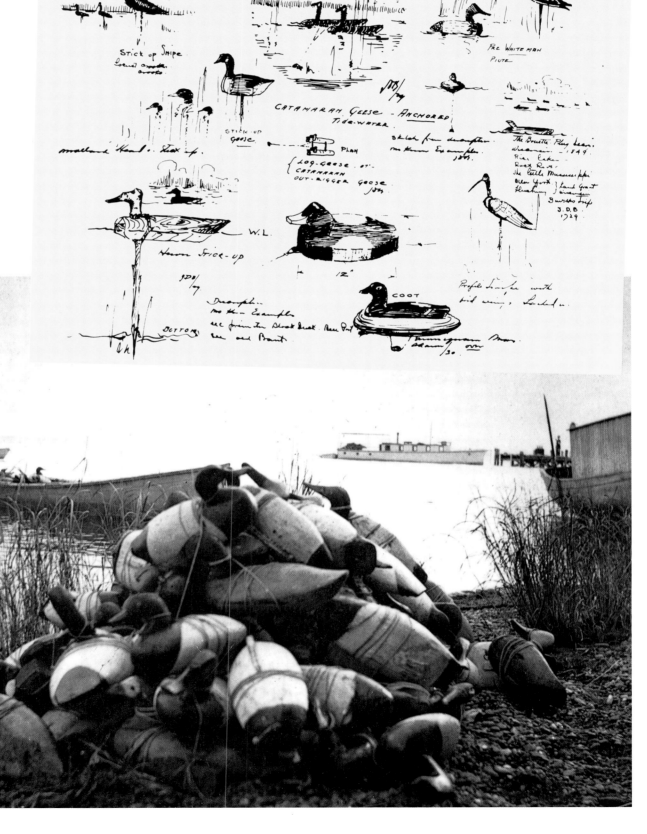

18

MASON'S DECOY FACTORY

MILFORD ST. & P. M. R. R.   DETROIT, MICH.

OPPOSITE: Cover of a mail-order catalogue distributed by the Mason Decoy Factory of Detroit; ca. 1910. The Mason factory was in operation from 1896 to 1924 and shipped decoys to sportsmen and market gunners all over North America.

RIGHT: Hudsonian curlew and robin snipe by the Mason factory. Mason made shorebirds, crows, and doves as well as ducks and geese.

BELOW: Black duck by Mason; ca. 1910. Mason decoys came in five grades. As this Premier grade example demonstrates, the company's best-quality decoys were carefully hand painted.

decoys, representing species not hunted for food, such as sea-gulls, were also sometimes added to a rig for the same reason. A variety of head positions added realism. In addition to the standard "straight heads," duck and goose decoys were made with their heads turned over their backs as if sleeping or preening their feathers or tucked low into their bodies as if resting. Occasionally, decoys were made with their necks extended upright into an alert position. Some were even made with no head at all and only half a body; these "tip ups" imitated bottom-feeding birds with their heads under water and tails in the air.

Shorebird decoys were sometimes made with bulging throats as if swallowing a minnow, with their heads bent down as if feeding, or thrust forward as if scurrying across the beach.

In the late 1700s and early 1800s, decoys were made in small numbers as an aid to family food gathering. But in the 19th century the tremendous expansion of economic opportunities and the improvement of the young country's transportation systems soon helped foster a consumer public eager and able to pay for goods and services that were not immediately available to them. Professional gunners supplied the public

20

demand for wildfowl for the table while professional decoy carvers, gunning clubs, and guides catered to city "sports" who traveled far and wide to enjoy the pleasures of different hunting areas. Hundreds of thousands of decoys were made by hand between 1850 and 1950 for use by market gunners and sportsmen. By the late 1800s, demand for decoys had grown so great that several "factories" began producing birds that were marketed through catalogues and national sporting magazines such as *Forest and Stream* and sold by mail order. Although these companies, most notably the prolific Mason Decoy Factory of Detroit, which opened its doors in 1896, were not factories

in the modern sense, they did employ simple assembly-line techniques by dividing labor between carvers and painters. The bodies of Mason decoys were turned on a lathe, while heads and painting were done by hand. Mason decoys were sold by the dozen and have turned up in every corner of North America.

As America's economy boomed, and the country shifted from a rural and agricultural way of life to an industrial and urban one, sport gunning became increasingly important. Gunning clubs and resorts throughout North America catered to wealthy businessmen, who traveled by rail and steamship to

OPPOSITE: Joseph Whiting Lincoln of Accord standing in the doorway of his workshop; ca. 1930. Like many decoy makers, Lincoln supported himself through a variety of handcrafts, also working as a shoemaker, clock repairman, and upholsterer.

ABOVE: Wood duck by Joseph Lincoln. When it came to auction in 1986, this decoy sold for $205,000, a record at that time.

RIGHT: New Jersey gunner poling his narrow sneak boat, loaded with decoys; ca. 1910.

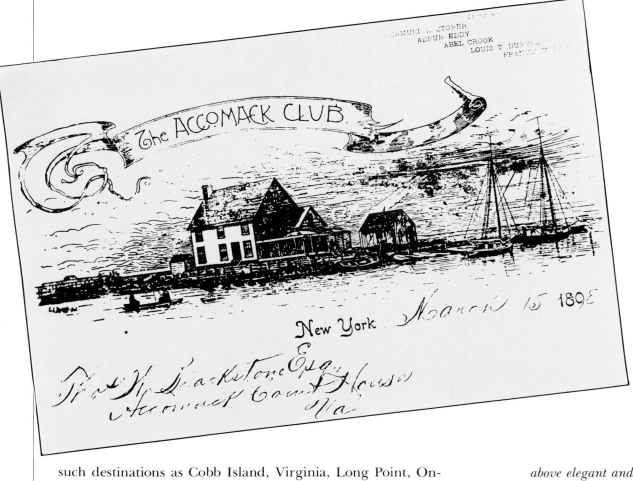

LEFT: Letterhead of the Accomack Club, one of the many private clubs and resort hotels that catered to wealthy sportsmen in the 19th century. BELOW LEFT: Engraving of ladies' feathered hats from an ad in Harper's Bazaar; *1888.*

such destinations as Cobb Island, Virginia, Long Point, Ontario, and Senachwine Lake in Illinois. These Victorian-era establishments offered dignified coat-and-tie gunning in the English tradition, plush accommodations, and fine local food and drink. Guest lists and members' rosters of the resorts and clubs are full of politicians and prominent capitalists; today, they read like a who's who of late-19th-century American society. A typical resort advertisement, published in 1881 in the *Peninsula Enterprise* by the Atlantic Hotel on Chincoteague Island, Virginia, tells the story:

> The undersigned beg leave to inform their friends and the general public that they have leased and refurnished the above elegant and commodious house, and are now prepared to accommodate permanent and transient guests in first-class style.
>
> Large, airy rooms. Home comforts. Fine Sea and Bay fishing, gunning and bathing, etc. The table is provided with wild fowl, terrapin, fish, oysters, crabs and all the luxuries of the season.
>
> Pleasure boats of all kinds, guides, fishing lines, decoys, ponies, etc., always ready for the use of guests.
>
> First-class Bar attached. Choice wines, liquors, ales, beers and cigars.
>
> Passengers for Chincoteague connect with steamer for the Island at Franklin City, the terminus of the Worcester Railroad, morning and evening. Connection may also be made daily at Nashville. All who visit the Atlantic may rest assured that they will receive courteous treatment and excellent fare.
>
> Your patronage is respectfully solicited.
> W. J. MATTHEWS & Co.

Incidently, many of the fine shorebird decoys Mr. Matthews provided for his guests to shoot over have survived.

The effect of the market and sport gunners of the 19th century on North America's wildfowl population was profound. The combination of hunting pressure and the inexorable loss of habitat brought about by Manifest Destiny doomed the passenger pigeon, once the most abundant species on earth, to extinction. It is less often realized that dozens of other birds also were in serious trouble by the turn of the century. Throughout the country, game and plumage species were gunned mercilessly for food and sport. Some species, including terns, spoonbills, herons, and egrets, were hunted strictly for their plumage, which was in great demand by the millinery trade for use in decorating women's headware. An early casualty of the plume-and-feather trade was the Labrador duck, a beautiful piebald seabird similar to, but more dramatically colored than, the oldsquaw. The Labrador duck, along with the larger and more numerous eider, was sought by early gunners for its down. The bird was already uncommon by 1851 when Audubon died: he never saw a live specimen and painted his

Poster announcing the opening of the hunting season and reminding hunters of birds under protection. The conservation movement was instrumental in creating laws regulating bird hunting.

Sportsmen! Shorebirds!

The open season for shorebirds is from August 16th to November 30th, inclusive, winter and summer Yellowlegs, Golden Plover and Blackbreasted Plover (beetleheads) *only.* **Daily bag limit 15 in aggregate of all kinds**

It is *Unlawful at anytime* **to shoot Peep, Ring-Necks, Sanderlings, Grass Birds or any other small Shorebirds not mentioned above. It is unlawful at any time to shoot Herons, Bitterns, Kingfishers, Gulls or Terns.**

Unlawful Shooting Spoils Sport for All

It should be reported to

DIVISION OF FISHERIES AND GAME

State House, Boston

MASSACHUSETTS AUDUBON SOCIETY

For the Protection of Birds

66 Newbury Street, Boston

These Cloth Posters will be Furnished Free on application to the Society

depiction of the species from mounts shot in the 1820s. The Labrador duck became extinct in the 1870s. By that time plume hunting was an industry in it own right. An 1886 bulletin, "Destruction of Our Native Birds," published by the American Ornithologist's Union, a forerunner of the Audubon Society, noted that 5 million birds were killed each year for use on ladies' headgear. Also in 1886 Frank Chapman, an early conservationist, observed headware while strolling the streets of Manhattan and counted 542 of 700 incorporating feathers, wings, etc. Ducks and plume birds were not the only victims; hats were adorned with the plumage (and sometimes the beaks and claws) of crows, owls, and various songbirds as well. In the 1890s a full-feathered sandpiper skin could be bought at Macy's Department Store in New York for a penny and a pair of gull's wings for 11 cents. Astonishing as it seems today, by 1900 plume hunting had reduced the now ubiquitous herring gull to a single East Coast colony.

As early as the 1840s, certain individuals began to recognize the need for restraint and conservation. But it was another forty years before these voices began to organize themselves

and affect public opinion. The American Ornithologist's Union was the seminal group dedicated to the protection of American birds. Provocative articles by members of the group published in the national sporting magazine *Forest and Stream* in the 1880s fostered the birth of what the magazine's editor, George Bird Grinnell, dubbed "the Audubon Society." By 1905 this group had grown into a national organization, incorporated as the National Association of Audubon Societies for the Preservation of Wild Birds and Animals. Throughout the 1890s and early years of this century, the new conservation movement gained strength and worked effectively to focus public attention on the destruction of the nation's birds and habitats. The public outcry grew in intensity until Congress passed the Weeks-McLean Act in 1913. This bill awarded to federal agencies all responsibility for regulating migratory game birds. Each state had previously set its own laws; Weeks-McLean made uniform protection possible. Also in 1913 the Federal Tariff Act closed the door on plume hunters by prohibiting the importation of wild bird skins, feathers, etc., for other than scientific or educational purposes. Finally, in 1918, the Federal Migratory Bird Act effectively brought an end to the market gunning industry by outlawing the sale of wild birds.

With these laws in place, wildfowl could no longer be exploited for profit. Demand for decoys was sharply reduced, and many professional makers were forced to turn to other pursuits. By 1924 the Mason Factory had closed its doors as well. A number of craftsmen continued to make decoys in the traditional manner either for sale or for their own use well into the 1950s, but slowly but surely the attention of carvers began to turn from function to form. Because most decoys made after 1920 were crafted by or for sportsmen, they tended to be more finely detailed than earlier working birds. In 1923 the first decoy-carving contest was organized in Bellport, Long Island,

by the collector and author Joel Barber. Over one hundred carvers entered the contest; the grand prize in the amateur category was awarded to Charles "Shang" Wheeler of Stratford, Connecticut, for a highly detailed pair of mallards he later gave to Barber as a Christmas present. (The prize-winning mallards, along with the rest of Barber's seminal collection, are now in the collection of the Shelburne Museum in Vermont.) Barber, a tireless promoter of the decoy as an important American art form, produced the first book on the subject in 1934 and loaned decoys from his collection to important early folk-art exhibitions at the Newark (New Jersey) Museum and the Museum of Modern Art in the early 1930s. His book *Wild Fowl Decoys*, which is still in print, has opened the eyes of

24

Broadbill Decoy

Folk Art USA

Mallard Decoy

Folk Art USA

Canvasback Decoy

Folk Art USA

Redhead Decoy

Folk Art USA

OPPOSITE: Carving contests, which fostered competition and exchanges of ideas among carvers, began in 1923. This pair of mallards by Charles "Shang" Wheeler won a blue ribbon in 1924.

ABOVE: Stamps with decoys issued by the U.S. Postal Service. The broadbill is by Ben Holmes; the mallard by Percy Gant; the canvasback by Bob McGaw; the redhead by Henry Keyes Chadwick.

several generations of collectors to the history and beauty of decoys.

The carving competition initiated by Joel Barber became an annual event that eventually moved from the Bellport library to larger quarters in New York City under sponsorship of the Schaefer Brewing Company. The idea of competition carving became increasingly common and popular, and carvers went to great lengths to outdo one another. Unlike "working" decoys, competition birds were made for and judged solely by human eyes. Nonfunctional details such as attached wings and extravagantly detailed plumage painting began to appear as the craftsmen became more sophisticated and self-conscious in their work. Inevitably, some of the more skilled craftsmen, such as Cape Cod's Elmer Crowell and the Ward brothers of Crisfield, Maryland, discovered they could make more money carving purely decorative birds designed for the mantelpiece than they could producing working decoys. The vast technological changes of the 20th century also took their toll on the wooden decoy tradition. By the end of World War II, effective mass-produced decoys made of inexpensive but durable plastics and other new synthetics had taken over a large and growing share of the market for gunning decoys, forcing many craftsmen either to change their approach or go out of business. Under these enormous economic and cultural pressures, the traditional handmade wooden decoy began to fade into history during the 1950s. By the mid-1960s it was, for all intents and purposes, a thing of the past.

This oil painting by an unknown artist shows A. Elmer Crowell carving a goose.

26

One of the many signs used by A. Elmer Crowell to advertise his decoys. Such signs and memorabilia have themselves become collectors' items.

From our late-20th-century perspective, American bird decoys hold a wealth of cultural, historical, and aesthetic value and interest. The best decoys are objects of great beauty, which in their simple symbolism capture the essence of the living birds they were made to lure from the sky. The great decoy makers, known and anonymous, rank with John James Audubon as the finest wildlife artists our country has produced. Through the work of these perceptive and talented observers of our wildfowl, we are linked with America's rich sporting history, with the days of unlimited and unrestricted natural resources, of market gunners and sportsmen's gunning clubs, and of wild game on the tables of the finest restaurants and the humblest home alike. We can imagine the thrill of watching the great migrations of canvasback and redhead, Canada goose and black duck, Eskimo curlew and golden plover, that in-

spired the decoy carvers. Through these hunter's totems we are connected with the twin legacy of awe and exploitation that has always defined our country's relationship to the natural world, from the earliest explorers to the present day, from Audubon and John Muir to the Audubon Society and the Sierra Club, from the Labrador duck and the passenger pigeon to the spotted owl and the ivory billed woodpecker and our current global concerns about whales, elephants, rain forest destruction, oil spills, and ozone depletion. The great flocks are gone, as is much of the undeveloped land they migrated over. But many of the decoys that lured the birds from the skies survive. Today they serve to remind us of our heritage as Americans: of the changes we have wrought in our land, of what we have lost, and of the importance and beauty of the natural world that remains for us to cherish, protect, and enjoy.

CHAPTER 1:

MAINE

by John Dinan

The great tollers from Down East represent species seldom seen, let alone gunned, except in those far-at-sea places Cape Cod, Nantucket, and eastern Long Island. Down Maine, loons, seagulls, and heron are the "Judas birds" put in rigs to ease the ducks' suspicions. Mergansers should be, but they were made in such great numbers that they were by definition the primary prey.

Joel Barber identified mergansers with Maine in his shanty poem book titled *Long Shore*. In the poem "Painter McGee":

And decoy ducks—why you ought to see him—
*   painting decoys:*
Shelldrake in full plumage—in beautiful patterns
*   of black and white,*
With speckled breast and crimson bill, and
*   markings like*
A pattern in a parlor carpet, with a belly white
*   as snow.*

If the great Maine carvers had a commonality it was that

ABOVE: *This sleeping brant by an unknown carver was found on a porch railing on a Maine island. It is covered with a* coat of white paint; *refinishing this decoy would do nothing to improve its wonderful form.*

OPPOSITE: *Merganser by George Huey of Friendship, Maine. Huey's mergansers were the best* on the coast of Maine. He often *signed his birds with a carved remarque on the bottom.*

they loved to make mergansers. Willie Ross of Chebeague, O. S. Bibber of South Harpswell, and Gus Wilson from the whole coast made superb mergansers.

George Raymond Huey of Friendship was the master. Huey (b. 1866) lived with his mother, Saltanny, for years and then in a shack with a wood stove and a chopping block and Martha Cronch. Huey had no electricity and no power tools, though he on occasion had a few decoy heads cut out at Winchenbach's lumberyard. He was a "water man" who clammed for food and cash, yet would keep only a certain size, which he perceived as being correct. He rowed the harbor for a 90-year-old lobsterman who no longer could pull an oar. Huey is known to have shortened his oars because "they rowed easier." He was a happy bachelor whose laugh was heard all across the Friendship harbor. Knowing this laugh, it is easy to accept the story of his live-in, Martha Cronch. She was 10 inches tall, carved by George, and was always introduced to the town children when they came to visit. Whether a lost love or just a gleam in his eye, Martha matched the carving George did of himself. A bit

eccentric, stories of this man abound. If it weren't for the quality of his birds, we would follow this town character aspect rather than "the merganser man." Given a railroad conductor's uniform, he wore it with pride with hat and brass buttons to the Adventist Church where he sat alone by the stove since he had no running water. George regularly stopped at local houses about suppertime and, if welcome, was given a special chair, which was easy to disinfect, and, if unwelcome, onions were quickly peeled that sent him flying.

George inherited his artistic ability from Saltanny, who made sought-after models of Friendship homes from shoe boxes. These models included curtains in the windows and were easily identifiable. He was known early on to take pride in his academic ability and was often described after successfully answering a spelling-bee word as saying, "Now, teacher, let me give you one."

Anyone turning one of Huey's mergansers over would recognize the signature, and it is said in Friendship that when he wrote a letter he would carry it around town before posting

29

Merganser by Willie Ross. This superb shelldrake illustrates Ross's ability to create a graceful decoy using simple lines.

30

it to show off his penmanship. He did this with his carvings also.

George made few species besides mergansers. A possible Huey eider has turned up, and several whistlers made with less care than the mergansers surfaced a few years ago. He made several miniature pheasants and raccoons, but nearly all his carvings showed the shell-drake influence.

The Huey seagull at the Shelburne Museum is essentially a merganser painted white. His birds, however, were honest, almost stark, and need no apologies. Some with carved crests, some with horsehairs or leather crests, they had carved eyes early and glass later on. The bevel at the waterline was all Huey, and when you see the poured weight, sometimes in the shape of a horse or even a thistle, you know how he treated special friends. They got more than just a decoy. If he liked you, he carved something special on the bottom, more often than not

George Huey showing off a small figure of himself.

only once, to work on a farm; he became ill from regular meals and had to return. The townsfolk nicknamed him Pokus, and though he died in 1947, they still remember George sitting alone in the Adventist Church in his conductor's uniform and sawed off rubber boots singing "Cleansing Wave." They thought George foolish when he would preen in front of a mirror and say, "Someday I will become famous."

William Everett Ross of Chebeague Island had only an axe, a spokeshave, and a jackknife to carve with. We can't say how many birds he made, but when he changed from painted eyes to glass eyes, he ordered them by the gross! Black ducks, mallards, and lots of whistlers were products of his talent. One-third-sized black ducks were probably either given away or sold at Bennett's store to people "from away." Willie made at least one robin for his wife, this robin standing in the window above the front door. But again, he made mergansers. Little souvenir mergansers are found as far away as Michigan. The classy shell-drake tollers that are thought of whenever one speaks of "Ross birds" grace many collections, and those giant birds that were part of one rig that were made by special order topped them all. Willie made birds for everyone on Chebeague, rigs of six or eight would do at a time when Willie charged $1 apiece or $10 a dozen. Bodies were either pine or cedar with heads usually of pine. He aged the wood in the loft of the shed, usually after cutting the trees himself. Ross did not use patterns, yet the birds are frequently mirror images. The finish of the birds was produced mostly by a skillful jackknife and a little sandpaper, then primed gray. Mrs. Ross helped with the painting.

Willie made oldsquaws and used a piece of ash for the long tail feather. Can you imagine finding a rig of those? Why not find them in a Ross half-bushel basket from Bennett's store?

The basketmaking began before marriageable age. Willie's grandfather, Freeman Ross, badgered him, saying, "The baskets would not hold a half bushel." This size was chosen because six made a barrel. Willie could and did dig a barrel of clams almost

including the great initials G.R.H. in scrolled lettering.

Concerning Huey's pride in his work, he was at one time commissioned to recane six dining-room chairs. George had for a time been in reform school as a boy when his father abandoned the family. He learned five different cane patterns and wanted to show his expertise in each. When the six chairs were delivered, only two cane seats matched.

This country character is known to have left Friendship

This oldsquaw by an unknown maker may have started as a now extinct Labrador duck: its paint gives both species.

32

every day in the winter. He received 75 cents a barrel from the shipper, Rufus D. Hamilton.

Just as he cut his own decoy wood, Ross cut the ash for baskets, and when he and Howard Curit pounded the trees to produce the basket material, it could be heard all over the island.

Willie Ross was born in 1878 and died in 1954. The Ross family began four generations before that with three brothers, Samuel, Walter, and John. So the islands of Casco Bay are filled with brothers and sisters and cousins. Willie's other grandfather, Joseph Upton, was a lighthouse keeper until he fell one night in 1935 while tending the light and was killed. It was Joseph Upton who talked so fondly of coot stew.

The edibility of seabirds comes up over and over. Willie's brother George shot a loon one winter to see how it would taste.

"When George carried that bird up the hill from the boat, he held its feet over his shoulder, and the beak dragged on the ground, but George was pretty short." No description of the taste was in the story, but "Gulls are a little strong, crows are even worse."

Besides building baskets and decoys and clamming, Willie worked on the Ballard farm for five or six years starting in 1928. Located at Indian Island Point, known as the Hook, the farm was owned by Philadelphians and allowed Ross a steady cash flow when he worked full-time. He helped on the farm, at their boat shop, and on the wharf. When the Ballards asked him to work only part-time, however, it became a nuisance, so he returned to his more satisfying ventures.

Willie hunted a lot, often accompanied by Billy Hill of Remington fame. Strangely, they would go to Little John Island to shoot teal. Those of you who have been to Chebeague know that the islanders' main quarry have to have been eiders and scoters and mergansers. Ross is not known to have made either scoters or eiders, but he hunted the bar between Big and Little Chebeague. If there was ever a place for dependable eider shooting, that bar is the spot. Who knows, maybe those big Ross mergansers were originally meant to have been eiders.

A member of the Ross family says that his last rig was eight mergansers, "just some old tollers that father fixed," and six black ducks that were an order no one came to claim.

OPPOSITE: Pair of mergansers by Os Bibber. Bibber made hollow birds that have a sense of style, perhaps reflecting his travels at sea. These birds are feather light and truly beyond compare.

Orlando Sylvester Bibber, "Os," of South Harpswell, was unusual among Maine decoy carvers. By his own statement, "I had a gentleman's position." Bibber was chief engineer on the Eastern Steamship Line ships that ran from Portland to Bangor or to New Brunswick and often from New York to Cuba. "Ollie" sat with the head purser at the captain's table.

Born in Harpswell in 1882, he died there on July 4, 1971, after a long career at sea and a productive retirement. The Bibbers came to Harpswell from Haskell's Island about the time Ollie was born. His mother, Cordelia, was an Orr, related to the Orrs of the island by that name. The youngest of four boys and two girls, he was preceded by Bernard, Winfred, Charles, Susan, and Annie. He was another who finished only the second or third grade in school before going on to the Portland Company for a technical education. Already a qualified engineer, he served as assistant engineer in the U. S. Merchant Marine in World War I.

34

Family closeness and his job at sea allowed him to live in the same house during his long life, even after he married Nellie Douglas. They shared mother Cordelia's home, and later, when Ollie was at sea much of the time, a nephew lived there to care for the ladies. The boy remembers spending long hours at the grinding wheel sharpening tools whenever Ollie came home from a voyage. He especially loved axes, and it is likely that the Eastern Steamship vessels had a high turnover in that equipment.

Bibber's birds are the best carvings on the coast. Thin and delicate, they do not have the inletted heads so often found Down Maine. There was a bit of Lincoln's influence in his work. The necks of his birds are thin, the bodies elongated, heads just a bit small, and more often than not, the birds are hollow. Os carried his hollowing beyond necessities since these birds were used from good-sized boats on the coast, where weight was not an issue. Found in his rig were several unfinished birds with only a primer coat of paint. These one-piece birds with necks thrust forward were either swimmers or meant to have wings mounted as flyers. They showed the eggshell-thin hollowing effect since no bottom boards had yet been added. Os used tiny square-cut nails to add bottom boards, and when you handle his birds, you can see the influence of his engineer's training. The calipers and other fine measuring instruments of his trade show their effect.

It is likely that Bibber differed from other high-output carvers in that he made decoys only for his own use. While making birds for your own use was reasonably typical, gunners who made their own rigs left only a few remaining examples of their work. In Bibber's case, we know that at least 75 birds survived, and it is likely that there are twice that many. Gorgeous mergansers with heads cocked right or left and with crests still in place brought attention to this Harpswell master. With their lines still attached, they cry to be back at sea. On a different day the whistlers would be used. Os seemed to give more attention to the hens, which had the grace of the shell-birds. The drakes are a bit bigger and do not sing the same siren song as his other decoys. Not many oldsquaws are known, and some confusion could exist over the origin of the old-squaws. Were it not for one particular bird, the other oldsquaws would still be attributed to a Cape Elizabeth carver, probably from Peebles Cove. They are, however, pure Bibber and were found in a Falmouth shed with the other more typical bird. When the contents of the loft were bought at auction, the intent had been to obtain just the nicely dried lumber stored there, but the dozen oldsquaws were ultimately included.

Bibber made black ducks, too, according to a family member, because black ducks came to Harpswell in late December when Portland's Back Bay froze over. He made no known eiders "because they weren't here then." There was a time, remembered by fathers of men who are now about ready to quit gunning, when seeing an eider duck was an occasion. On the other hand, these same men can remember seeing rafts of eiders from West Brown Cow to Halfway Rock Lighthouse! There is only one big bird, lacking a head, painted white, which was found on a summer-house porch on Long Island, Maine. Possibly a goose, but again, the head is broken off, the bird is a Bibber, and has the grace of a Phineus Reeves of Long Point, Ontario. Oh, to have seen the bird while it was intact.

This superb oldsquaw with a real tail feather is by Os Bibber. It shows clear kinship with the pair it flanks, once thought to be by an unknown carver from Cape Elizabeth.

Os hunted with a 10-gauge, lever-action, full-choke Winchester model 1901, and while he was a temperate man, befitting his place in life, he hated crows. Possibly because he raised strawberries and chickens after he retired, he considered crows as threats to the family's well-being and would use the same 10 gauge out the bedroom window if a crow were unwise enough to trespass.

After the Eastern Steamship Line closed down, he lobstered from a Hampton that he rebuilt, putting in a new four-cylinder engine. Os lost his shirt during the Great Depression. He had developed a habit of depositing his Steamship Line paycheck in a bank wherever payday happened to be. The bank losses and the premature closing of the steamship line made continued work at least a perceived necessity. He was always a gentleman, however, putting on a coat and tie whenever he went to the village. He was proud of being Chief Engineer Bibber and was not, in his own mind, old Os sitting by the wood stove in Harpswell Neck smoking Blackstone Junior cigars.

What about Monhegan? All the early articles about Monhegan eiders and scoters eventually raised doubts about the possibilities of so many birds being carved by so few carvers. Granted, we have seen photos of eiders piled high as a man's head and ten feet across. That is a lot of eider shooting even on Monhegan. But, then again, you didn't need many decoys so far at sea, and, besides that, the Monhegan lobstermen are preparing to start their season on January 1. There was probably little time of idle eider carving. The explanation could be that Augustus Aaron Wilson, who was keeper of the Marshall's Point Light at Port Clyde, was responsible for a large number of the so-called Monhegan sea-duck decoys. Gus was already carving then,

36

and, of course, the mailboat leaves Port Clyde for Monhegan all year long. Gus Wilson spanned the 19th and 20th centuries, as did the other great carvers in Maine. Ross and Huey and Bibber specialized in mergansers. Gus had a broadness of interest and an artist's eye that allowed him to come up with birds of such merit that they rivaled the best of the others. There were rocking-head shell-drakes, at least one turned-head preener, and that great pair owned and written about by the late George Ross Starr. Gus Wilson looked at waterfowl much the way the Ward brothers did. There was a similarity in their ability to capture an unusual pose and to produce a decoy that continues to enthrall even seasoned gunners who have spent their lives observing waterfowl.

Gus, of course, carved so many marvelous "folk pieces" that he is not owned only by decoy collectors. Robins, bluejays, Baltimore orioles would be produced when Gus looked out of the window, saw a bird, and felt inspired. The great full-sized tigers and the superb 32-inch miniature tiger were the result of Gus's interest in the circus. One brother was a toymaker in Bar Harbor, which probably inspired Gus toward items besides waterfowl. Gus made his five great blue herons while living on Preble Street in South Portland. Our knowledge of him is largely the result of his befriending Fred Anderson, who lived next door as a boy. Fred remembered being sent to a maple thicket to bring home legs for those five birds and appreciated Gus long before he became the local decoy guru.

Born Down East in Tremont, Maine, on Mount Desert Island, Gus spent much of his life in the lighthouse service. He served on the lighthouses before they became part of the Coast Guard. One of his first duty stations was at Great Duck Island Light. He arrived there only to find that they had no Parchessi board, so he promptly made one, and typical of his "make-do" approach, it is painted sky blue simply because such paint was available to him at the time.

His Marshall's Point connection has been discussed by all students of Wilson lore. It is probably birds that were made there that started the Hans Berry stories, even though the birds marketed as being Berry's from the Cross Island Light were found in South Portland. Gus's last duty station was at the Spring Point Light in Portland Harbor. He tended the light in association with his brother, Otto, and it was there that he did most of his carving, both on the light itself and at home on Preble Street.

After the death of his second wife, Gus needed someone to talk to and said one day that he was going to carve a full-sized lady and sit her in the parlor in his wife's clothes. Ander-

OPPOSITE TOP: Augustus "Gus" Wilson, whose carving career spanned two centuries and included the creation of many varieties of birds.

OPPOSITE BOTTOM. Half-size blackducks and a mallard by Gus Wilson. You'd have to take a measure to these to tell them from real decoys.

RIGHT: This Gus Wilson robin, part of a weathervane, graced the roof of Fred Anderson's woodshed. Wilson made it while working at Spring Point Light, his last duty station.

son said it took all he could do as a 12-year-old to tell the respected grown-up that they might think he was crazy if he did that. Anderson, therefore, had the heavy burden of knowing that he may have prevented the construction of one of the great folk pieces of our time.

Then there was the new Browning automatic that Fred convinced Gus to buy. He had always had an old 12-gauge double with a simple safety, and when they went hunting the first time with the new gun the more complicated safety of the Browning failed to do its work. A great hole was blown in the bow of the dory just above the waterline. Fred and Gus stuffed their hats in the hole and rowed for shore. The Browning was returned that very day!

Gus had a big Chrysler that he had trouble managing. He seldom was able to put it away without hitting one side or the other of the garage until Fred painted a target on the back wall of the garage and showed Wilson how to line it up with the hood ornament.

Fred said that Wilson never used good patterns for his birds, preferring to draw them out on paper that was allowed to fall to the floor no matter how good, be swept up, and burned. One day Fred saved some of the best patterns and traced them onto wood, which he dutifully cut out and presented to Gus. These too eventually fell to the floor, were swept up, and also placed in the wood stove.

Gus is one of the few carvers from Maine who we know sold his decoys through an outlet. Edwards and Walker were longtime hardware specialists in Portland. Gus sold his birds there, and wouldn't it be a treat to see the old invoices if the company still existed?

The typical Wilson decoy was large and had an inletted head, often turned left or right, or was preening. The birds had carved eyes just as the early Ross and Bibber birds, but Gus

LEFT: This flying goldeneye by Gus Wilson hung in a gunning camp at Hockomock, Maine, for many years. Wilson modeled his flying birds after illustrations by sporting artist Lynn Bogue Hunt.

ABOVE: This superb eider with a mussel in its mouth was collected by the late Dr. George Ross Starr on one of Maine's coastal islands. The maker is unknown. The mussel was not added to the carving and was instead formed from the same wood as the decoy.

Almost all of George Huey's carvings were mergansers, and, in fact, this Huey seagull is essentially a merganser painted white.

40

never changed. Interestingly, some of the eyes were raised, especially on his songbirds, which indicated the heads were carved away from the eyes. The wings on Wilson's birds were usually raised and occasionally pieced on. Several of his mallards and black ducks actually had wings elevated away from the body in a flapping position. Telltale marks are seen beneath the tail from Gus's half-inch chisel, and more often than not, the flat bottoms of the birds are unpainted unless repainting has been done.

Few of Wilson's birds were hollowed, though at least one hen eider is known and a rig of six oldsquaws were hollowed but spent their prior lives as black duck decoys. Two or more of these birds exist today, and they were the result of a Wilson experiment. Gus had made six black ducks and hollowed them before applying bottom boards. Poor caulking resulted in the birds quickly filling with water, and the customer returned them. Gus instructed Fred Anderson to strip the bottoms. They then reshaped the tails and heads, and after painting them as oldsquaws, left the bottoms open, which worked fine. Most of Gus's oldsquaws were more delicate, with large nails driven through drilled heads, allowing them to swivel. Such adaptability and innovation was a Wilson trademark as seen in the rocking-head mergansers and coots. Gus even made a few sleeping black ducks from one piece of wood. Doctor Starr identified one of these birds as made by Trefethen of Yarmouth, Maine, but George was no different from Joel Barber,

*This eider decoy was made by
Phineas Alexander, one of
Maine's earliest decoy makers.
Although few of Alexander's
decoys remain, the excitement
of this eider duck makes the
hunt worthwhile.*

who originally identified a Ben Holmes black duck as being from Long Island.

It was Barber who first called a Wilson coot a Monhegan bird. A great scoter with a finely sculpted head, the bird's body was pegged together laterally. Pieced bodies are trademarks of Gus's work. Even the best work may have a strip tacked on one side. More often than not, this was not a repair but part of the original construction. This make-do attitude, however, did not extend to Wilson's decoy heads. Even the preening scoters with bills down on the chest had mandible carving beneath the bill. Said carving existed only because it was important to Gus.

A few of the later Wilson decoys carried a stamp on the bottom as follows, "Made by A.A. Wilson, South Portland, Maine." Rigs keep turning up, some of which are still being used to gun over, but as is true of most of the great carvers, no identifying mark or signature is required. Once you have handled a Wilson decoy, you will never have difficulty identifying another.

Merrymeeting Bay should have had a typical decoy, but if such ever existed not enough remained to be classified. Superb black-duck and teal hunting exists in Merrymeeting even today, but most of the decoys are "factory birds." Many were made by George Soule and his successors and often sold by L.L. Bean. Mr. Soule is a superb carver, and his wooden-head, cork-bodied birds are among the best "real" decoys available today, but the old hand-carved tollers are our subject.

LEFT: *This preening merganser by Gus Wilson is folk art at its best. The form and paint combine to make this one of Wilson's finest creations.*

ABOVE: *This oversize hen eider by Amos Wallace of Harpswell, Maine, with a horseshoe keel weight, exemplifies the simple beauty of Maine tollers.*

One rig made by Scribner warranted considerable praise. This man left a half-dozen fine black ducks that resembled Wilson's in posed style and paint. Who knows who followed whom and, in fact, possibly they were simply more innovative Wilsons.

As one surveys the coastal birds, names like Alexander, the Wallaces, and Maurice Decker keep turning up. This brief discussion of Maine decoys does not attempt to list all the great men but simply some of the high-volume carvers whose work graces many collections. Omission of a particular carver only reflects the author's lack of enough details about that individual to impart even a smattering of new information.

Something that pleases all of us, however, is that tollers are still being made in the old way down the coast. Some of us have noted that on a bright day the eiders really do not toll to Clorox bottles or to silhouettes but need a rig of finely crafted birds to make the difference.

One family that possibly takes the longevity award for decoy making is the Whitneys. Grandfather John, son Jim, and grandson Harold span over 100 years of decoy construction. John and Jim turned out birds in the same boathouse on the Presumpscot estuary in Falmouth. Harold has moved up country but makes birds so close to the ones of his forebears that only the bottom brands identify the difference. The Whitneys made superb geese and mergansers, fine black ducks and whistlers, but sadly never made eiders or scoters. It is a shame that some of Jim's giant geese or blacks couldn't have been eiders. Simple as the divers from the upper Chesapeake, the Whitneys' decoys still are in rigs where they belong. In that old boathouse heated by decoy scraps with the smell of oakum, paint, turpentine, and new cedar, it is quite apparent that the hand-crafted decoy does not need to be decades old to carry on the legend.

I refer you again to Joel Barber's *Long Shore.* No more quotes because you should find a copy and treasure it. Read Barber's "Gramps," and you will learn what decoys represent, the people, the places, and the time.

CHAPTER 2:

MASSACHUSETTS

by Jackson Parker

The "sacred cod" hangs high in the legislative chamber of the State House on Beacon Hill to remind the lawmakers that the Commonwealth of Massachusetts depends on the products of its waters for its livelihood. If that symbolism is lost on citizens, they are reminded daily by the news media that they live in the "Bay State." From their arrival in 1620, the Pilgrims and later the Puritans fished and fowled in the waters using techniques they brought with them and some learned from the local Indians.

With the growth of cities and the consequent increased demand for food, market gunning thrived. The long coastline with its bogs and marshes and the inland lakes and ponds attracted ducks, geese, and shorebirds by the tens of thousands. The decoys that were needed to lure the wildfowl into range of the guns were made by professional gunners and after them by sportsmen for their own use. Among them were craftsmen who supplied both groups with superior decoys.

Decoy making began very early in Massachusetts. When asked who made the first decoy, Joel Barber, in his landmark book about decoys, quoted an 1842 story told by a Fire Island, New York, gunner about his great grandfather, who had been "one of the first settlers that come down from Massachusetts . . . the first man that made wooden stools for ducks." While we do

not take this story literally, it is significant in that it dates the earliest decoys to well before the American Revolution and traces their origin to Massachusetts. A historic parallel for the idea that Massachusetts was the source of decoy making comes from Virginia, where the finest decoys were made by the Cobb family, which, like the gunner's decoy-making great grandfather, had "come down from Massachusetts."

The decoy-making tradition was so strong and inventive in Massachusetts that it gave rise to a great diversity in form, size, and style. Massachusetts decoy makers made solid-bodied ducks and geese as well as hollow-carved examples, also with slats and canvas-covered frames. They made their decoys flat-bottomed but also round-bottomed. They made silhouettes, either singly or mounted together in rigs. Shorebirds were made solid and hollow, full-bodied and flat. They used cork, tin, and papier-mâché as well as wood; they even floated stuffed bags to lure ducks. And they made them in every form: floating, standing, preening, sleeping, hissing, calling, turned head, even some with mechanized movements, such as flapping wings. The sizes ranged from tiny three-inch-long peeps to six-foot-long loomers (giant slat geese).

In his *American Wildfowl Decoys,* Jeff Waingrow, a New Yorker, sums up the Commonwealth's decoy-making activities

Preening hollow-carved Canada goose with detachable neck, one of a rig of five made by or for Captain Osgood of Salem.

Captain Fabens had a rig of
hollow scoter decoys with
distinctive keels. The scoter
(below) has his brand; the
goldeneye (above) has no brand
but its form and identical keel
indicate it was Fabens's.

with the words "Massachusetts, whose carvers may have produced more beautiful decoys than any other state, represents one of the most fertile locales for development of the decoy arts."

Massachusetts honors this tradition with its annual duck stamp, the sale of which goes to support Ducks Unlimited's wildfowl conservation efforts. Other states and the federal government issue duck stamps, but only the stamps of Massachusetts annually picture decoys, a different one every year by a deceased Massachusetts decoy maker, known or unknown. Annual competition decides which decoy will grace the next year's stamp.

At the earliest stage of an area's decoy development, crude lures evolve into what can be called "floating sculpture." Three 19th-century makers (or owners) of decoys with artistic merit are known from eastern Massachusetts: two sea captains on the North Shore and a clerk in the Boston area. Decoys crafted with distinctive style were owned by the sea captains and the clerk, and the three are assumed to have been the makers, but it is possible that the decoys were made by some gifted unknowns, such as the captains' ship carpenters or cabinetmakers in the shop of the clerk's father. Until more is known about the making of these decoys, they will be considered to have been the work of their owners: captains Fabens and Osgood and the clerk Stephen Badlam.

Captain Samuel Fabens (1814–99) of Marblehead was skipper of the clipper ships *Golden Eagle* and *Challenger*. He was later known as Judge Fabens because when his sailing days were over he served as a trial justice. His decoy fame rests on a rig of scoters with the name "S.A. Fabens" branded into their bottoms; one of them is on the 1984 Massachusetts duck stamp. He is known to have had a rig of mergansers, and there is a goldeneye that looks like his work, but little else is known about his decoys.

Even less is known about Captain Osgood. His home port was Salem, and the date 1860 was a sort of midpoint in his life. All that remains are his splendid hollow-carved decoys (Canada geese and mergansers) and the oft-told legend of the Osgood goose decoys. It is said that he sailed west in 1849, and, while waiting in a California port for his return cargo, he carved five geese (three sentinels, a preener, and a feeder). Upon his return they were taken to a friend's hunting lodge up the Rowley

ABOVE: This early oldsquaw decoy, with an "S.B." brand on its bottom, was in the rig of Stephen Badlam. He may have made his decoys in the family shop, which closed in 1847, or the decoys may have been made for him at another time.

LEFT: Shorebirds by Lothrop Holmes. In front is a feeding yellowlegs; at left is the famous ruddy turnstone that was sold out of the Starr collection for $67,000, setting a record for the sale price of shorebird decoys at auction; at right is a black-bellied plover.

48

ABOVE: Joseph Lincoln, who was probably the finest carver of his time, a master of symmetry and smooth, spare forms.

OPPOSITE: Oldsquaw and yellowlegs decoys by Lincoln that display his elegant simplification of form.

River, where they remained for one hundred years. It's a nice story with absolutely no proof, but the geese are undeniably first rate and are now on display at the Shelburne Museum in Vermont. At least four Osgood mergansers are known, two at the Museum of American Folk Art in New York City and two in private collections in Michigan and Texas.

Stephen Badlam was unknown to decoy collectors until a rig of seven old duck decoys, branded "S.B" and with hand-forged nails holding the lead weights, came to auction in 1987. The consignor's father had acquired them in 1948 from a Dorchester lady and had hunted over them. The lady, Elizabeth Nichols, said she was the grand-niece of the maker, whom she identified as Stephen Badlam of Dorchester. Fortunately, a Badlam family genealogy enabled researchers to trace the line from Ms. Nichols back to Stephen Badlam (1822–92), her grandfather's younger brother, who had descended from a line of cabinetmakers also named Stephen Badlam. His grandfather (1751–1815) was famous not only as a lieutenant-major in the Continental Army and as a general in the Massachusetts militia but also as the maker of one of the most important pieces of early American furniture, the Derby chest-on-chest in the Garvan collection at Yale University's Art Gallery. His father (1779–1847) continued in the family furniture-making tradition, specializing in mirrors. The "decoy maker" broke the tradition, becoming a clerk and remaining a bachelor.

The Badlam ducks at auction—four oldsquaws, two black ducks, and a white-winged scoter—raised questions of who made them and when. Two of the oldsquaws were expertly made and two were less so. Were the former made by one hand and the latter by another, or were the latter a first effort and the former the result of experience, both by the same hand? Were they made in the father's shop before he died in 1847, and by whom? Did Stephen Badlam buy the good ones from some unknown craftsman and then try to duplicate them? Was the brand "S.B," which appears in a smaller version on a tea table from the family shop, used only on shop products before 1847, or was it used after the shop closed? These still unanswered

50

questions are typical of those that arise when good old decoys are discovered. In this case, whether Badlam made them or not, they are mid-19th-century decoys and will be known as the Badlam decoys unless evidence turns up pointing to another maker.

One of the greatest Massachusetts decoy makers was Lothrop Holmes (1824–99) of Kingston on the South Shore. He came from a family that ran a shipyard on the Jones River, which flows through Kingston into Plymouth Bay, and was superintendent of the local cemetery. His occupation apparently gave him ample time to go duck hunting and to make decoys. Along with his family's shipbuilding tradition, he inherited the craftsmanship that enabled him to turn out the very finest decoys that had been made up to his time. The Holmes reputation is based on five species he made: a rig of oldsquaws with canvas covering an ash frame that brings to mind an inverted ship's hull; splendid mergansers, a pair of which sold in 1985 for what was then a record auction price ($93,500); and three types of shorebird: mostly yellowlegs, including feeders, some black-bellied plovers, and a beautiful ruddy turnstone that holds the record ($67,000) for any shorebird sold at auction and is the subject of the 1979 Massachusetts duck stamp.

Also making decoys in Kingston was Holmes's nephew, Clinton Keith, a surveyor who made mergansers that are such good copies of his uncle's work that they put some attributions in doubt. Keith also made canvas-covered scoters.

Born in southeastern Massachusetts within three years of each other around the beginning of the Civil War were two of the greatest decoy makers who ever lived: Joseph Whiting Lincoln (1859–1938) of Accord in Hingham, and Anthony Elmer Crowell (1862–1952) of East Harwich on Cape Cod. This claim of greatness is not a personal bias, but is based on the collective opinion of those who attend decoy auctions in person or by phone and vote with their checkbooks.

TOP: Two forms of brant decoy by Joseph Lincoln. At left is a solid-body example; the one at right is self-bailing.

52

The highest price yet paid at a decoy auction was $319,000 for a Crowell preening pintail. The second highest was $205,000 for a Lincoln wood duck. And the third highest was $165,000 for a Crowell hissing, spread-wing Canada goose. All three were sold in 1986. So far nothing else has sold for six figures at a decoy auction.

In the three-year period 1986 to 1988, decoy prices at auction reached record levels, eight lots selling for over $70,000 each. Seven of them were made in Massachusetts (four by Crowell, two by Lincoln, and one by Lothrop Holmes). Those who bought them based their opinions on esthetics, certain that they were buying the best of their kind.

What brought these decoy makers to their high level of excellence? Their natural ability and the period into which they were born. They grew up in the heyday of market gunning, which came about in response to the cities' demand for meat and the lack of conservation laws to restrain the hunters. And gunners need decoys to attract wildfowl.

Both Crowell and Lincoln had been gunners and made decoys for their own use. Because they made decoys better than anyone else, they also made decoys for sale to market gunners and for the sportsmen who came along later. Both worked full- and part-time at making wildfowl, either decoys or decorative examples.

They knew each other and each other's work, but there is little evidence of one's influence on the other. Even so, Lincoln is known to have influenced Crowell to make miniatures. Crowell's earliest miniatures resembled Lincoln's but soon changed direction. All they had in common was the same high degree of craftsmanship. Otherwise, their decoys were different, Crowell's more natural and Lincoln's more stylized. Both were master carvers, with Lincoln perhaps having the edge. Both were fine painters, but Crowell was a master painter. Crowell moved from making decoys to making decoratives. Lincoln is not believed to have ever knowingly made a decorative, aside from his miniatures, but hunters impressed with the

53

OPPOSITE TOP: A. Elmer Crowell.

OPPOSITE BOTTOM: Early preening pintail made by Crowell for Dr. John C. Phillips; ca. 1914. This set a record price when sold at auction in 1986.

ABOVE: Two forms of Crowell shorebird, a feeding black-bellied plover decoy (left) and a yellowlegs (right) decorative for the mantel.

beauty of his decoys would occasionally pick one out for the mantel. They were innovative, but in different ways. Crowell's innovations were mainly in head style: preening, sleeping, feeding, turned, extended. Lincoln's heads were usually straight, but his body innovations ranged from solid to hollow (self-bailing), from canvas-covered to slat-type.

Joseph Whiting Lincoln of Accord in Hingham on the South Shore was perhaps the finest carver of his time. His decoys were simple, yet elegant. Critics marvel over the symmetry of his carvings. His decoys are smooth and spare, free of any excess touch. These days he would be called a "minimalist," and yet his decoys have beautiful form.

He is said to have cut cedar in the dead of winter to prevent the splitting of his decoys. It didn't work. So many Lincoln decoys have cracked bottoms that collectors routinely turn them over to smell the cedar emanating from the crack. The cracks seldom affect the value of the decoys.

Lincoln's painting was not natural, like Crowell's, but stylized, usually hard edged but sometimes brushed for feather effect. It looks deceptively simple, but close examination often reveals wondrously subtle effects, especially in his miniatures.

Joe Lincoln must have inherited his woodworking skills from his father, who was a cooper. He began to make decoys in his teens and was in his twenties when he sold his first. Whatever he put his hand to was made with skill, even the making of his own camera in his late thirties. He worked in shoe factories, where, like George Boyd of New Hampshire, he learned skills later used in making canvas-covered decoys. Convinced the

55

shoe-factory machines were producing shoddy work, he quit to work at home on clock repair, upholstering, and making decoys.

Captain Ellery H. Clark, Jr., whose family shot over Lincoln decoys for generations, summed up Lincoln as "a perfectionist. He never made a poor decoy." Lincoln must have been a crusty character, claiming he was too busy to smile for photographs and observing that "No man is worth more than fifty cents an hour," according to Clark. Although Clark included Lincoln "in the top three of the great old-time carvers and painters," George Ross Starr, Jr., the leading collector and historian of his day, went one step further. When interviewed on television and asked who was the greatest decoy maker, Starr answered without hesitation, "Lincoln!"

Joe Lincoln's major decoy output appears to have been Canada geese and coot (scoters). He made the geese in all sizes, from solid life-size to loomers (giant slat geese, some as long as six feet). He made three kinds of scoter: solid, self-bailing, and canvas-covered. He made brant both solid and self-bailing, one of which is on the 1989 Massachusetts duck stamp. Among his solid species were bluebills and black ducks, wigeon and wood ducks, mergansers and oldsquaws, ruddies and pintails. He was known to have made shorebirds because of a diary kept by a friend of his, but there was uncertainty about which shorebirds were Lincoln's. Some plovers and yellowlegs can now be identified as Lincoln's work, but a good many similar shorebirds are still listed as doubtful.

A. Elmer Crowell of East Harwich on Cape Cod was a master carver of solid, flat-bottomed decoys and decoratives. Most are made of cedar bodies with pine heads. Some have cork bodies with pine heads, but these are rare. He also made oversize slat goose decoys. Although Crowell worked to achieve a lifelike look, he didn't sacrifice strength at key points (bill, neck, and tail).

Crowell's earliest shorebird decoys are often breathtaking in their beautiful form and carving detail. When shorebird shooting was outlawed in 1918, legs were applied to some of these decoys, and they were put on mantels as decoratives. Crowell responded to this by making standing shorebirds, perched songbirds, game birds, and other decoratives for the market.

As fine a carver as he was, Crowell was a better painter, probably the best decoy painter of all time. He could bring a wooden bird to life with his natural feathery painting. The only painting lessons he ever had were said to have been two dozen at a dollar a lesson from a Massachusetts lady who summered on the Cape.

Elmer Crowell began early, making a rig of black ducks for his own use when he was 14. Details of his hunting and decoy making can be pieced together from his recollections

Sleeping Canada goose by A. Elmer Crowell. He is thought to have made this decoy around 1920 to show off his carving and painting skills.

Rare cork-bodied wigeon by Elmer Crowell. His cork decoys were made with pine heads.

56

written for Eugene Connett's book *Duck Shooting Along the Atlantic Tidewater* in 1946 when Crowell was 84. He recalls the days he worked at hunting camps, handling the live decoys, particularly the ten years (1898–1908) he managed Dr. John C. Phillips's camp at Wenham Lake in Beverly and a camp at Oldham Pond in Hanover. When live decoys were outlawed, it ended for Crowell the "good shooting," and he gave up hunting to begin "making decoys out of wood." He either forgot about the earlier decoys he made or he meant that now it was a serious business—more likely the latter.

Crowell tells of making decoys for the ten years 1908 to 1918 and then decoratives (ducks, shorebirds, songbirds, game birds, and miniatures). He said, "I worked at making decoys nearly forty years" and had to stop in 1943 when rheumatism affected his fingers. This means that he began making decoys in earnest while he was still working for Dr. Phillips, who was the first to buy one of his decoys. The decoys and decoratives he made for Dr. Phillips and Dr. Cunningham were among his very best, judging by the record prices they brought when they came to auction in the mid-1980s.

Crowell's earliest decoys had the most carving, and it extended right down to carved primaries, crossed wingtips, and tail feathers. They were unsigned and unbranded, but can be identified by their distinctive bold form, the rasp marks on the breast and back of head, and their wonderful paint. Some were slightly oversize.

Crowell began identifying his work around 1915 with a large oval brand on the bottom that read "A. Elmer Crowell / Decoys / East Harwich, Mass."

In the next stage, there was less carving, no wingtips, but continued tail feathers and rasping and still the oval brand. Later work was plain and uncarved as to details and was branded with the oval or, later, was stamped with a small rectangle that read similar to the oval. There were sometimes different grades for a species: his best work and a simple gunner's grade. But whatever the carving, there was always good paint, more or less detailed depending on the grade or perhaps on his mood at the time.

Crowell's son, Cleon, joined him upon his return from World War I and continued the work for two years after Crowell's death, so the later decoys and decoratives are suspect. Cleon's work was very good, so it takes a trained eye to distinguish between their work.

Distinguishing between the decoys Crowell made for gunning and the decoratives he made for the mantel is often a problem in some borderline cases. One way to tell the difference is to examine the bottoms. His decoys have painted bottoms and his decoratives shellacked bottoms, but not always.

A *Boston Globe* reporter showed great foresight when he interviewed Crowell in 1914 and showed some expertise as well when he pronounced Crowell's work "the best decoys produced by hand in any workshop."

Many decoy makers north of Boston followed in the tradition of the ship captains Fabens and Osgood, but three of them rise above the crowd because of the high quality of their decoys: Fred Nichols, Charles Hart, and Tom Wilson, all three born around 1860.

Fred Nichols (1854–1924) of Lynn is remembered today for two of the finest yellowlegs ever made, one of which (a feeder) graced the 1982 Massachusetts duck stamp.

Charles Hart (1862–1960) of Gloucester was a stone contractor who did not hunt much but made decoys, mostly of black ducks but also of mallards (solid and hollow, some hollows with no bottom boards) and Canada geese (standing hollow and floating solid). They were handsome decoys with intricate wing carving and detailed painting. Hart made them for his brother Nat and friends who were gunners. One of his younger friends, Henry Oakes (1900–73), copied his black-duck patterns and style so faithfully, sometimes improving upon them, that it is difficult to tell the difference between a Hart and an Oakes black duck unless you know what to look for. Later in life, Hart carved decoratives such as penguins from shelf-size to four feet high. One medium-size penguin was given in 1935 to Admiral Richard E. Bird by Atwater Kent, the early radio manufacturer. Hart made other decoys, such as goldeneyes and other decoratives (miniatures, and possibly wood ducks). One of the more interesting Hart decoys was a standing black duck that would flap its wings when the hunter pulled a string.

An exciting discovery was made in 1951 when the noted folk-art scholar Nina Fletcher Little came upon 13 unused shorebirds, ducks, and a Canada goose by Tom Wilson (1863–1940) of Ipswich. Wilson worked as a market gunner and guide, operating two gunning camps and a blind in Portsmouth, New Hampshire. He is said to be the subject of Frank Benson's etching *Old Tom*. Wilson decoys are as fine as they are rare.

The Hinckley family of Beverly consisted of dapper father George (1853–1929) and his three sons: Elmer (1885–1953), Harry (1895–1954), and Clarence (1896–1981). George is known to have made duck decoys, and Clarence is believed to have made the somewhat bulbous greater yellowlegs decoys. They are also known for their Canada geese, which appear to be copies of Lincoln's.

Marblehead, the home port of Captain Fabens, was alive with decoy makers. Research has unearthed at least 19 who followed in the tradition. Most notable were James Bowden

(1849–1910), whose scoters worked best and whose furniture brings a premium price in today's antiques market; Arthur Bamford (1864–1938), taxidermist and boatbuilder, who made oversize black ducks and goldeneyes; and William "Doc" Harris (1870–1938), a high-school custodian who is remembered for his wonderful mergansers.

Stephen Badlam may have been the earliest known South Shore carver (Dorchester is in the southern part of Boston, the dividing line), but there is no doubt that Lothrop Holmes and Joe Lincoln were the foremost decoy makers of this area. Another two dozen can be counted, including such outstanding decoy makers as the Baileys, the Burrs, and several from Duxbury.

The Bailey brothers of Kingston were Boston harbor pilots. Captain Clarence expanded the Lothrop Holmes technique of canvas stretched over an ash frame when in 1902 he built a rig of four-foot-long Canada geese, each with ten lateral ash splats covered by canvas. He is also known for his oversize hollow-carved oldsquaws and mergansers. All that is known of Captain Fred's decoy-making abilities is a canvas-covered Canada goose he made.

The finest decoys were often made by gifted unknowns. The Eskimo curlew at left was found in a carriage house in Easton; the goldeneye at right was found in Osterville.

The Burr family of Hingham is noted for making distinctive shorebirds with carved wings extended past a dropped tail. Three members of this family are said to have made decoys: brothers Elisha and Carl, and Carl's son Russ (1887–1955). The conventional wisdom is that these shorebirds are by Elisha and Russ, who copied his uncle's work; no decoys by Carl are known. A minority opinion, however, holds that Russ made them all. As they all appear to have been made by one hand, this opinion is growing. However, so long as birds said to be by Elisha bring higher prices than those said to be by Russ, more will be ascribed to Elisha, and the conventional wisdom will prevail. More is known about Russ because he lived closer to our time. He made shorebirds, some bluebills, a few content black ducks, and miniatures. Elisha's decoy making is largely supposition.

Research unearthed at least ten old-time decoy makers from Duxbury. The earliest may have been George Winslow,

about whom nothing is known except for a circa 1840 date. The other nine are either dated circa 1890 or have no dates. Duxbury's outstanding decoy maker was most likely David Goodspeed, who commuted to his "business" in Boston. He is said to have dressed as a businessman because he did not want it known that he was a bartender in a Boston hotel. Goodspeed made yellowlegs, goldeneyes, mergansers, and some remarkable oldsquaws with real oldsquaw tail feathers.

There is a rig of fine buffleheads by John Winsor, and a beautiful feeding dowitcher is attributed to William Henry Weston. Both were circa 1890 Duxbury carvers. A pair of the Winsor buffleheads and the feeding dowitcher are in the Museum of American Folk Art in New York.

Charles W. Thomas was a gunner from Assinippi who made somewhat elongated shorebirds around the turn of the century: long curlews, shorter black-bellied plovers (including one rig of balsa plovers), and other species.

OPPOSITE: Miniature wildfowl from Massachusetts (clockwise from lower left): Running red-breasted merganser and feeding canvasback by Crowell; pair of mallards by Russ Burr; pair of goldeneye and sleeping Canada goose by Joe Lincoln.

Two decoy makers who gunned with Lincoln were his neighbor Alfred Gardner, who made Canada geese, and Gordon Mann, a Rockland railroad man who made black ducks. Both worked in the Lincoln style.

Benjamin Franklin Torrey of Braintree was a blacksmith, wheelwright, and fiddle maker who made small shorebirds around 1860.

A fine rig of oversize hooded mergansers was made by Arthur Tuell of Westport Point, one of the southernmost towns of mainland Massachusetts. He repainted them at the beginning of hunting seasons, which reduced their present-day market value to collectors, who rate original paint higher than repaint even when it's been done by the original maker.

So dominant was Elmer Crowell in decoy making on the Cape that one tends to overlook the other carvers who worked there, especially the Nickersons and the Wrights. The Nickerson family of Cotuit produced decoys worthy of note, such as

ABOVE: Yellowlegs decoys from the North Shore. The decoy at left is by Fred Nichols of Lynn; at right is one by Tom Wilson of Ipswich; in the middle is one by the Hinckley family of Beverly, probably son Clarence.

60

the mergansers of Luther Nickerson. Among the finest mergansers made were those by a Cape carver named Wright. They were originally considered to be the work of Franklin Pierce Wright, but recent research has confirmed Captain Preston Wright as the maker. In addition to decoys by known makers, many decoys of unknown origin, some of them pretty wonderful, turn up on the Cape from time to time.

Henry Keyes Chadwick was one of the best decoy makers on Martha's Vineyard and is the best-known among collectors. In his pioneering and excellent book on the island's decoys, Stanley Murphy says there were other carvers in Chadwick's class and one better. We assume that one better was Ben Smith, Chadwick's teacher and the man he called the "best."

A great variety of decoys was made by this island's known and unknown carvers. Murphy listed the island's decoy output as mainly bluebills, then redheads, black ducks, goldeneyes, and brant, but the carvers reached their heights of expression in their racy mergansers, particularly those by Smith and Chadwick, and Frank Adams, Matthew Mayhew, Frank Richardson, and some gifted unknowns. Martha's Vineyard redheads were almost as stylish, particularly when made by Chadwick, Jim Look, and Ben Pease.

Although Murphy's book identifies 18 decoy makers on Martha's Vineyard, the following seven were selected for brief descriptions here because they are in Chadwick's class:

Frank Adams (1871–1944) was a carpenter and wheelwright in West Tisbury who made furniture, ship weathervanes, paperweights, doorstops, and decoys. Among his decoys were solid and hollow, flat-bottomed goldeneyes, mergansers, and wigeon, and solid shorebirds.

Henry Keyes Chadwick (1865–1958) was a professional decoy maker in Oak Bluffs, but he thought of himself primarily as a fancy poultry raiser and diploma inscriber. All his decoys were solid and flat-bottomed with a distinctive 1³/₄-inch-diameter flush-poured circular lead weight. It is estimated that Chadwick made around 2,000 decoys of every type made on the island, except for Canada geese and shorebirds; he made hundreds of bluebills, many of which were for the well-known Foote rig and are so stamped.

Matthew Mayhew (1847–1940) was a carriage painter of West Tisbury whose one rig of a dozen solid, flat-bottomed mergansers shows the neat, hard-edged lines expected of a painter in his trade.

Jim Look (1862–1926) was a shipbuilder, fisherman, and guide of West Tisbury. Among the 200 or so solid and hollow, flat- and round-bottomed decoys he carved were redheads and bluebills, and possibly some Canada geese.

Benjamin Warren Pease (1866–1938) was a builder, farmer, and fisherman of Oak Bluffs who made solid, flat-bottomed redheads and bluebills.

Frank Richardson (no dates, but contemporary with Ben Smith or earlier) was a fish buyer in Edgartown who made solid and hollow, flat- and round-bottomed mergansers, brant, and bluebills.

Benjamin D. Smith (1866–1946) was a carpenter and market gunner of Oak Bluffs who made solid and hollow, flat- and round-bottomed mergansers and canvasbacks that look more alive and alert than any other of the island decoys.

Because Nantucket was a rest stop for curlews and plovers on their long migrations, the making of shorebird decoys became a high art on this little island. The distinctive Nantucket shorebird decoys were usually hollow with whalebone bills and had carved wings and tails. They were mostly Eskimo curlews and golden plover in spring and fall plumage. The best were

OPPOSITE: Red-breasted merganser decoy made by Captain Preston Wright of Osterville.

ABOVE: Henry Keyes Chadwick made 2,000 decoys, but his earliest were his best. The brant (top) is one of a dozen he made; the red-breasted merganser (below) is one of his earliest known works.

62

the mid-19th-century birds made by the Folger family, specifically Franklin Folger and his son, Frank, Jr. Another fine shorebird decoy carver was Charles Fred Coffin, circa 1875. As Canada geese stopped at the island too, there were goose decoys and loomers, some by Wallace Gardner (1859–1937). It was an active decoy-making community, with about two dozen makers identified, plus examples by gifted unknowns.

Some decoy makers also made decoratives for the mantel, and some produced wildfowl miniatures. The outstanding Massachusetts makers of miniatures were Joe Lincoln, Elmer Crowell, and Russ Burr.

When Joe Lincoln was a boy, he carved his first wildfowl miniatures as toys. He continued to make them for fun as he grew older, but when orders started coming in, their production became part of his decoy-making business. Lincoln miniatures are small decoys. Paint patterns that are usually simple on the decoys become more complex on some of the miniatures. An examination under a bright light of one of his miniature black-duck bodies, for example, reveals a subtle, intricate feather pattern. Most Lincoln miniatures are rubber-stamped on the underside, reading "Joe Lincoln/Accord/Massachusetts."

Lincoln took credit for influencing Crowell to make miniatures, and Crowell's first efforts in this direction resulted in small decoys similar to Lincoln's. In time Crowell miniatures came to look like real ducks, geese, shorebirds, and songbirds. He made them in singles and in pairs, usually standing on the distinctive round mound with webbed feet painted on the mound, and in various positions of the live bird.

Crowell made miniatures in sets of 25: ducks and geese,

shorebirds, songbirds. Often the birds were numbered on their bases (side and bottom). Crowell's miniatures were beautiful, with a live look and some with a humorous touch such as the feeding canvasback and the tipsy bufflehead. Lincoln may have been the first to make miniatures, but Crowell was the most prolific. There are thousands of Crowell miniatures, so many that the later ones are often suspect, some probably made by his son, Cleon, and some by other imitators.

Crowell's miniatures can be dated by their bases and the markings on the undersides from the earliest, which were like decoys and unsigned, to standers on flat bases with signatures, then on to the round mounds with circular stamps, then blue paper labels, and finally rectangular impressions. It is thought that the handwritten species name in printed letters is Elmer's handwriting and that in script is Cleon's.

Crowell's miniatures were made in four sizes: micromini "decoys," medium (about 2 to 3 inches high), large (curlews and Canada geese, 5 to 5½ inches from bill tip to tail tip), and half life-size.

The Shelburne Museum in Vermont has an extensive display of Crowell miniatures and decoratives in addition to his decoys.

According to Russ Burr's niece, Burr carved miniatures strictly for his own pleasure and gave them to his friends. He must have had a lot of friends because he made a lot of lifelike miniatures, in singles and in pairs, standing and flying, most rubber-stamped "Russ P. Burr/Hingham, Mass." The Shelburne Museum in Vermont has a display of over forty miniatures by Burr.

OPPOSITE: Massachusetts is the
only state whose duck stamps
annually picture decoys. To
date, 16 decoys have been used.

ABOVE: Hollow stickup Canada
goose made in the sentinel
position by Charles Hart, a
stonemason of Gloucester.

CHAPTER 3:

NEW HAMPSHIRE

by Jackson Parker

The coastline of New Hampshire is less than 15 miles long. Sandwiched between the long, decoy-rich coasts of Maine and Massachusetts, it too produced decoys of note, not as many as its neighboring coastal states, but of great significance.

There was market gunning all along the New Hampshire coast to provide the Boston market, around fifty miles away, with meat for its restaurants and feathers for its hatmakers. The center of decoy making for the gunners appears to have been the town of Seabrook at the southern end, about two miles from the Massachusetts state line. Seabrook is known today as the site of a controversial nuclear plant, but once it was known as the home of the Seabrook carvers.

Among the Seabrook market gunners who made their own decoys were the Randalls, father and son. The father made decoys of one piece of pine with an oak bill for strength. He made them for himself and also sold them to other gunners for a few dollars apiece. His son, Herbert, followed in the tradition, gunning and making decoys for the family and other gunners. With the end of market gunning in the late 1920s, he turned to making decoys for sportsmen and decoratives for mantels. Herbert Randall used seasoned wood: cedar railroad ties, cedar and chestnut telephone poles, and fence posts before the days when they were creosoted and tarred. When he died in 1971, it was the end of the Seabrook carvers.

Contemporary with the Randalls was George Boyd, truly one of the greatest decoy makers and wildfowl miniaturists of all times. He lived his whole life in Seabrook (1873–1941) and produced beautiful and unique decoys and exquisite miniature game birds.

In the early days of decoy collecting, the 1960s and early 1970s, little or nothing was known of George Boyd, and his works came to auction labeled "unknown carver." We are indebted to the late collector-dealer Winthrop L. Carter of Portsmouth, New Hampshire, for most of what we know about George Boyd today. Win Carter wrote a monograph on Boyd's shorebirds in 1978 and produced a Boyd decoy show at the art galleries of the University of New Hampshire in 1979. It was at the opening of this show that he introduced me to Boyd's daughter, Mrs. Elvira Boyd Thompson, who told me stories about her father and his miniatures.

After grammar school, George Boyd worked in the Seabrook salt marshes, market gunning and farming. When he married Alice Fowler in his early twenties, he went to work in one of the local shoe factories, where he became a foreman. He built a shop behind his house for shoemaking homework and making decoys. Like Joe Lincoln in Massachusetts, who also did shoemaking, Boyd combined these skills to make canvas-covered decoys that are masterpieces of neatness and precision, not to mention their great form.

Boyd made both solid and canvas-covered black ducks and Canada geese. He made solid red-breasted mergansers, goldeneyes, and shorebirds (black-bellied plovers and yellowlegs). Boyd may have made bluebills, but we've never seen any. But I did see two extremely rare teal drakes, one blue-winged and one green-winged, probably the only teal he ever made.

When I saw these teal in a private collection, I asked the owner where they came from. He said that he had told the previous owner, who got them from Boyd, that if money was ever needed for a special project he would buy them. When he

OPPOSITE: George Boyd.

ABOVE: The only known teal ever made by George Boyd are these two drakes, green-winged (below) and blue-winged (above).

told me that one day the previous owner offered the teal in exchange for money for a trip for him and his wife, I said that I hoped it was at least a trip to China. "Exactly so!" said the new owner with a satisfied smile.

All Boyd's decoys, canvas-covered and solid, have the distinctive appearance of an alert, proud bird. Their heads are often slightly turned, adding to their lifelike look. Their form is graceful, almost to the point where some could be faulted for being too pretty. We have no record of how successful they were at luring wildfowl, but we do know of their great appeal to people, particularly collectors. Like Randall, Boyd used seasoned railroad ties and telephone poles made of cedar. Because he did not follow patterns in his carving, no two birds of a species by him are exactly alike.

The canvas-covered black ducks and Canada geese were made the same way: wooden head, neck, and breast connected to a body made of a frame covered with tightly drawn canvas tacked into place with a shoemaker's neatness, and a wooden tail (turned up for the blacks and flat out for the geese).

Boyd was a perfectionist in his painting as well as in his carving. His painting technique was to sand, prime, sand again, and paint. To reach every area, he worked with the sandpaper wrapped around his finger. His paint patterns were precise, almost geometric, and never overdone, a perfect complement to his carving.

Boyd made two types of shorebird—plover and yellowlegs—and they had two distinctive characteristics of form and paint. Their heads were flat-topped "beetleheads" with upturned bills. Their paint was an overall pattern of many short strokes done with brushes he made himself for that purpose.

Win Carter dated these shorebirds to around the turn of the century. They were sold at the Iver Johnson store in Boston, beginning in 1915, for an unbelievable $17.50 a dozen, a fraction of the $3,000 price the good ones average today. Carter noted that you rarely find Boyd's shorebirds with shot marks, "suggesting little use or meticulous care." Or perhaps they were "too pretty" to be hunted over and were displayed on mantels. Such early collectors as Adele Earnest tell of shying away from these shorebirds, which were unknown and cheap around thirty years ago, because they looked too new.

George Boyd retired from shoemaking by the early 1930s and devoted his time to making miniature wildfowl. His daughter estimates that he made around 700 of them, which he sold for 50 cents apiece. When she suggested he raise the price to a dollar, he rebuked her. He must have done so gently because she remembered him as patient and never angry.

We were able to see almost the full range of Boyd miniatures at a 1977 auction near Seabrook of the collection of Philip Drake of Rye Beach, New Hampshire, who had acquired it from Edward Papin, who is said to have encouraged Boyd to make miniatures.

There were over 150 miniatures in this collection, representing over 65 species of wildfowl. The catalogue opened with loons and closed with quail. There was about every species of duck, goose, and shorebird, swans and puffins, cormorants and turkeys. The top price was $800 for a great blue heron, and the average price was $217. Win Carter bought 31 minis for display at the University of New Hampshire exhibition planned for the following year.

Pair of red-breasted mergansers made by George Boyd; the hen is at left.

68

In form, Boyd's miniature ducks and geese were made as floating decoys, resembling Lincoln's. All other Boyd miniatures stood on two legs like natural birds, more like Crowell's, except that Crowell's miniatures were more natural in form and paint. Boyd's are more stylized, more of a geometric than natural line. Looking at these little birds and at photos of Boyd's large hands, it's hard to realize that he made them two-piece, joined at the neck. As for Boyd's paint, it's at its best in his miniatures, detailed and subtle.

Boyd never signed his decoys or miniatures, but he would write the species in pencil on the underside of his miniatures, using the old names like "baldpate" for wigeon and "northern diver" for loon.

Boyd's miniatures were sold in New York City by Macy's and Abercrombie & Fitch. He also gave some away as gifts. His daughter told me that in his sixties he liked to put some in his pocket and go to town to visit with the pretty shopgirls. When he found one that took his fancy, he'd give her a miniature as a gift. Think of all the Boyd miniatures now sitting on the knick-knack shelves of retired shopgirls in the area!

A collection of 43 miniatures, mostly pairs, turned up in the Midwest some ten or more years ago. They were said to have been made by Boyd for exhibition in the New Hampshire building at the 1939 New York World's Fair. They were acquired by Easterners, Win Carter taking half.

Values of George Boyd decoys reached a new high at a 1988 auction where his canvas-covered Canada goose in a swimming or hissing position sold for $38,500. The previous auction record for a Boyd decoy was $10,450 for a merganser at a 1986 auction. Boyd miniatures now sell for around $1,000 each, depending on rarity of species and condition, a Boyd loon with some crazing of paint selling for $2,700 at a 1987 auction.

Fifteen years after George Boyd died, the Seabrook carving tradition was taken up by the Beckman family for a decade. Harvey Beckman made shorebird decoratives from 1956 until his death in 1963. His son, Emery, continued the work until his death in 1966.

OPPOSITE: *George Boyd made two kinds of shorebird, black-bellied plover (left) and yellowlegs (right).*

ABOVE: *Boyd also made two kinds of black duck, canvas-covered (below) and solid body (above).*

LEFT: *These Boyd miniatures include a yellowlegs (left), pair of wigeon (center) and Canada goose (right).*

CHAPTER 4:

VERMONT

by Dr. Loy S. Harrell

Quietly guiding their canoes close along the shoreline, "thirty to forty savages" accompanied by Baron Lahotan eased out of what is now called the Missisquoi River into Lake Champlain. Paddling into a large, marshy cove, the Indians quickly assembled a number of "floating huts" made of branches and leaves of trees. Three to four of the "savages" entered each hut.

For a decoy they had the skins of geese, bustards, and ducks, dyed and stuffed with hay. The two feet being made fast with two nails to a small place of light plank, which float around the hut. The place was frequented by wonderful numbers of geese, ducks, bustards, teals, and an infinity of other waterfowls—see the stuffed skins swimming with their heads erected as if they were alive. They repair to the same place and so give the savages an opportunity of shooting them either flying or upon the water, after which the savages get into their canoes and gather them up.

The French explorer Baron Lahontan cannot have imagined the significance of this written account, which he made in 1687 while exploring North America: it is the first recorded mention of the use of decoys on this continent and thus designates Lake Champlain as historically important in what is now considered a major folk art—the decoy.

There is little doubt that American Indians employed decoys to hunt waterfowl. Various tribes inhabited what is now Vermont, notably the Abnakis, but no recorded Indian lore or artifact documents the use in Vermont of decoys.

Vermont presents a wonderful expanse of water and ideal coastlines on which to hunt. Lake Champlain was discovered in 1609 by Samuel De Champlain, and the first white settlement was on Isle La Motte in the northeast corner of the lake in 1666. The lake is approximately 110 miles in length and extends

from Whitehall, New York, in the south into the province of Quebec, Canada, in the north. It covers a surface of 440 square miles and forms the boundary between New York and Vermont for much of its border.

Today, significant wildlife management areas (WMA) stretch the length of the lake on both the New York and Vermont sides. The oldest such area in Vermont is the Sandbar, established in 1920 and situated next to the "entrance" to a group of islands that lay off Vermont's shoreline. These islands—South Hero, North Hero, Grand Isle, and Isle La Motte—have always produced the major abundance of waterfowl for the gunner. Demands for conservation required opening of other WMAs, the largest being Dead Creek WMA in Addison, Vermont, covering 2,578 acres. This particular WMA is the major stopover for thousands of migratory Canadian and snow geese, which travel between Canada and the southern United States. Besides geese, all major puddle ducks, including mallards, blacks, pintails, teals, and wood ducks are found on the lake. Divers, including goldeneye or whistlers, redheads, bluebills, canvasbacks, and mergansers, are also seen.

It is of little wonder then that waterfowl hunting has been so important on the lake for over 300 years. Obviously, as the number of hunters increased, so did the demand for decoys. These were made from locally available material, such as cedar, pine, and basswood.

Most were made by local craftsmen, many of whom were carpenters and boatbuilders. Design was influenced by artistic inclination, ethnic origin, and use. Specifically, those decoys originating from carvers near the Canadian end of the lake have the French-Canadian influence; that is, the heavy wing and head carving characteristic of decoys from the St. Lawrence River area of Quebec. More notable, however, is the use of a simple, conservative style, epitomized by the decoys of

OPPOSITE: *Vermont whistler decoy by Frank Owen.*

ABOVE: *Goldeneye decoy and miniature by David Harrington.*

George Bacon (1861–1925), from Burlington, Vermont. His decoys are now considered the most important from Lake Champlain both to the collector and the historian. With their smooth lines and simple paint style, Bacon's decoys are part of the most important collection of decoys in the world, housed at the Shelburne Museum, Shelburne, Vermont.

However, George Bacon decoys are not the first documented on the Vermont side of Lake Champlain. Also housed in the Shelburne Museum collection are decoys by Frank Owen of South Burlington, Vermont. Owen is thought to have been a stonemason living in Vermont during the mid-19th century. A "Stone House," reconstructed on the grounds of the Shelburne Museum, is attributed to this artisan. Only five of Owen's decoys are known, one being pictured on page 46 of "Decoys of Shelburne Museum," 1961. To the knowledge of this author, Owen's decoys are the oldest documented decoys attributable to North America.

Starting with Owen and extending to the present period, over eighty decoy carvers have been documented on Lake Champlain, the majority being on the Vermont side of the lake. Some of the more notable ones are Wellington Aiken (1879–1954), a 1901 graduate of the University of Vermont and later a professor emeritus in English; Archibald "Archie" Bodette (1900–82), West Addison, Vermont, who made over four hundred whistlers; Adolfo Comolli (1894–1965), Barre and Hog Island, Vermont; Phillip Gregory (1911–69), Essex Junction, Vermont, who carved beautiful decoys; William Austin Hill (1873–1951), Isle La Motte, Vermont, a descendent of early 18th-century settlers who was minister of the Methodist church on the island, which was built in 1843; Charles "Tom" Holloway (b. 1920), Monkton, Vermont, a commercial carver who made thousands of decoys for sporting-goods stores; Charles W. Kirby (1879–1958), Burlington, Vermont, a member of the Modern Woodsmen of America, boatbuilder and prolific decoy carver; Rupert King (1892–1972), Burlington, Vermont, who carved large, hollow decoys with relief patterns; Ford Patno, (b. 1905), Burlington, Vermont, one of the "old-timers"; Thornton Penrose, Jr. (b. 1913), Burlington, Vermont, who, in 1930, began carving many stylized, well-constructed decoys; Royal Perry (1916–83), Burlington, Vermont; Gerald Tremblay (b. 1918), Alburg Springs, Vermont, who made working decoys for gunners and stores throughout the country. Tremblay claims to have made 5,000 decoys, which are characterized by their chipped carving. Raymond Poquette, (1905–81), Alburg, Vermont, a former state's attorney and guide who raised Chesapeake Bay retrievers, made over 400 decoys and contributed articles to *Field and Stream;* and David Harrington, (1934–88), Underhill, Vermont. Harrington was a noted historian of the folklore of the decoy. His prolific output of decoys prompted him to open a shop to sell his wares. Unfortunately, he contracted diabetes, lost his eyesight, and died of complications in 1988. He carved hundreds of decoys, marked by many styles and exquisite paint. Included were over one hundred miniatures.

Undoubtedly, new carvers will come along to perpetuate this great folk art—the decoy—and the tradition of the Vermont carvers of Lake Champlain will remain.

Goldeneye decoy by George Bacon, considered the most important carver of the Lake Champlain area.

CHAPTER 5:

RHODE ISLAND

by Jackson Parker

Jewellike miniature pairs by Allen J. King. Clockwise from top left are bluebills, black ducks, green-winged teal, and harlequin ducks.

Little Rhode Island is just over 1,000 square miles in area, and knifing up from the south into its heart (Providence) is Narragansett Bay, which is about one quarter the size of the state. One would think that all that coastline would have produced many market gunners and their need for decoys, but it just didn't happen here. Not even the strong decoy traditions of its coastal neighbors, Connecticut and Massachusetts, had any influence. The only known duck shooting on the Bay was done by well-to-do sportsmen of Newport and other coastal towns who bought their decoys from nearby carvers like Elmer Crowell of Cape Cod or ordered them from faraway factories like Mason of Detroit.

However, one name in wildfowl art stands out in this state, and it's not that of a decoy maker but of a wildfowl miniaturist, Allen J. King of North Scituate (fewer than ten miles west of downtown Providence). His miniatures are unique in that they are one half the size but twice as detailed as those of the other great New England miniaturists, Burr, Crowell, and Lincoln of Massachusetts, Boyd of New Hampshire, and Gilley and Morse of Maine.

King miniatures are jewellike in their precision and beauty. He made ducks, geese, and other game birds in singles and pairs, mounted on burl bases, or in shadow boxes of wildfowl scenes, or on plaques, all signed "A.J. King." He was a naturalist who worked with his son. While Allen specialized in wildfowl, son James carved animals, especially dogs.

The work of A. J. King was largely unknown until a major collection of his work was donated to the Massachusetts Audubon Society in the mid-1970s. The society's questionable decision to sell the collection resulted in it being consigned to Crossroads of Sport, a sporting-arts store in midtown Manhattan. As there were no or few sales at the prices being asked, the collection was withdrawn and consigned to the Skinner auction gallery in Bolton, Massachusetts, where it was sold along with Crowells and other decoys, decoratives, and miniatures in November 1975. There were 60 pairs of wildfowl, including 31 of ducks and geese, 21 singles, 13 shadow boxes, and one magnificent plaque of 17 raptors (birds of prey), and other items.

All those wonderful miniatures in one place was both stimulating and depressing, stimulating to the eye and depressing because of the prices. The Skinner prices were less than half the Crossroads asking prices, and the Crossroads asking prices, while considered high then, were about half of what they sell for today.

Current values of King miniatures are difficult to determine because they rarely come on the market. Recent private sales of pairs were as high as $1,100 (gadwalls); recent auction sales of pairs were as low as $468 (woodcocks). Today's prices are much higher than the 1975 Skinner prices: pairs $100–225, singles $65–225, shadow boxes $150–375, and the raptors plaque $750. Those prices are ancient history.

CHAPTER 6:

C O N N E C T I C U T

by Dixon MacD. Merkt

AMERICAN DECOYS

THE CENTENNIAL BROAD-BILL
BENJAMIN HOLMES ~ MAKER, STRATFORD, CONN.

1876

Courtesy of Capt. Charles D. Wicks.
(Young Cappie)
STRATFORD, CONN.

Joel D. Barber, 1923.

Evidence indicates that decoys were neither brought here from Europe nor based on European traditions. The Continent used other methods to attract and capture waterfowl. In fact, Europe learned about the decoy from us. To quote Adele Earnest, "Of all our folk art none is more American than the decoy. Indigenous to this country, popular in use, created out of native woods and material formations—what could be more expressive of the people, their needs and their individuality?" Decoys are truly American folk art.

During the 17th century, Indians along the East Coast used duck skins stuffed with hay to attract waterfowl. Over the years, our innovative ancestors improved upon those early lures. By the last half of the 18th century, a new industry had evolved and matured called market gunning. Market gunners shot scores of birds a day for both home and restaurant. The great kills common to the extensive marshes of the South Shore of Long Island, the Barnegat Bay area of New Jersey, and the Chesapeake created a large demand for decoy makers who could produce in quantity.

Thus, the rise of the market gunner brought a tremen-dous increase in the production of decoys. The development of the breech-loading gun (the shotgun in particular) coupled with rapid population expansion made it possible and accept-able for the market gunner to feed a hungry America.

Just as guns, boats, blinds, and decoys were an essential part of the hunter's equipment, his demand for effective equip-ment brought about the development of a trade that has made the collecting of decoys possible.

By 1913 the government felt compelled to respond to the mass slaughter of ducks that had been going on for about fifty years. The Federal Migratory Bird Act of that year prohibited all spring shooting, all night shooting, and the shipment of birds. In 1918, the Migratory Bird Treaty Act between the United States and Canada protected wildfowl over the entire range of their migratory flight and brought an end to shore-bird shooting.

Connecticut forms the northern coast of Long Island Sound. This large body of water and the rivers feeding into it have had major economic and social impacts on the people living along its shores. Shipbuilders, oystermen, gunsmiths,

OPPOSITE: Page with sketch of early decoy type from the notebook of Joel Barber.

and pattern makers in the textile industries, familiar with the sound and the rivers, were the men who became involved in duck hunting and decoy making.

The compact Connecticut marshes could not yield the great kills necessary for market hunting. Though a few gunners did hunt for market, sending their birds to New Haven, Hartford, Bridgeport, and New York, the pressure by the market gunners for large numbers of decoys to support their daily activity never developed. Here, the occasional shooter and sportsman predominated. Not seeking large kills, they wanted decoys of quality, not quantity. Connecticut carvers made decoys for their own use or the use of their friends. Seldom did they carve for sale. On the whole, they were gentlemen carvers. Typically, they provided quality birds in limited numbers.

As in other geographical areas, a distinctive look evolved over the years that says, "made in Connecticut." Regardless of their origin within the state, three basic characteristics are normally found in decoys made by Connecticut carvers. First, a full breast that noticeably slopes away from the bow of the decoy. Second, a pronounced tail, which had two purposes—to

ABOVE: "Noank" merganser; ca. 1900. This attractive decoy may be the work of Ira Baker, a turn-of-the-century carver known to have made decoys with unusual head positions.

78

provide a stern "handle" to hold when the gunner was picking up his rig after a hunt and to provide a turning spot for the anchor line, which was stored on the decoy. Hunters accomplished this by wrapping the line across the back of the bird in the shape of a figure eight. The base of the neck became the top of the eight and the tail the bottom. Any excess line was looped around the neck before the circular anchor was placed over the head. The third characteristic was the location of the platform on which the head rested. It was normally located below the highest point on the back and parallel to the surface of the water.

Prior to the Civil War, the hunters used heavy, low-floating wooden birds referred to as "rocking horses." The last part of the 19th century saw the evolution of the decoy into a beautiful, abstract, and refined shape, due largely to the talents of Albert Laing (1811–86) and his followers.

From about 1860 to 1925, the making of decoys was at its height. The demand for decoys was so strong the local gunners and carvers could not keep pace. Thus, between 1880 and 1920, several decoy factories appeared and flourished.

Though not an important source to market gunners, factory-made decoys frequently found their way into the rigs of the casual hunter, often referred to as a "sport." The market gunner felt his own handiwork, or that of a local friend coupled with local knowledge of the hunter's particular needs, resulted in the creation of superior decoys. Factory-made decoys are distinguished from handmade by two features. First, the bodies of factory decoys were made by being turned on a lathe. Second, the maker advertised his wares for sale to the general public.

Several decoy factories flourished in Connecticut. Tux

Ducks, located in Madison, never enjoyed national recognition but did supply inexpensive, serviceable, and effective cork-body decoys that were used by many local hunters.

Located in Old Saybrook and founded by Ted Mulliken in 1939, Wildfowler Decoys enjoyed an outstanding reputation for quality gunning decoys. This fine reputation was enhanced by Ted's success as a competitive decoy carver. His decoys won numerous blue ribbons in the professional machine-made and handmade class at the Sportsmen's Shows during the 1940s in New York City.

The Wildfowler Decoy Company made a variety of ducks, but black ducks and broadbill were the most common. The bodies were made with either balsa or pine. The pine bodies were occasionally hollowed out. Most important to the collector, however, was the circular brand. Besides having the company name, the brand states the decoy's origin—Old Saybrook. Not all of Ted's decoys carry the brand. Its omission does not necessarily mean an inferior decoy. In 1957, a fire destroyed the building and brought an end to Ted's involvement with Wildfowler Decoys. Subsequently, the name passed through several owners. All have maintained the classic Wildfowler look, but all production was outside Connecticut. The company's departure from Old Saybrook brought an end to the original Wildfowler Decoy Company. From a collector's standpoint, the decoys made in Old Saybrook have more value.

The steps in constructing a handmade decoy and the tools used were simple. A small hatchet, drawknife, spokeshave pocketknife, wood rasp, and sandpaper were all that was needed. Though many decoy bodies were solid, some carvers preferred to make them hollow. The hollow bodies were often constructed of two pieces of wood of equal thickness pinned

together and then shaped to size. After achieving the desired shape, the pins were removed, the two halves hollowed out with a gouge or adz, and then nailed together with white lead and caulking rope in the joint to keep it watertight. More delicate work, using a pocketknife and sandpaper, was employed in the carving of the head.

American decoy carving was considered utilitarian. Again quoting Adele Earnest, "Not all the carvings are good, worth saving, or deserving of the name of art. Thousands are not—they are simply blocks, awkward and expressionless. The astonishing fact is that so many are excellent." Adele Earnest goes on to say, "The one question was and is: Does the decoy catch the bird in body and spirit? If it does, we may truly call it art." In decoys, Joel Barber found exciting examples of form following function. Simplicity, not exact duplication, was the mark of the great decoy makers. As the father of decoy collecting, Mr. Barber talked and wrote endlessly on the subject. His book *Wild Fowl Decoys*, published in 1934, started the decoy collecting craze that has driven the value of fine decoys to incredible heights.

As the collector becomes more knowledgeable, an objective evaluation guides him in his acquisitions. What are the most important factors in making an evaluation of a decoy? Aesthetics is the most general factor. However, the decoy will have a different appeal to each individual, as individual tastes differ. Yet each will receive his or her aesthetic impressions from the sculpture, paint, condition, origin, and rarity. Origin, or maker, is usually the most clear-cut evaluation. If the maker of the decoy is known and admired in the collecting world, the decoy has more value than one of comparable quality but whose origin is unknown. Regarding sculpture, most people

OPPOSITE: Albert Laing broadbill drake; ca. 1865. Laing believed an effective gunning rig should include birds in a variety of poses.

ABOVE: Albert Laing surf scoter drake; ca. 1865. Like many Laing decoys, this was repainted by Shang Wheeler after it joined his rig.

have some artistic sensitivity and can judge the shape or form of a decoy. Does it have pleasing lines, is it symmetrical, is it graceful? Are the body and head in proportion? Is the bill well carved? Paint: is it original? Is it crude or light and beautiful? Is it worn, is it an overpaint? Another important factor is condition. Perfect condition means unused original condition —often referred to as "mint." Worn paint, gouges or cracks on the surface, broken bill or tail, unattractive repairs, all detract from the condition. Rarity frequently has to do with species. A wood duck by an important carver would be a rare decoy. Wood-duck decoys are seldom found because the friendly woodies are attracted to any decoy setting on the water. Other rare species are ruddy ducks, ringbills, or eiders.

The first decoy was collected in 1918 by Joel Barber. Found in an old sail loft in Babylon, New York, it quickly received a place of honor on the mantel of his home. With this acquisition began the pastime of collecting decoys or "floating sculpture," as he so aptly called them. In the 1940s, after having spent his working years as an architect in New York City, Joel Barker retired to Wilton, Connecticut. It was here that the first decoy museum on record was founded. Located in an old dilapidated chicken coop on the property of his son, David, Joel Barber established the Shanty Museum of Old Decoys. After his death, the entire collection, including his drawings and other documentary material, was purchased by the Webb

80

family for their museum of American art in Shelburne, Vermont, where the collection remains today on public display.

Up until the mid-1960s a small closely-knit group of collectors pursued their hobby in a low profile, swapping and trading. Highly desirable birds were exchanged for other birds—rarely did cash change hands.

It was William J. Mackey, Jr., who was most influential in ushering the hobby into its current level of sophistication. Mackey's book *American Bird Decoys*, published in 1965, was an instant success and remains an important reference even to today's expert collector.

Over the years, oystermen had learned that spawning oysters preferred to sit on clean and "soft" Housatonic oyster shells. During the latter part of the 19th century, rivermen of the Housatonic who called themselves "shellers" began foraging the rivers and creeks and then storing their shells on the banks of the Housatonic. In the spring, the shells would be transferred by boat to the spawning grounds in the sound and on eastern Long Island.

More than any other, the oyster industry was most influential in spreading decoy-carving knowledge. These oystermen, who were often duck hunters, would travel Long Island Sound by boat, talking hunting, fishing, oystering with the local shore residents. Their familiarity with local currents, tides, and weather made an intimate knowledge of nature and waterfowl. When the talk came to duck hunting and decoys, the men from the Housatonic were proud to elaborate on their achievements in decoy making. Others listened with interest, for all the gunning along the shore was subject to the same conditions. The construction and design features proven successful on the Housatonic River, its tidal marshes and swift currents in Long Island Sound adjacent to the mouth of the river, were enthusiastically applied by the hunters of the Connecticut and Mystic rivers as well as the many small rivers piercing the coastline.

By disseminating their decoy knowledge to fellow carvers, the men of Stratford were most influential in the development of a classic look that says "made in Connecticut." We must not, however, allow the success and notoriety of the Stratford school overshadow the achievements of the Connecticut River school, Mystic River school, and isolated carvers of distinction.

During the 1800s the area of the Mystic River at the eastern end of Long Island Sound was a hub of economic activity. Situated about halfway between Boston and New York, the area prospered from the flourishing industries of ship building and fishing. Ducks were plentiful, and many of the local fishermen and boatbuilders enjoyed spending their free time in pursuit of waterfowl, using black-duck, broadbill, scoter, merganser, and occasionally goldeneye decoys. Unique to this area was the fact that hunters of the Mystic River actively pursued mergansers. To find numerous shell-drake decoys is therefore not surprising. The slender bodies and long narrow bills of this diving duck provide an interesting and exciting subject.

The largest and most picturesque river feeding into Long Island Sound is the Connecticut River. With its headwaters just south of the Canadian border, this mighty river carves its way through the heart of New England. Many factories were founded and flourished along its banks. Farther south near the mouth of the river, major social and economic impetus came from farming, fishing, boatbuilding, and recreation.

Essex, a lovely riverfront community located about five miles north of the mouth of the river, has produced fine decoys carved by fishermen or carpenters employed by local boat-

BELOW: Ben Holmes black duck; ca. 1875. Holmes succeeded in making a large number of quality decoys that were well accepted by local gunners. Many were still in use in the 1960s, a tribute to their quality.

OPPOSITE: Black duck by Shang Wheeler; ca. 1940. Blue-ribbon winner at the 1941 National Sportsmens Show, this is Shang— a master of black ducks—at his best.

yards. Normally solid in construction, the decoys from the Connecticut River school have a distinctive look. On decoys in other parts of Connecticut, the breast was fully expressed in the body and the base of the head set back from the breast and "faired" into the body. The Connecticut River school, on the other hand, completed the breast by utilizing the base of the head. This was done by making the base full and locating it as far forward as possible. The body and base of the head were then shaped together to form the breast. Black ducks, broadbill, goldeneye, and mergansers were the species most frequently carved on the Connecticut River.

Sam Collins, Jr. (1856–1948), a sea captain by trade, is credited with fine decoy carving and fine-tuning the Connecticut River look. His friends Bertram Tooker and Ned Pratt (1885–1970) also produced distinctly "Connecticut River" decoys.

A number of very attractive decoys have been found in Deep River, a town just north of Essex, but at this time very little is known about their origin.

Of the three schools, the Housatonic River school is the most important. Decoys from this school are held in high esteem and are among the most valued of all decoys. Included in this group are Albert Laing (1811–86), Ben Holmes (1843–1912), and Shang Wheeler (1872–1949).

From the time of the Civil War, the hunters of the Houstatonic evolved into a concentrated gunning society bound together by a compulsive desire to accept and follow the general decoy-making principles of the area.

Laing introduced and developed the basic style. Ben Holmes, outliving Laing by about fifteen years, maintained the momentum of the school. During the last few years of Holmes's tenure, a new generation of carvers was developing its skills. Shang Wheeler became the leader of this third generation.

Whether gentlemen of leisure, skilled craftsmen, or old salts, they developed a common pride in their decoys. And since the majority of Stratford carvers worked for personal pleasure rather than profit, they showed an unusual willingness to share the secrets of their craft. Thus, the general principles of decoy making pioneered by the three leading Stratford carvers gained wide acceptance in the area. The work of Roswell Bliss (1887–1967), Willard C. Baldwin (1890–1979),

Louis Rathmell (1898–1974), C. Ralph Welles (1895–1978), and Reginald I. Culver (1897–1975), plus a host of lesser-known carvers, demonstrates the profound impact of the Stratford style. As decoy historian William J. Mackey, Jr., once commented, the spirit that moved them was never "how many, but how good!"

What separated Laing, Holmes, and Wheeler from their comrades was certainly not the quantity of their work. Neither Wheeler nor Laing produced in excess of five to six hundred decoys; only Holmes, who supplied market gunner Cappy Wicks, had anything approaching large-scale production.

What is noteworthy about Laing, Holmes, and Wheeler is that each made fundamental contributions to the design and the look of the Stratford school. They are to decoy carving what trend-setting artists are to stylistic schools. They made the major breakthroughs, while the others followed in their paths. In decoy carving as in painting, writes Mackey, "The copy always honors the original." Holmes, Wheeler, and their imitators all followed the basic ideas that Laing pioneered. Only Wheeler's work could be said to surpass Laing's in quality of appeal.

After Albert Laing's arrival in Stratford, the bodies of most Housatonic decoys were made of two pieces of wood. This was done so the carver could make the body hollow. Although hollowing was technically more difficult and, of course, more time consuming, it was the preferred method of the Housatonic carvers. They had several good reasons for using the technique. The birds were lighter in weight and rode higher in the water, making them much easier for the ducks to see. Furthermore, gunners preferred carrying baskets with a couple dozen hollow decoys to carrying the much heavier solid decoys.

During the last half of the 19th century, within the Housatonic school, another look became popular, the "Milford" look. Some speculate it was popular with the Stratford carvers who were not influenced by Laing and Holmes. Others theorize that these decoys originated on the eastern bank of the Housatonic. Some decoys of this type have been found with the brand "S and S." These were made by the Smith brothers from Milford.

The birds of the classic Housatonic school can be easily identified by certain characteristic features: elongation and

82

sleekness in body shape, slimmer in the forward third before flairing, like shoulders, into the main body section. In contrast, the "Milford" decoys are ovoid and chunky. The body line from the breast aft is continuous, not interrupted by shoulders. Furthermore, the "Milford" tail is short and stubby compared to the sleek, long tail characteristic of the classic look.

A native of Rahway, New Jersey, Albert Laing was 52 years old when he settled in Stratford. Judging from his will and testament, and the home he lived in, we can assume he was a man of some wealth. Exactly why he came to Stratford is unknown. However, it is generally agreed among decoy historians that Albert Laing did the most to establish the Stratford look.

As was customary in New Jersey, Albert Laing made most of his decoys from two pieces of wood of equal thickness. Before assembling the body, he would hollow them out. The two halves were then brought together with white lead and copper nails. Careful analysis of Laing's decoys vividly illustrates the imagination, skill, and artistry of this innovator. This gentleman carver set the stage on which all future Stratford carvers performed. The slim, distinctive tail, elongated body, and full breast of all his decoys were designed with a purpose in mind. The current was swift at the mouth of the Housatonic. The slim body and full breast reduced resistance to the current while simultaneously adding buoyancy to the "bow." This extra buoyancy was important in the current, which had a tendency to make the bow ride low in the water. As the current swept by the decoy, it would put a strain on the anchor line, thus causing the bow to dip. The full breast and elongated body therefore helped to keep the decoy "trim."

That an effective gunning rig should include birds in various postures was Laing's greatest contribution. Most carvers did not attempt to make decoys simulating turned-head sleeping ducks. It was just too difficult. This was not the case for Albert Laing. He must have enjoyed making them. Compared to the output of other carvers, Laing's ratio of sleepers to straight heads was unusually high. They are sculpturally spectacular. The peace and tranquility these sculptural beauties brought to a rig must have been equal to their artistry.

Demonstrating what a man could accomplish when he attended to the aesthetics as well as the practical qualities of a decoy, Laing had a profound impact on the history of Connecticut carving.

The gentlemen decoy makers of Connecticut were not prolific. Most concentrated their production on black ducks, broadbill, and scoters, the birds most common to the area. Laing, however, was known to have made canvasbacks, pintail, and swans. Laing's total output probably did not exceed 200 decoys. In fact, his will stated that his rig of 111 decoys was to sell for $45.

After Laing's death, the leadership in Connecticut carving passed to Ben Holmes. A carpenter by trade, Holmes apprenticed under Laing. By his attention to quality of construction, sculptural form, and utility, Holmes was most effective in solidifying the innovations associated with Laing. Holmes made a decoy that looked pleasing to the hunter's eye, was durable, and worked well. The use of his decoys by local hunters continued well into the 1960s. This alone offers quite a tribute to his craftmanship.

Holmes was one of Stratford's more prolific carvers. To estimate his total production is difficult, but a production reaching into four figures is realistic. As a carpenter, Holmes did not enjoy the leisure time that wealth allowed Laing to pursue. To supplement his income, Holmes often took orders for decoys. As a result, many of his birds have a similar look, normally with the head in a straightforward position. Structurally, Holmes's method of construction differed. Where Laing made many of his hollow bodies from two slabs of equal thickness, Holmes consistently used two unequal pieces, hollowing out the larger body piece and then nailing on a 5/8-inch-thick bottom board.

The quality of his work, along with assuring the popularity of the Connecticut look, was acknowledged in 1876 at the Philadelphia Centennial Exposition. Holmes had entered a dozen broadbill decoys for competition. Records of the competition indicating other competitors are not available, but we do know that Holmes's "Centennial Broadbill" won top honors.

This event alone guaranteed Ben's reputation along with bringing widespread recognition to the Stratford style.

The Holmes style continued long after his death in 1912. By purchasing all the unfinished blocks from Holmes's widow, Reg Culver, a leading third-generation Stratford carver, started his own carving career influenced by the style of Holmes's decoys. Two other contemporaries of Culver, both fellow Connecticut pattern makers, Willard Baldwin and Roz Bliss, copied Holmes's pattern in their own work. Though the Holmes style has been copied by many carvers, few have managed to recapture his strong interpretation of form in cutting out his basic body patterns. Holmes took pains to eliminate any sharp angles and rounded off the prominent lines to create a very pleasant, yet simple decoy incorporating numerous curves.

By the early 1900s, several young men were about to swell the ranks of the Housatonic school. As a group, these men represent the third generation of Stratford carvers. The leader of this new generation was unquestionably Charles E. "Shang" Wheeler.

Shang knew the decoys of the Housatonic because he had grown up using them and had hunted with many of the old-timers who made them. He drew upon the traditions of largely anonymous pre–Civil War carvers and upon the work of the two great Stratford decoy makers who preceded him, Albert Laing and Benjamin Holmes. He personally melded Laing's artistic flair and Holmes's practical and sculptural sense with his own extraordinary skills. To the next generation of carvers—Roz Bliss, Ralph Welles, Reg Culver, Willard Baldwin, and others—he was a friend and mentor. Shang made himself readily available to all members of the area's hunting and carving fraternity. He took real pleasure in assisting newcomers. If their decoys began to resemble his (a perplexing

OPPOSITE TOP: Shang Wheeler
mallard hen and drake; 1940.

OPPOSITE BOTTOM: Wheeler
shoveler hen and drake; ca.
1935. This rare pair was part
of Wheeler's exhibition for the
National Sportsmens Show.

ABOVE: Wheeler whistling swan;
ca. 1935. This graceful
carving was also part of
Wheeler's exhibition at the
National Sportsmens Show.

RIGHT: Wheeler surf scoter hen;
1940. Wheeler made this decoy
as a gift for a friend.

LEFT: Shang Wheeler passenger pigeon; ca. 1940. In addition to waterfowl, Wheeler carved songbirds, shorebirds, seagulls, and various kinds of upland birds.

OPPOSITE: Black ducks by Lew Rathmell; ca. 1941. Rathmell carved one of the finest rigs of black ducks ever made, all with cork bodies and heads in varying positions.

86

problem for decoy collectors), he took pride in the quality of his fellow carvers' work. Shang's willingness to share his patterns and techniques with carvers throughout the country further broadcast the Stratford look. His business and political activities linked him with prominent public figures, and his acquaintance with pioneering decoy collectors Joel Barber and William J. Mackey, Jr., exposed the Stratford style to a national audience.

Too often the folk artist is viewed as an unsophisticated rustic, working in isolation, his art the product of a solitary, often eccentric, genius. This stereotype hardly fits Shang Wheeler. He was a successful businessman and a widely respected figure in the public life of Connecticut. His life story is as fascinating and as varied as his artistic works.

Born in Saugatuck (now part of Westport), Connecticut, on July 15, 1872, Wheeler came from old Yankee stock. His mother died before he was five and by the age of 16 he had left home. For the next ten years he knocked about as a fieldhand, fisherman, pipe fiter, boatbuilder, fishing and hunting guide, and crewman on racing yachts. Shang was also a market gun-

ner, one of those late-19th-century hunters who supplied restaurants and retail shops with a variety of wild duck. Up and down the Connecticut shore, Shang learned the ways of fish and wildfowl—where they lived, what they ate, and how they behaved under every natural condition.

In his twenties Shang began to settle down. He completed his education at New Britain High School, where as starting fullback he led the football team to the state championship. Throughout his life, he continued his interest in athletics as an amateur boxer and as umpire for local football clubs. Around the turn of the century, Shang moved to the Stratford area, where he discovered the work he loved and at which he spent his life—oyster cultivation and harvesting. Oystering was an ideal calling for a man like Shang: it gave him a chance to work out-of-doors; it was physically demanding, posed a variety of risks, required extensive knowledge of the environment, and generated a great deal of good fellowship. In 1912 he became general manager of the Connecticut Oyster Farms in Milford and worked there until his retirement in 1946. He was already boarding across the river in Stratford at the home of Chick and

Fanny Bond. With the Bonds, their children, and grand-children, the dedicated bachelor found the family he never had. Shang remained with them, a devoted friend and adopted family member, until his death in 1949 at the age of 77.

Once established in Stratford, Shang became an active participant in the life of his community. After World War I, his concern for conservation led him into politics. Shang's political career was remarkable for its single-minded preoccupation with the public interest and a corresponding disregard for personal advancement. As an oysterman, he was alarmed to see Connecticut's pure waters so polluted that the oyster beds were threatened. As a sportsman, he was sadly aware that intensive land development and uncontrolled hunting were endangering the state's forests and wildlife. Running on the Republican ticket, he won two terms in the state House of Representatives (1923–26) and another in the state senate (1927–28). There he secured the passage of pioneering antipollution and wildlife conservation legislation and was instrumental in creating a state commission to regulate water quality in Connecticut's streams and rivers. Having achieved these objectives, Shang retired from public office. At one point his political allies urged him to run for the governorship. To their entreaties he replied, "A governor should be married—I'm not married. A governor should attend church—I like to fish on Sundays!" In 1939 he did return to the senate for a single term to help manage the legislative programs of his good friend and political protégé, Governor Raymond E. Baldwin.

As Shang became more involved in his business and in politics, he used his free time for fishing and decoy carving rather than for active hunting. His pastime soon won him recognition that extended far beyond his town and state. In August 1923 a group of conservation-minded sportsmen held the first decoy show in Bellport, Long Island. Competitive carving was a feature of the show, and to the Long Islanders' surprise the first prize in the amateur category went to an outsider—Shang Wheeler.

Wheeler took the top prize at Bellport because he intro-duced a new style of naturalism to decoy making. Old-time carvers had never been sticklers for detail. Their decoys were carved quickly and painted in solid colors with only an ab-stracted suggestion of feather patterns. Wheeler took the time to put in all the details. During the next twenty-five years he carved almost every variety of wildfowl seen along the Atlantic coast. For twelve consecutive years his decoys won first prize in the amateur category of the International Decoy Makers Con-test held annually in New York City. He hit his peak in 1941 when he took 24 firsts, 19 seconds, 8 thirds, as well as a special prize for the best bird.

Wheeler approached decoy making with the eye of a hunter, a naturalist, and an artist. In this sense he was akin to John James Audubon; his birds, like Audubon's, are at the same time faithful reproductions of nature and accomplished works of art. Wheeler's keen eye observed all the nuances of each species' anatomy and feathering. Such was his skill as both

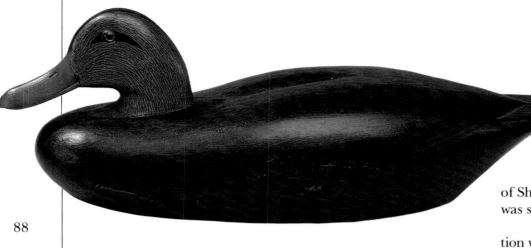

Black duck by Roswell Bliss; 1947. The heads and bills of Bliss decoys have a distinctive look, but the overall shape and construction are reminiscent of the work of Ben Holmes.

88

carver and painter that he could recreate what his eye had seen, giving each decoy a relaxed, natural, lifelike look.

Wheeler used no special equipment. Until the late thirties, when some friends gave him a power saw and a drill press, he worked with the same simple hand tools used by carvers of the past. He continued to do all his finishing by hand. Holding the bird in his lap, he could turn it and examine its planes from several perspectives. That gave him a better sense of how successfully to integrate all the parts.

Anyone who carves decoys knows that the head is made separately from the body and that the body is often made from two hollowed-out parts. A Wheeler decoy appears to be a seamless whole: bill flows into head, head into body, which sweeps out to the tail. Wheeler used his remarkable painting technique to emphasize the natural flow of his carving. One might say that for him painting was a process of unraveling. He began with a mental picture of how he wanted the finished decoy to look and worked backward in his mind to map out the plumage patterns. He then conceived a series of layers and zones of color that would lead up to the desired look. Where one zone merged into another, he blended the shades to achieve a subtle gradation rather than the sharply delineated areas found in much primitive painting.

No detail escaped his attention. A decoy can be spoiled by a seemingly small matter like the placement of the eyes. For every bird the best possible placement is different. The eyes on Wheeler's birds are watchful and alert. With an apparent twinkle, they complement the whimsical smile that enlivens many of his decoys.

Wheeler made three grades of decoy: flat cork-bodied working decoys; fuller-bodied cork and balsa decoys; and decorative birds, most of them made of wood. Shang carved for personal pleasure and refused to sell his birds, even when the industrialist Walter Chrysler offered to buy a group of sixty decoys for $250 apiece (an unheard-of price in Wheeler's day).

During a lifetime of carving Wheeler probably produced no more than 500 to 600 birds. Adding his pen-and-inks, his political cartoons, a few oil paintings, and the carved fish, the total body of his artistic work would not exceed a thousand pieces. By comparison other notable carvers like Elmer Crowell, the Ward brothers, or Ira Hudson, all of whom carved for resale, turned out decoys in the thousands. Decoy collectors will tell you that they rarely find more than a few Wheelers on the market. This is because so many of them were distributed as gifts to friends and remain in their families as treasured heirlooms. Only one museum has a significant body of his work on display, the Shelburne Museum in Vermont.

Without exception, every third-generation carver spoke of Shang Wheeler with affection and admiration; his influence was significant.

Like the men before them, members of the third generation were, on the whole, gentlemen carvers. Without exception, decoy making was an avocation that first and foremost brought enjoyment. In most cases the Stratford carvers enjoyed financial stability. They did not make decoys for profit.

Much had been accomplished before the 20th-century carvers began their work. Following in the footsteps of three of the greatest decoy makers of all time, the fine work of many of the third-generation carvers is often overshadowed.

Charles Disbrow (1885–1955), Stratford's game warden, most closely copied Wheeler's work. Even the experts have trouble distinguishing Disbrow's black ducks from those made by the master. Few examples of this gifted carver remain in circulation. We must, therefore, assume his production was very limited.

An active gunner, Ken Peck (1887–1961) spent the summer months sailing yachts owned by the wealthy. The fall and winter months were spent gunning. The bulk of Peck's decoy production was 25 black ducks made in 1933 with Bill Bedell (1904–66), another carver of this generation.

Roswell Bliss (1887–1967) was probably the most prolific carver of the third generation. He continued to make decoys until his death in 1967. A pattern maker by trade, Bliss spent many of his working years self-employed, doing patternwork and making decoys in the shop behind his house in Stratford. Of all the carvers, Bliss was most dependent on the sales of decoys as a source of income. He was one of the few carvers to make decoys of species uncommon to the area: geese, teal, pintail, and even some crows.

The most underrated of all third-generation carvers was Lou Rathmell (1890–1976). Rathmell moved to Danbury, Connecticut, after marrying a woman of wealth. His production may not be much more than 100 decoys. However, every decoy was outstanding. In 1941 he made a rig of about fifty-five black ducks that must be considered one of the best gunning rigs ever made. Constructed with cork bodies and wooden heads, these decoys were so lifelike that whenever Rathmill set up, the black ducks would pass by other gunners and head right for him. No two heads were identical: the position or height of the head always differed. In addition to these fine cork black ducks, he made several remarkable pairs of mallards, canvasbacks, redheads, broadbills, teal, and buffleheads. These beautiful decoys were hollow and made of pine.

Reginald I. Culver (1897–1975) was from an old seafaring Stratford family. Following the family tradition, he spent many years at sea. When Reg was ashore during gunning season, most of his time was spent in the marsh, gunning black ducks. An accomplished carpenter, Reg made excellent black ducks, broadbills, goldeneyes, and scoters, almost all hollow

and made from pine. Structurally, his work is reminiscent of Ben Holmes's. In the area of painting, Culver learned much from Wheeler.

Probably the best "technician" in the art of decoy making in this generation was Willard C. Baldwin (1890–1979). Baldwin was a respected pattern maker at the Singer Company in Bridgeport. He lived by the idea that "the best tools are the ones you make yourself." He made just about everything—from canoe paddles, gun stocks, and boats to chisels, knives, and drills—all of superb quality. His decoys are equally high in quality. Around 1920 Baldwin made a lovely rig of black ducks. Varying in shape, size, and head position, these decoys remain in original paint and outstanding condition even though they were regularly gunned over by Baldwin until the early 1960s. It was then that they began to circulate through the world of the collector. They are now prized possessions of many decoy enthusiasts.

Another of Stratford's fine gentleman carvers, Charles Ralph Welles (1895–1978) graduated from Yale in 1917. His family had substantial land holdings in the northern part of Stratford along the river. Highly influenced by Laing and Wheeler, Welles made some outstanding decoys in the 1920s and 1930s. More than most of his fellow carvers, Ralph employed several basic body shapes. This has resulted in some confusion that makes identifying his work difficult. As with all carvers, subtle carving and painting characteristics in all his decoys allow experts to identify his work.

Broadbill drake by Reginald I. Culver; ca. 1920. By trade a pattern maker, Culver was a member of the third generation of Stratford carvers.

CHAPTER 7:

UPSTATE NEW YORK

by Walter C. Hallbauer with Sue A. Bauer

For centuries, decoys of various shapes, sizes, and types have been made by skilled craftsmen for the sole purpose of attracting live prey. Blocks of wood were carved to assume a most tranquil and reposed appearance, and many folks have found this art form most appealing.

The definition of what constitutes Upstate New York depends on where one hails from within the state. For the purpose of this chapter, it means the triangle from Buffalo, on the shores of Lake Erie, through central New York, north to the Thousand Islands and St. Lawrence River—a distance of over three hundred miles. As one might expect, the terrain varies considerably, from the fertile lake plains bordering lakes Erie and Ontario to the more rugged, rock outcropping areas of the St. Lawrence.

Regardless of the topography, waterfowl were and still are found in abundant numbers throughout this area. In the late 1800s and early 1900s, market hunting was a way of life for many sportsmen and decoy carvers. Barrels of waterfowl from this area were shipped to New York City, Philadelphia, and other East Coast cities. Unlike some other famous waterfowl regions, this area had few duck-hunting clubs. This is not to say that duck hunting was not popular in this region. In the St. Lawrence area, many wealthy people owned islands with large summer homes, and these "retreats" sufficed very well for the duck-hunting interests of their family and friends.

Throughout this area there were hundreds of decoy carvers, a few well-known prolific carvers, and many who made but a rig for themselves. The greatest concentration of carvers in Upstate New York was in the small town of Alexandria Bay on the St. Lawrence River. It has been said that at one time there were over fifty decoy carvers in this town alone. This cadre of carvers made a significant contribution to our rich heritage of hand-carved decoys. With the similarity in carving style of many of these "whittlers," confusion can run rampant when present-day collectors try to positively identify these art pieces of the past. Within the boundaries of Alexandria Bay, the most famous of the local carvers lived on Holland Street and were referred to as the "Holland Street Whittlers."

Few will dispute that Chauncey Wheeler, the originator of the "Holland Street Whittlers," was the headmaster of the lot. Born May 14, 1862, in a log cabin on Wellesley Island, he was a bay boy and never moved far from the river. His mother was a Patterson girl from Wellesley Island and, by no surprise, Chancy Patterson, a decoy carver in his own right, and Chauncey Wheeler were cousins. Making decoys seemed to run through the veins of the relatives. Whittling was so natural to Wheeler that by the age of eight he had carved his first pair of miniature decoys.

As was typical back then, Wheeler learned the basics and then left school after completing a few grades—the river was calling him. In a recent conversation with Wheeler's daughter, Marie Tousant, she described her father as a kind, up front, gentle, and humble riverman who would give the shirt off his back to another man. In reciprocation, he expected honesty and consideration.

Wheeler was a licensed St. Lawrence pilot and from time to time worked as a guide, overhauled boats, and also was in the employment of several summer estate owners. The latter helped him to gain prominence and earned his carvings recognition. A collector's item, highly sought after today, is the flying duck that is reportedly an "original Wheeler creation." One full-sized flying decoy, cut in half from bill tip to tail tip, yielded two exquisite wall plaques. Some folks encouraged Chauncey to patent this unique idea, but his compassion to share his techniques with others won out.

One of Wheeler's more famous customers was John Philip Sousa, who purchased a flock of Wheeler doves. He was so enamored with Wheeler's finished product that he requested and received the first-known correspondence course in decoy making. The "76 Trombone Band" leader's carving abilities are not known; we are unaware of decoys made by Sousa. Abercrombie & Fitch was interested in retailing many more than Wheeler could possibly carve. Actually, he was happiest selling his decoys to island people and others in and around his beloved river area for $3.50 each. Chauncey used Sherwin-Williams paint, and mixed his own colors to suit the many species native to the region. His workshop down by the water had many purposes and was the scene of the greatest ideas and discussions. The "Holland Street Whittlers" and their compadres all had responsibilities, and each was attended to faithfully. While the boys whittled, the sitters, watchers, and conversationalists were responsible for tending fire, sweeping,

OPPOSITE: *This turned-head brant decoy with outlined wings is one of the rarest Chauncey Wheeler decoys. Wheeler made most of his brants on special order for Long Island clients.*

and other routine tasks to keep the carving room impeccably neat. Sexism reigned, as the shop remained off-limits to anyone of the female gender. A bell was rung from the main house to summon the shop inhabitants.

In the late 1880s, Chauncey married the first of his three wives. His offspring, two sons and two daughters, never developed their dad's carving ability or talent for painting.

With the summer sun retreating and fall approaching, hunting and carving fever commenced. Each winter, flocks were made to fill special orders. The last group of decoys whittled by Chauncey, in 1933 to 1934, were made of cedar wood from the forests at Fort Drum, New York.

ABOVE: Classic canvasbacks by Chauncey Wheeler; 1932. This pair of decoys shows the excellent combing and blending that are indicative of Wheeler's finest workmanship.

ABOVE: The long-necked style of Frank Coombs is evident in this pair of bluebills. The hen shows the reverse feather painting pattern Coombs and Chauncey Wheeler used.

Chauncey was the captain of the decoy makers in northern New York, and some of the characteristics of his decoys are quite specific and identifiable. Unique to Chauncey's decoys was the rounded tip of the feathers, which were painted pointing toward the front end rather than the tail of the decoy. Carving outlined the decoy's mandible and distinguished the bill from the rest of the head. A simple jackknife, drawshave, and paintbrush were the master's main tools. Additional identifying features are found on the bottom of the decoy. During construction, a vice securely held a block of wood to which the decoy was affixed by two screws. These screw holes were later filled with small, square plugs. A small gouge in the bottom held a staple to which a swivel and anchor line could be attached. Wheeler prided himself on carving beautifully shaped heads and lifelike decoys. The indented nostrils and carved groove line through the head where the eyes were placed add to their classic simplicity. The fine feather combing and painting can be appreciated by the novice and discriminating collector. Wheeler's forethought and planning were vividly displayed in his finished product. In the authors' opinions, there is little doubt that the Chauncey Wheeler decoys rank as the finest of the St. Lawrence carvers.

OPPOSITE: Goldeneye and bufflehead drakes by Roy Conklin; ca. 1945. Conklin was the most artistic painter of the St. Lawrence River carvers, as is clear in these two.

Chauncey Wheeler was active in his world, teaching the young the rudiments of making and sailing a boat, helping townsfolk refurbish boats, or most anxious to share his decoy knowledge and life experiences with others. It is no wonder then, that during his final bedridden days in March 1937, in his home on Holland Street, these folks did not forget or forsake him. His talents were endless, and our lives were richly enhanced by them.

Those long-necked decoys will spook rather than attract wild birds, scoffed the natives of Alexandria Bay. These were the comments heard in the 1920s when they first saw the new-style decoys carved by Frank Coombs. The actual results were quite the opposite, and thus Coombs became known as the father of the Alexandria Bay "long-necks." The catalyst for designing the long-necked style came from Coombs viewing a movie. He noticed that a group of ducks already on the water would look up as flying ducks descended to join the flock. The long-necked decoys had an advantage in that their bills would not ice up in the cold weather as did some of their low-headed counterparts. The concept paid off handsomely as Coombs could sell more decoys than he desired to make over the next twenty years.

Abercrombie & Fitch was interested in selling Coombs decoys, but the home market was so strong that the big store's orders were never accepted. Coombs copied Chauncey Wheeler's reverse-feathering paint style and some of his blending techniques, but he did not carve a line in the bill to indicate a mandible. He was known to be able to carve a decoy from start to finish in a twenty-minute period—a feat accomplished by very few decoy makers. He was an avid hunter, even though he was involved in a hunting accident in 1916 when a companion shot off part of his hand. Born in 1882, he lived in St. Lawrence County until his death in 1958. Coombs's decoys are highly desirable to collectors because of their unique style and excellent paint patterns.

Another bay boy, Roy A. Conklin, was born on January 10, 1909. Conklin was one of Chauncey Wheeler's many students. For a short time, he attended Columbia University's Art School to further develop his artistic proficiency. The St. Lawrence had a strong influence on him, so he returned home to work as a boat captain, guide, and carpenter. An ambitious and brilliant man, with a superior artistic talent and an innate ability to carve wild fowl as they are, Conklin could have made a fortune carving decoys.

His rendition of a decoy was completely different from that of Wheeler, his teacher, or his whittling colleagues. Eventually, he developed his own style, which depicted the birds with longer and thinner necks, and his painting was much more bold in color brilliance, with paint combing dominating feather blending. The "comb," a special toothed appliance, was squiggled over the back of the decoy to simulate feathers.

His carving career spanned about thirty years, beginning around 1930, with small, decorative, and very desirable decoys. In a few years, he hired people to help him meet the demands of his customers, which included Harrods of London and Abercrombie & Fitch.

Some of Conklin's finest works are miniature decoys in a flying position, many of which were unusual species like whistling swans and emperor geese. Conklin's many talents included the making of full-size decoys, miniatures, half-bodies mounted on plaques, and painted canvas scenes of the St. Law-

rence with attached carvings of small waterfowl in flight. All of these are eagerly sought by today's decoy collectors.

Heading west from Alexandria Bay lies Clayton, New York, Samuel Denny's lifelong hometown. Born on September 25, 1874, Denny married in 1896 and died on May 23, 1953. He and his wife, Salina, had fifteen children. Beginning around 1900, Denny was a commercial decoy maker for more than half a century. Like many of the carvers in his region, his life was interspersed with other jobs. Fishing, painting boats and houses, cutting ice and wood, tying flies, guiding, and rowing boats for fishing patrons kept him busy. Still and all, he found time to teach himself to play the violin and share his musical talents at local dances.

The style of Denny decoys varies from the early deep-chested form to the later, longer, sleek-bodied profiles, frequently carved in a lowhead position. His decoys have the deep eye grove so characteristic of other makers from the area. Sam

developed his own painting techniques, which produced a more flat finish than seen on many decoys. Collectors vehemently discuss the attributes of the various St. Lawrence River carvers, and time and again Denny decoys are near the top in desirability.

Weedsport, New York, was home to the famous Stevens decoys. It is difficult to know just when the first Stevens decoys were made by their founder, Harvey A. Stevens. However, an advertisement for Stevens decoys appeared in a 1880 issue of the *Forest and Stream* magazine. This outfit can be considered, in the broadest sense of the term, a commercial decoy factory. The last Stevens decoys were made in about 1902, when a fire destroyed the decoy workshop. With the national exposure received from advertising, the Stevens decoys were sold throughout the United States. For a period of time eight employees were needed to fill the demand for these classic decoys.

The style of the Stevens decoys varies from the early flat-bottom style to the much more pleasing and collectible oval body with the paddle tail. Stevens decoys have characteristics that make them more identifiable than many other early decoys. The oval-body-style decoys have a wooden dowel toward the back of the top of the head extending through the neck and

ABOVE: Lowhead bluebill drake carved by Sam Denny that shows the prominent breast found in his 1920s-style carving. The deep eye groove was a characteristic employed by other carvers in the area.

96

down into the decoy body. The bottom of Stevens decoys holds a wealth of information: toward the front is a ⅞-inch hole with a recessed staple for attaching an anchor line; also, there are one or more ⅞-inch holes containing recessed poured lead used to correctly balance the decoy. Not having an exposed staple and lead weights eliminated much of the marking and wear that is commonly found on decoys with these features. In addition, most Stevens decoys are identified by one of three types of labeling. The most common is an applied stencil that reads, "H.A. Stevens, Maker, Weedsport, N.Y., Standard Decoys." Based solely on speculation it is believed this stencil was used until August 28, 1894, at which time Harvey A. Stevens died at the age of 47. Harvey's brothers George and Fred continued making decoys until the fire of 1902. Decoys produced during this time have a brand in the bottom with the lettering "G.W. Stevens, Weedsport, N.Y." On some examples a paper label was attached under the bill that reads, "Geo. W.

Stevens, Weedsport, N.Y." It is easy to understand why few original paper labels remain: exposure to water and the elements quickly removed the fragile labels. One can conjecture that since the Stevens advertisements indicated all their decoys were identified, and many presently on collectors' shelves lack identification, that at one time those decoys had a paper label affixed to the underside of the bill. A few mint examples even have a pencil signature on the bottom in what can be considered excellent penmanship.

Stevens decoys were constructed of cedar. Often, cedar knots had to be concealed with a wood filler as clear cedar was at a premium in the Weedsport area. Calling the Stevens operation a factory seems inappropriate, as each decoy was hand constructed using a hatchet, chisel, rasp, and drawshave. One can take a step back in time to the Stevens "factory" while visiting the Shelburne Museum in Vermont, which has the original Stevens decoy-maker's horse on display. The realistic

OPPOSITE: Outstanding examples of the oval body and paddle-tail style of Stevens decoys. This pair of redheads has excellent combing on the drake and feather blending on the hen.

BELOW: Rare species of Stevens decoys produced at the Weedsport decoy shop. The bufflehead drake is in normal plumage; the goldeneye is in rare eclipse plumage.

painting patterns exhibit excellent combing, feathering that frequently extends to the bottom of the decoy, and distinctive wing speculums. When filling orders, the salesmanship of the Stevens boys is further indicated by the inclusion of directions on how to rig the decoys as feeders. Stevens decoys sold for $10 per dozen, a healthy price for the era in which they were produced. Stevens decoys were sold at early sporting-goods stores such as Von Lengerbe and Antoine in Chicago. Because of their age and attractive form, Stevens decoys rate at or near the top as the most collectible decoys from Upstate New York.

In the western region of Upstate New York, the name Julius Edward Mittlesteadt is the most prominent of the local decoy carvers. Born on July 3, 1888, he lived in the Buffalo area until his death in 1957. His stylish decoys were made from cedar bodies with white-pine heads. A few examples of Mittlesteadt decoys are made with cork sandwiched between a bottom and top piece of cedar in the construction of the body.

While the bodies of the Mittlesteadt decoys appear somewhat heavy in design, the proportions and free-flowing styles of the total decoy make them appealing even to the most discriminating collector. Mittlesteadt decoys were produced primarily for the Mittlesteadt family's hunting trips, with a few lucky customers being fortunate to have a rig made for their own use. Mittlesteadt carved most common species of decoys, with mergansers and canvasbacks being the class of the flock. A few decorative turned-head sleepers and decoy lamps excite the decoy-collector world when they are discovered.

One of Mittlesteadt's sons, J. Robert Mittlesteadt, produced decoys in the style and paint pattern of his father.

The list of notable decoy carvers from Upstate New York also includes such names as James Stanley, Frank Louis, Fairman Davis, Wally Bishop, Moses Semmel, and such recent carvers as Ken Harris and Chet Schutte. All have made significant contributions to the decoy-collecting world.

CHAPTER 8:

LONG ISLAND

by Fred Dombo

Long Island, New York, is a unique bit of geography. It juts out easterly into the Atlantic Ocean, while the rest of the continent heads northeast. Approximately 118 miles long, its width varies from twelve to twenty-three miles. Long Island has over 280 miles of coastline. And this coastline is what drew the birds: "Flights of birds that darkened the sky" is a comment that comes up in several old-timer tales.

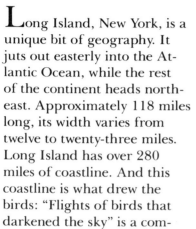

While it may not readily appear so, Long Island is a true island, completely surrounded by water. Nearly half the length of its South Shore is paralleled by a sandy barrier beach. This barrier beach buffers the mainland from the Atlantic Ocean. In doing this, it has formed many interconnected bays and marshes. The bays are relatively shallow and are open to the ocean only by several inlets widely dispersed along the length of the barrier beach. At one time, these bays contained hundreds of square miles of salt marsh rich with aquatic animal and vegetable life.

On the North Shore, there is a sound between the Long Island coast and the Connecticut coast. This is a relatively deep body of water, with harbors boring in along the length on both sides. The eastern end of Long Island becomes two fingers, with Orient Point on the end of the northern one, and Montauk Point on the end of the southern finger. Between the two is a series of deep bays and many islands, some of them quite large (one, Gardiners Island, is 3,300 acres).

To the west is the East River, which separates Long Island from New York City. In fact, the western end of Long Island is made up of two counties, Kings (Brooklyn) and Queens, which are boroughs of New York City.

That was the stage: a sizable body of land surrounded by water, different types of water, which must have presented a compelling environment for nearly every species of eastern duck, goose, and shorebird. There also was the largest city in the country demanding tasty morsels in huge quantities on a regular basis for its hotels and restaurants.

So it was that a certain type of man who chose to live away from that city went from using waterfowl as part of his table fare to using it as a crop to be harvested and sent to the nearby market, providing an important source of income. Indeed, the crop became a very important part of the income of the men who worked the bay. The "sports" came later, also providing the locals with a way to earn a living.

The photographs in this book are of the tools these men

used. Not all of the examples selected are decoys of the market hunters, but many of the oldest ones are.

This chapter does not cover the entire field of decoys used on Long Island. The examples of Long Island decoys presented here were selected because they are good examples of well-made Long Island decoys used long ago to bring birds within range of a hunter's weapon. They are not necessarily the best, or even the best examples of a carver's work, though in some cases both statements would be true.

What these photographs have in common is that they are of decoys that are all well done. They go beyond what was necessary for the job at hand. There is no question that something less graceful or less realistic—requiring much less work—would have sufficed. There are many more examples of decoys that fit this description and were used effectively. But here are "stool" made by many different men, none of them formally trained to do it. They just needed tools to make a living, and obviously some of them had talent.

They needed tools and went about making them, each to his own standard, interpreting what the living bird looked like into a form that would work.

That might be taken as a rough definition of folk art, and it is one of the things that attracts me to decoys. Another is their age and the fact that they were used—and used hard and often—by their makers and others to bring birds to the gun. Many of these decoys existed long before you and I and will be here after we are gone.

In the range of Long Island decoys, these photographs attempt to illustrate the following: shorebirds of various species; cork and its importance in this part of the country in decoy use; feather hunting; wooden ducks; spring shooting and the brant; and, in general, the sheer beauty of Long Island decoys.

Shorebirds are certainly the most important category of Long Island decoys. They go from the very realistic examples of William Bowman's curlew, dowitcher, and golden plover to the more impressionistic work of William Southard's yellowlegs and Obediah Verity's plovers and peep. Even the cork shorebirds cover a range of detail. It is a wonder that they have survived more than a century, since they were shaped and stuck on a stick to attract their live counterparts. Long Island is noted for its shorebird decoys, and some collectors consider them the finest examples.

OPPOSITE: Setting out stickup shorebird decoys.

ABOVE: Curlew by William Bowman of Lawrence. A truly fine example of a shorebird decoy.

Long Island shorebird decoys. Left to right are a peep, curlew, and black-bellied plover. The plover and peep are by Obediah Verity; the curlew is by John Henry Verity.

100

Cork was a very important material to the Long Island decoy maker. Cork was light, readily available, and it was free! Old worn-cork life preservers that might otherwise have been thrown away yielded their cork to the decoy maker. So did the waves of the ocean. Cork was used for dunnage. Whether it was blown, washed, or thrown overboard from the ships that plied the route to and from New York Harbor, a good quantity found its way ashore along the barrier beach and into the inlets and bays. It was easily shaped, and the color was especially good for black ducks. In such cases, all that was needed was some kerosene and a match, a finely carved and painted head, a keel and a weight to make it ready for the next trip. Other species were painted.

Little is known about John Carter of Jamaica Bay, one of the many Long Island carvers to employ cork. A seagull by

him, with the "C" carved under the face, is pictured in the January-February-March 1964 issue of *Decoy Collector's Guide.* It was found in the rig of feather hunter Don McKeeman of Freeport.

A mason by trade, Eugene Wells made mostly black ducks, but he did make other species. He lived all his life in the Port Jefferson-Stony Brook area and took great pride in the decoys he made for himself and friends.

Andrew "Grubie" Verity of Seaford was the son of Smith Clinton Verity. A bayman by trade, he made many decoys of all species. He also carved and sold many heads, so it is not unusual to find a Grubie head on another man's block.

In addition to being an avid gunner, Jimmy Ketcham of Amityville also worked at the Life Saving Station on the beach. He made many decoys of all species, with heads that had

Feeding ruddy turnstone (left)
by Obediah Verity and (right)
peep attributed to Verity (it was
made by a member of the Verity
family, if not by Obediah).
Feeding ruddy-turnstone
decoys are rare for Long
Island; this may be the only one.

consistently clean lines and an alert look.

John Boyle of Bellport came from a wealthy family, and as the story goes, he preferred to carve and hunt rather than tend the family business. Apparently, the feeling was mutual, and he was paid to stay home and do what pleased him. A detailed account of this arrangement is given in the Museums at Stony Brook book *Gunners' Paradise*.

Born in Brooklyn in 1866, Ralph Cranford spent his adult life in the village of Babylon, where he died in 1948. A wealthy architect, he built several boats. His own gunning boat was named *Plover*. He made particularly nice black-duck decoys for his own use and probably for friends. Brant by him are also known, and he did at least one decorative carving.

In addition to hunting for meat, some of these baymen set their stool for feathers. The same city that had a seemingly insatiable appetite for fresh meat also housed a large millinery trade. Many hatmakers and department stores had a need for huge quantities of feathers from many different birds for use on women's hats. The seagull by Frank Kellum of Babylon, circa 1890, and tern by Obediah Verity, circa 1880, were used for this purpose. Kellum was a painter by trade. He was often encouraged to pursue his artistic ability, but he never did, preferring to spend his time on the bay.

I have wondered, more than once, how necessary these decoys were. The nature of seagulls and terns has probably not changed in a hundred years, and today almost anything edible—fish entrails, small baitfish, or ground fish doled out into the water—will bring flocks of both species within easy shooting range. But there is no question that these decoys were used. And knowing how pragmatic these hunters were, we have

LEFT: Cork black ducks. From top center and then clockwise these are by John Carter; Eugene Wells; Andrew Verity; James Ketcham; John Boyle; Ralph Cranford.

TOP: Seagull (left) by Frank Kellum and tern (right) by Obediah Verity. These are examples of the decoys used by feather hunters during the late 19th and early 20th centuries.

ABOVE: Yellowlegs by William Southard of Bellmore. Southard was a wheelright and made decoys in what has become known as the Seaford style.

Cork shorebirds, including a curlew by Thomas Gelston; plover and small peeps by William Cornell; peep by Obediah Verity; and peep by an unknown maker.

Broadbill hen (above) and drake (below) by Obediah Verity. Long Island was home to several Obediah Veritys; the one intended here was the son of a bayman of the same name and was born in 1850 and died around 1910.

to also assume that these decoys were indeed necessary, for the hunters would not have expended the time and energy to make them, let alone use them, if they were not important to a successful day on the bay.

As for wooden duck decoys, the pair of broadbill by Obediah Verity show form and wing carving similar to the detail on his shorebirds. The merganser hen by William Southard has similarities to the style of his yellowlegs. The American merganser pair by Thomas Gelston, 1900s, are also examples of wooden decoys made with considerable talent.

Prior to 1913, when spring shooting was banned, the brant decoy was very important to the market hunter. It is said that they decoyed better in the spring than in the fall. Perhaps one explanation could be that in the spring the birds are inter-ested in mating and grouping up for the long flight to their nesting grounds on islands in the Arctic Circle.

There is very little information about the maker of the shorebirds that are referred to as John Dilley's. The first find was made by William Mackey, and, as he relates in his book *American Bird Decoys,* he was given six by the widow of Captain Jesse Birdsall of Barnegat, New Jersey. At that time, he believed that they were made by Birdsall. After that, others were found. A group turned up in Amityville, Long Island, about fifteen years after Mackey's original find. Since then, dozens more have been found on Long Island. The only ones found in New Jersey were those original six given to Mackey by Jesse Birdsall's widow.

One group was found in a box marked "John Dilley, Quo-

gue." There is no proof that this person made the decoys, and there is no information on who this person was. They are nevertheless beautiful shorebird decoys and testimony to someone's skill as a carver and painter. The plumage on these decoys is very accurate and skillfully blended. Imported glass eyes were used to complete these little beauties.

In collecting circles, they are generally accepted as "John Dilley" and as Long Island. Many are found in mint condition, while others are found that were heavily shot over and shot at.

Thus on Long Island as elsewhere decoys began as an implement used casually to supplement the family diet and became a serious tool used to provide large quantities of birds to the market, both for meat and plumage, as well as a significant part of the income of the men who did the work. Later, some of the men who carved decoys turned to caring for the estates and hunting rigs of the wealthy. They became guides to the less experienced sport hunters, and they got involved with the hunting clubs that developed along the island as guides or rig tenders or decoy makers, or all three.

Whether the attraction to these objects is their folk-art appeal or the allure of the hunt that they conjure up, or a little of each, there is no doubt that they are the source of great satisfaction to the collector.

108

OPPOSITE TOP: *Shorebirds by John Dilley of Long Island. Left to right, these are a ruddy turnstone, black-bellied plover, and dowitcher, all in spring plumage. Little is known of Dilley, but collectors suspect* *that the reason many of his carvings have survived in pristine condition is that the beauty of his paint patterns made hunters hesitant to shoot over them.*

OPPOSITE BOTTOM: *Roothead brant decoys. Left to right: by Emery Ackerly, ca. 1850; by David Cochran, ca. 1900; by Jack Donnelley, ca. 1870.*

ABOVE: *Oldsquaw (below) and broadbill hen (above) by Abrem Smith. The wing carving is typical of the Seaford school.*

CHAPTER 9:

NEW JERSEY

by Gary Giberson

Along the direct line of the great Atlantic flyway, the New Jersey coast is home to more species of wildfowl than any other area in the country, and thus more types of decoys are found in this region than any other. The area's most prolific decoy maker, Harry Vanuckson Shourds, is known to have created more than thirty different species of wooden bird decoys.

The South Jersey area, rich with large tidal bays, salt-marsh ponds, clean streams, and swift-flowing rivers, was long a haven to birds, hunters, and decoys. New Jersey's earliest form of tourism involved the guiding of hunting parties in these areas with their abundant bird populations. Locals profited from the guiding of gunners, and market hunting flourished.

Among the areas visited by these Victorian market gunners were Sandy Hook south to Manasquan Inlet, Barnegat Bay, Manahawkin Bay, Great Bay, the Mullica River, Great Egg Harbor Bay, Corson Inlet, Townsend Inlet, and Cape May Point. Each of these areas had its own decoy masters. Many carvers copied the masters and turned out examples of seaworthy decoys.

The decoys of New Jersey can thus be divided by area, and the styles that emerge can be separated into Barnegat, Tuckerton, Manahawkin, Mullica River, Absecon, Head of the River, and Cape May. The masters for each area include John Dorset, Henry Grant, Captain Jesse Birdsall, and Taylor Johnson for Barnegat; Henry V. Shourds, Bradford Salmons, and Roland N. Horner for Tuckerton; Joseph King, Lloyd Parker, and Liberty Price for Manahawkin; Gideon Lippincott, Captain John McAnney, John Updike, and Benjamin Maxwell for the Mullica River; Captain Daniel Showell, Harry Boice, William Hammell, Levi R. Truex for Absecon; Samuel Corson, Townsend Godfry, Mark English, Dan Lake Leeds for Head of the River; and Ephrim Hildreth, Otis Townsend, Jonathan Cresse for Cape May. Great shorebird decoys also come from the Cape May area, with carvings by John McCarthy and William Stites.

Several factors were important to the make-up of New Jersey's decoys. The first of these is the wood used. The counties of Burlington, Ocean, Atlantic, Glouchester, Cumberland, and Cape May were once rich with stands of Eastern white cedar, a tree nicknamed swamp cedar. Huge stands of these trees lined the rivers, from the coast inland. New Jersey's first industry was the cutting of these great forests to provide lumber for the area's flourishing ship-building industry. At one time cedar sawmills outnumbered village stores.

The development of New Jersey's decoy tradition can be seen as a development from the area's abundant waterfowl, rich marshlands, and large quantities of cedar, the wood from which all Jersey decoys were made.

The cedars grew straight, like stalks of celery, with all the limb growth at the top third of the tree. The straight grain, uninterrupted by limb or knot, provides a perfect wood for planking a ship. It also has the great quality to resist rot or the attack of wood-eating insects and worms. The average full-grown white cedar stood eighty feet tall and had a diameter of three to four feet. Such trees no longer exist.

The stands of these trees were "clear cut," meaning they were cut down entirely. This was done because the trees grew very close together, with their tops intertwined so much that a tree chopped through at its base would not fall. Thus, one could not simply go into the swamp and cut down a few large trees. Instead, the entire stand was removed—it was "clear cut."

The smallest trees, those growing around the outside of the stand, would make the best bean poles or net markers. The next size tree, two to four inches in diameter, would be used for fence posts. The six-inch-diameter trees would be used for cedar shingles. Working in toward the middle of the stand, the next size tree would be cut for weather boards or small trim material. These logs would be around eight to ten inches in diameter. The remaining large trees were used as boat lumber.

Crude corduroy roads were built into the damp swamps to help remove the downed trees. The logs were brought back to mills where they were sawed into lumber. The thick-butted cedars would yield broad slabs because of the bell-bottom shape of the log. These thick slabs of straight-grain soft cedar were an excellent wood for the creation of light, buoyant decoys.

OPPOSITE: *Mallard drake by John Updike; 1925. This is a rare species of decoy for New Jersey; mallard drake decoys were said to scare off black-duck hens, the predominant species in New Jersey's wetlands.*

ABOVE: *Canada goose (above) and Atlantic brant (below) by Gideon Lippincott; ca. 1860. These pieces show the primitive decoy style that was used along with single-barrel muzzle-loading shotguns.*

Decoys by Joe King: a long-billed dowticher (left) and curlew (right) with a high-tailed swimming Atlantic brant (center). King was one of the first New Jersey makers to earn his living carving decoys.

112

The New Jersey decoy, or "stool duck," as they were called in the South Jersey area, is uniquely crafted in three pieces. The bodies were made in two halves, and the head was carved separately. The two halves were hollowed by means of a gouge or special decoy-hollowing adz. The carved head was attached by way of screw, nail, or sometimes dowel. Hollow decoys ride higher on the water, affording a more visible shape to high-flying game birds. They also float more buoyantly with lifelike movements. They were lighter to transport and easier to carry on the smaller gunning boats used in the New Jersey region.

In the shallow marsh ponds and stumpy creeks, a shallow-draft boat was required. A good, stable seaworthy design was also necessary for bay front gunning. Around 1840 the perfect hull was designed. It was ten to twelve feet long and had a beam of one-third the length. It was shaped just like a pumpkin seed with the rear-end cut off. A cockpit was cut out of the center top portion where the hunter could fit. It was said as to the amount of water required to float one, "They could follow a sweating mule up a dusty road" and "You could sail around the world in one." They were simply called a sneakbox. With their

OPPOSITE: Canada goose (above) and Atlantic brant (below) by Lloyd Parker, a man whose decoys were eagerly sought by Victorian market gunners.

RIGHT: Pair of buffleheads by Roland Nathaniel Horner. This excellent pair shows why Horner's work was considered among the very best.

BELOW: Geese by Henry Grant. Few decoys ride the water as well as those by this maker: their flat bottoms took the roll and fooled the true fowl.

Shorebirds by the prolific Harry Shourds. From left to right, these are a wimbrel curlew, greater yellowlegs, dowitcher, black-bellied plover, knot (in rare winter plumage), and sanderling.

low profile they were easily hid from view of flying birds. The deck was covered with sedge grass or salt hay or one could pull the sneakbox ashore, walk back on the meadow to the high-water mark, and grab up a couple armfulls of bay trash. Decoys were held on the back of the boat by means of removable side boards. After the decoys were set out the boards were un-hooked and stowed under the bow. The oarlocks could be folded down also to make the whole rig resemble a portion of the surrounding bank or the mass resemble a bunch of floating bay trash.

The first-known New Jersey decoy maker was Gideon Lippincott of Wading River. Born around 1820, he was a boat-builder working the local shipyards in Chestnut Neck. His decoy production was not great in numbers, but enough of them are still turning up to be considered collectible. They have an almost primitive quality that makes them an interesting addition to any collection. Gideon resided on Turtle Creek Road in Wading River; three other noted decoy makers lived a stone's throw away: Benjamin Maxwell, John McAnney, and John Updike. Turtle Creek Road meanders out to the north-side of the Mullica River at its widest point in an area known as Swan Bay.

The Wading River, a major tributary of the Mullica, lies just a half mile to the north of Turtle Creek Road. Here wild rice still grows and some of New Jersey's finest duck hunting is carried out to this day. Captain John McAnney, a sea captain and farmer of salt hay, created decoys in the traditional man-ner. They can be recognized by their long, pointed tails and nearly flat backs. The decoys of Benjamin Maxwell are among New Jersey's finest. They are often mislabeled as the work of Roy Maxwell. The Maxwell decoy resembles the well-known style of Harry Shourds. They can be distinguished by the shoulder groove at the back of the neck area on the decoy. This groove is referred to as the "ice groove." The recessed lead counter weight on the bottom has rounded ends, as Maxwell drilled out the wood on each end and then used a straight chisel to remove the wood in between.

John Updike was a great decoy maker. He later moved from Wading River up the Mullica to Lower Bank. Here John, better known as Jack, built sneakboxes, garveys, and bateaus. He purchased cedar from my grandfather Alonzo Giberson and took many a thick cedar slab home from grandpop's to build his decoys. He was a good friend to my family.

John Updike was probably one of the first true decoy collectors. He was truly in love with the Mullica. The striped bass, better known as stripers or rock fish, went past his house by the ton each year. Black ducks, green-winged teal, mallards, wigeon, gadwalls, and many other species of wildfowl would sit on his doorstep awaiting a hand out.

One of his closest friends was Chris Sprague of Beach Haven, New Jersey. Chris was a fine decoy maker in his own right and used to paint a lot of decoys for Jack. Another close friend was Somers Headly of Leeds Point, New Jersey, who now resides in Wilmington, Delaware. Somers tells of their warm relationship and how Jack Updike helped him start what is one of the best collections of decoys in New Jersey. William Mackey, the well-known collector and decoy author, spent a good deal of time at Updike's home on the Mullica not only to gather rare decoys but decoy knowledge as well.

118

ABOVE: Red-breasted mergansers by Harry Shourds. Among the best examples of this master's work, these show the excellent quality of his carving and his skill at applying paint to cedar. Shourds was one of the first decoy makers to define feathers on decoys.

RIGHT: Harry Shourds.

Ephrim Hildreth of Cape May and Joe King of Parkertown were born in 1835. Hildreth was a grain dealer and market gunner. He is the creator of great early Jersey decoys but more famous for his "camel-head" shorebirds. The spring and fall migrating shorebirds filled the point at Cape May each year. Joe King is considered by many to be the true father of the New Jersey decoy as we know it today. King was one of the first carvers to make decoys for a living. He made a likeness of just about every bird, goose, brant, and duck that flew the great Atlantic flyway. His brant are among this collector's favorite decoys, and I am the proud owner of a very rare ringed plover in original paint, a priceless decoy to a collector of New Jersey shorebird decoys. Many well-known carvers follow the decoys of Joe King.

Lloyd Parker also made decoys for a living. A master carpenter and boatbuilder, his decoys reflect close ties to the decoy patterns of his predecessor, King. His carving skills are hard to beat, and his decoys are great prizes to any collection. Many of the professional hunting guides of the day gunned their parties over his stools.

Harry Vanuckson Shourds, the most prolific decoy maker in Tuckerton, New Jersey, is said to have created 200,000 decoys. This figure is astounding and hard for the layman to imagine. Shourds used a unique push bench to hollow and shape his decoy bodies. He could carve a decoy head almost blindfolded, or so it has been told. Shourds, like his counterpart Joe King, carved all species of bird decoys. I have seen his black-bellied plover decoys painted in nine different plumages. I recently was curator of a decoy exhibition at the Noyes Museum, located in Oceanville, New Jersey, that featured the decoys of this carver. It was entitled "The Prolific Master." I gathered the finest Shourds decoys for the show, thanks to all the great lenders, and the day it was finally installed—with all the exhibition cases polished and the decoys resting on handwoven silk or dark navy worsted wool—I could not hold back a tear of wonder. Before me stood over one hundred decoys created about one hundred years earlier all by one man, and every one of them had at one time been gunned over. The great gathering of decoys included over thirty species. The Shourds family were all invited, an undertaking almost as hard as finding the decoys for the show. When you stood in the gallery and looked across the room you could somehow feel a reverence for this very talented creator. Shourds was an artist who became a house painter and then became a master artist. Shourds and a few others draw from King, but literally hundreds copy the style of Shourds. His decoys were sent all around the country. It is as easy to find one in California as it is in Tuckerton.

About three miles north of Tuckerton is the town of West Creek. This rural community was home to Roland Nathaniel Horner. His family and friends called him "Rolly," but by any name he was surely New Jersey's finest decoy creator. A master at boatbuilding, his skill at designing, carving, and painting was unrivaled in New Jersey. Family members claim his father-in-law, Ellis Parker, from Barnegat, a well-known decoy maker himself, got Rolly started carving. He carved low, elongated bodies in the same manner as his in-law teacher. His painting was taught by a third-generation decoy maker, Chris Spraque, of Beach Haven. He took Spraque's painting a step further, a pure case of student outshining teacher. Chris had a way of

painting many carvers decoys and also repainting them with his name placed on the bottom. His own decoys are easily identified by those who study Jersey decoys. Horner decoys in my opinion rival the works of Crowell, Ward, or any other master of the craft.

The Barnegat area had Jesse Birdsall as its early master, along with John Dorset. Birdsall was a sea captain, market gunner, commercial fisherman, and carver of decoys. Taylor Johnson took up the Barnegat style after him. Dorset's decoy style is kept alive by Henry Grant. Birdsall lived in Barnegat, a town located between the Barnegat Bay and the main north-south highway of Route 9. The town flourished in the time of these great artisans. Great sailing ships were built and launched from there. The Chadwick family, world renowned for making sails, lived here. Howard Perinne built one of the best sneakboxes there. Taylor Johnson was from Bay Head, an area rich with tradition and nautical activities. Henry Grant also made many decoys. His production cannot be counted as great as that of Shourds, but many still exist. They were skillfully created, and many would say they look more like the real duck on the water than any other decoy.

Barnegat-style decoys all had flat bottoms and would not roll as hard as their Tuckerton-style counterparts. Inland farther, but still carving in the Barnegat tradition, Louis Barkelow created many fine decoys, including shorebirds. He resided in the town of Toms River. Near Toms River was the town of Silverton, home to William Beardsley, boatbuilder, fire warden, and decoy maker.

The town of Port Republic, along the southern shore of the Mullica River, was home to Calvin Hickman, a member of the United States Life Saving Service. Port Republic hosted nine sawmills around the turn of the century.

Just seven miles to the south is the city of Absecon. This was home to a unique style of carvers. Its earliest known carver was Captain Daniel Showell. His carvings are uniquely halved in the center of the tail, and all carry the unique carved eye so prominent in this area. Showell carved great shell-drake decoys. They are known to most as mergansers. Harry Boice also lived in Absecon. A market hunter and sport shooting guide, he made all species of duck, goose, and shorebird decoy. His works are very hard to collect as he made decoys only for his own gunning pleasure.

William Hammell was a bayman, boatbuilder, and skilled decoy maker. His decoys have alert, turned-up bills and can be spotted from across a room. Levi Rhodes Truex lived in nearby Atlantic City. Bridge tender by profession and decoy maker while awaiting a ship to require his skill to open the roadway, Truex made great decoys. He created all the species of duck, goose, and shorebird that frequented Absecon Bay and also Great Bay to the north, where he enjoyed the hunt. Truex's decoys have the same carved eye as do others from this region.

The area of Somers Point was home to decoy carvers Mark English and Jake Barrett. Mark English decoys have a distinct appearance. Short choppy bodies with a sudden sharp drop under the tail are sure clues to his work. He too was a builder of sneakboxes. His decoys were very round with lead pad counter weights on them. He used a woodrasp to shape his decoy bodies, and perhaps this is how they take this form. The carvers would usually chop their decoy bodies with a hatchet and then

120

ABOVE: *Red-breasted mergansers by Harry Boice; ca. 1890. These are painted in spring plumage, indicating they were hunted over in that season.*

RIGHT: *Shorebird decoys by Dan Lake Leeds; ca. 1880. Left to right are a yellowlegs, black-bellied plover, ruddy turnstone, red knot, and long-billed curlew. These are five of the six species Leeds made: missing is the sanderling.*

shape the finish line with a drawknife. This tool being drawn lengthways along the decoy body creates an elongated form, whereas the rasp, as it is pushed across the grain, produces the choppy round form. Jake Barrett was a tall, thin man with good woodworking skills. His decoys are very flat on the top of their bodies as well as their bottoms.

Just a bit north of Somers Point is the city of Linwood. Here two neighbors made decoys from the same patterns. Mark Kears was a skilled boatbuilder. His decoys reflect very good carving and painting abilities. His neighbor was Eugene Hendrickson, also a boatbuilder and housebuilder. Hendrickson's decoys as well as Kears's all have a very distinct look. The back of their bodies are flat from the base of the neck rearward and drop off very suddenly to the tail. Hendrickson later moved to a very large farm on the Mullica River at Lower Bank. Gene was a good friend and started me carving decoys back in the early

forties. He gave me secret glue developed during World War II to glue the decoy bodies together. He was a foreman at the Ventnor boatworks where plywood PT boats and wooden mine sweepers were being built. Gene also bought cedar from my grandfather for his boats and decoys. Some of his decoys in later years were painted by Armand Carney of Mathistown. Just directly east to the ocean lies the city of Longport. At the south end of Longport is Great Egg Inlet. This area was an excellent area for hunting shorebirds. Some of the finest shorebird decoys that were ever stuck in the sand were gunned over here. The hunter and decoy maker that made them was Daniel Lake Leeds, a carpenter by trade and a master artisan by hobby. His decoys have a look similar to that of the best New England carvers, and his painting detail has a very distinctive character. His shorebird decoys were used only by himself, and most have been purchased from his family descendants. Along with the duck decoys of Roland Horner, Dan Lake Leeds shorebirds are the best.

One of the oldest towns in Cape May County is near its center. Its history starts in the 1600s. It was called Head of the River. Townsend Godfrey resided near here as well as a shorebird maker by the name of McCarthy. Many good shorebirds were made from Sea Isle City south to Cape May. Ephrim Hildreth, William Stites, and Jonathan Cresse are among the makers of these fine decoys.

In no place in the United States can so many different types of shorebird be found. The point was a favorite haunt of many hunters. If the sands could only speak . . .

New Jersey duck hunting, decoy carving, and now decoy collecting have been rich and rewarding experiences for many. Information about decoys has been available primarily from among those of us who collect the decoys and pass on what we, as lovers of all this history, have learned. The fascinating charm and folk-art quality of this area's decoys draw more people into the fold each day. How strange it would seem to the creators of these decoys—and how very proud they would be—if they could somehow see how the simple blocks of wood they created to draw a flying duck or fast-flying shorebird to within range of their guns have become recognized as collectible art forms.

LEFT: Cape May shorebirds; ca. 1895. This feeding black-bellied plover (left) and preening yellowlegs (right) are the work of two unknown carvers.

ABOVE: Green-winged teal, a species of decoy rare in New Jersey, by Charles McCoy; ca. 1925. This pair was found abandoned on Little Beach Island, which has since disappeared under the area's changing tides.

CHAPTER 10:

DELAWARE RIVER

by Bruce Williams

No less practiced an eye than the noted decoy collector and authority William J. Mackey revealed in his famous 1965 book, *American Bird Decoys,* his partiality to Delaware River decoys. He appreciated the delicate care with which they were carved and the realistic and detailed manner in which they were painted. Mr. Mackey lavished praise on decoys used on the Delaware River as being as close to perfect as possible and the finest the country has ever seen. Of comparable stature among decoy historians, Joel Barber, in his equally famous 1934 book, *Wild Fowl Decoys,* discussed at great length and with great enthusiasm the Delaware River decoys of John Blair, which date back to 1866.

Despite the limited quantity, several compelling factors capture the fancy of collectors of Delaware River decoys. These include an exceptional beauty, the extra workmanship, the early historic leadership, and the preponderance of good-condition original-paint decoys.

In no geographic region is the quality of the decoys produced as consistently high as in the Delaware River region.

This is a result of early artistic leadership and the personal, painstaking pride of the rivermen. Carvers of the region were fortunate to have the extraordinary craftsmanship of John Blair in the lower Delaware River (decoys circa 1866–1900) and of precision-carver John English in the upper Delaware (decoys circa 1875–1910). Right from the start, these men set an elevated standard of achievement that basically stated: no clunkers allowed on the Delaware River!

John Blair created magnificent, sleek decoys beginning right after the Civil War, 1866, with feather-painting detail that was not even approached by others in accomplishment before 1900 and has never been surpassed in the minds of his many boosters. Considering the times, John English was quite a ways north on the river. He is credited with creating the raised wings and carved feathers on body and tail that were of unmatched precision in a decoy and set the standard to this day for all Delaware River carvers to follow.

Delaware River decoys have an above-average historic interest because, with few exceptions, carvers were constructing

OPPOSITE: *Mallard drake by John Blair; ca. 1866. From the 1880s rig of the Philadelphia lawyer-sportsman A. Mercer Biddle, Sr., this decoy was later in the collection of William J. Mackey.*

ABOVE: *Green-winged teal drake by John Blair; ca. 1870. This decoy's head is in the very desirable swimming position.*

RIGHT: *Bufflehead decoys by John English, ca. 1880 (left) and John Blair, ca. 1875 (right). The bufflehead is the most rare species for both carvers; the one by Blair is in his "classic" style.*

126

ABOVE: American merganser hen carved by John English, ca. 1880, and painted by John Dawson, ca. 1910. This belonged to Dawson's rig and then to William J. Mackey.

RIGHT: Pintails by John English; ca. 1875. This rare and superb pair of decoys is in its original form as made by the master carver of the Delaware River.

decoys for use within their personal hunting rigs (or for friends) and, accordingly, lavished extra-special effort to the very best of their ability.

While John Blair and John English must have produced many decoys, perhaps 600 to 700 each, this was before 1900, and most have long since disappeared. Those remaining are quite rare, particularly if still graced with strong original paint. Many Delaware River carvers produced only one or two rigs of hunting decoys in their lifetime, so there is a limited supply of quality work of most carvers, even in the 1900 to 1950 era. Fortunately, decoys from this region have been well preserved. The Delaware is a fresh-water river, the rigs have been relatively small, and carver-hunters have felt protective toward their own decoys. This has led to a generalized situation where, to the extent of available supply in the region, there is a preponderance of quality-condition original-paint decoys.

In the Delaware River region, taking an arbitrary cutoff year of about 1950, decoy production by better-known carvers has been estimated as follows:

About 50 decoys or fewer (10 carvers): Sam Archer, Howard Bacon, John Baker, John Blair, Jr., John Dawson, David Downey, David Faulks, Joe King, Joe Morgan, John Updyke

About 100 decoys or fewer (7 carvers): Charles Burkley, August Glass, William Kemble, William Quinn, Al Reitz, George Runyan, Joe Savko

Perhaps 250 decoys or fewer (6 carvers): Charles Allen, Antonio Bianco, Jack English, Ridgway Marter, Larry McLaughlin, Joe West

From 250 decoys to perhaps 1,000 (6 carvers): Charles Black, John Blair, John English, Dan English, Harry Fennimore, Claude Trader

Over 1,000 decoys (3 carvers): Tom Fitzpatrick, Jess Heisler, John McLoughlin

The estimated decoy production of all these carvers from 1865 to 1950 is roughly equal to the lifetime production as forecasted for Harry V. Shourds (East Coast, circa 1880–1920), a dedicated loner who by himself carefully selected all wood, and hand carved, hollowed, sanded, painted, and weighted all of his own decoys.

Back in the late 1960s, Bill Mackey referred in articles to the Delaware River as one of nature's masterpieces, with a magnificent past, but he predicted that the end was near for duck hunting, due to pollution, the impact of dredging by the Army Corps of Engineers, and the shoreline developments that

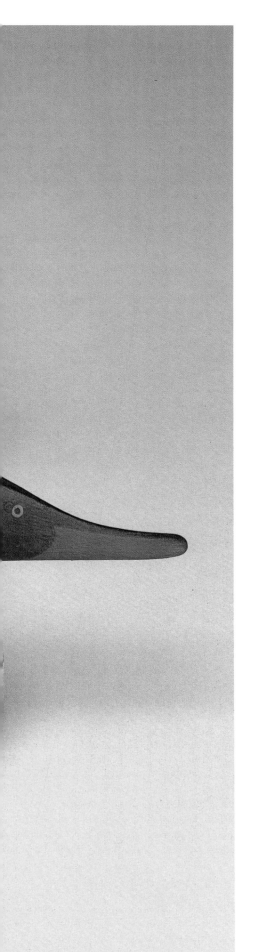

destroyed wildfowl habitats. The hunting area herein discussed stretches on the Delaware River from Trenton, New Jersey, in the north to Philadelphia, Pennsylvania, and into the Delaware Bay to the south. Midway between these two cities were three prominent decoy-carving communities, Bordentown and Florence, in the state of New Jersey, and the Bristol area of Pennsylvania.

In the early 1900s, the depth of the Delaware was 10 to 15 feet with many little inlets and waterways and tall grass feeding grounds for ducks along the water's edge. But over the years, the Army Corps of Engineers has deepened the river to depths of 40 to 50 feet, straight-lining the water's edge by dredging. All that was captured from the riverbottom was dumped onto the farmland at river's edge, destroying feeding and nesting grounds for ducks while creating bulkheading for commercial and residential property. Lush wetlands of wild celery and wild rice were replaced by sludge.

Long gone are the full-time market gunners, the hardy souls, descriptively but affectionately called "river rats," who fished in the summer and hunted in the winter along the Delaware for a livelihood. They could no longer maintain their carefree but demanding lifestyle. This could be said for the ducks also, who lost their happy feeding grounds. As the supply of ducks has diminished, so has the "sport" of hunting; the famous hunting clubs for "deep pockets" members are mostly a thing of the past. Such is progress.

Hunting on the Delaware River has entailed a technique called "sculling." A sneakbox or sculling boat is for one or two hunters, is about 14 feet long, wooden, and has a low profile. It has a limited foredeck draped with camouflage of some kind—frequently marsh grasses—to hide the hunter. A sculling oar

LEFT: Goldeneye hen (above) carved by John English, ca. 1880, and painted by John Dawson, ca. 1910, and American merganser ice-duck (bottom) carved and painted by John Dawson. The goldeneye's tucked-in head gives it a contented look in the water.

ABOVE: Black ducks carved by members of the English family. John English, credited with originating the raised-wing style, made the decoy in the center, ca. 1880; the decoy on the left is by his son Jack, ca. 1900, and that on the right is by Dan, ca. 1910.

juts out through the stern or an oarlock on the aft deck is used to propel the boat toward ducks resting on the water.

The technique involves setting up a rig of hunting decoys, perhaps 30 to 45, out in the water, and then rowing upstream with two side oars to quietly await the arrival of ducks to the placed wildfowl lures. When ducks were attracted to the decoy rig, the hunter, hiding low in the boat, ever so carefully moved up toward the ducks by sculling with the single oar, which is hidden from view in the rear of the boat. This procedure required good boatsmanship and great patience by the hunter to carefully sneak up on the ducks for the shoot. Once the shoot is completed, the procedure is repeated by returning upstream. This technique is more active and much more subtle and cerebral that sitting in a duck blind banging away at ducks on the flyby. Importantly, the sculling technique required Delaware River decoys to not only attract ducks but, by necessity, to hold the ducks in the water until the hunter could close in. This demanded carvers from this region to create decoys with extra realism—more tailored carving of wings and feathers and more embellished paint patterns.

To review the carvers' styles in the Delaware River region, it is helpful to subdivide them into several broad groupings: the John Blair school, the John English school, the Bordentown school, and, separately, the unique work of John Dawson.

Many consider John Blair, Sr. (1842–1928) the elder statesman of decoy carving. Family history records that he made his first hunting rig—17 mallards—right after the Civil War, 1866. John Blair was a prosperous carriage maker outside Philadelphia until about 1900 when, at age 58, he retired and moved to a big spread in Elkton, Maryland. He became a gentleman farmer and sportsman, hunting and fishing on the Elk River and north to Andalusia, Pennsylvania, on the Delaware River.

As a carriage maker, he owned the best tools available, had precision work habits, the best knowledge of woodworking, paints, and painting techniques. Early carriages (and sleighs) had especially elaborate paint decorations. In my childhood, we had three unusually fine, 1900-era sleighs in the barn, and I am aware of several large and valuable collections of these beautiful old vehicles. Decoys made in Blair's shop were probably a seasonal fill-in project, and the prestige-enhancing product produced was more than likely given to close friends or customers who also belonged to his two elite hunting clubs. For example, Bill Mackey and others have reported that the hunting rig of the well-known Philadelphia lawyer-sportsman A. Mercer Biddle, Sr., was prominently represented by John Blair classic decoys, and these were used on hunting trips in the 1870s with Ulysses S. Grant.

130

OPPOSITE: *Decoys by Jess Heisler. The "rocking-horse" black duck in the center was part of a special order of eight, ca. 1925, made for use on rough water; at left is a wigeon hen; at right a turned-head black duck.*

There are several styles of Blair decoys, but family members recall only the decoys known as Blair "classics"—plump, round-bottomed, large double-dowels, hollow, two-piece construction, rectangular lead weights skillfully beveled and secured with a dozen small nails, a neck-shelf for the head placement, tack eyes, and rounded head-top. A second class of Blair decoys comprises all of the above characteristics but are flat-bottomed; a third class are solid. Blair "classic" carvings have conservative, gracefully flowing lines. All Blair carvings have the extraordinary, exclusively Blair-style paint. Close inspection reveals realistically detailed and stylish feather patterns and delicate blending techniques. They are simply masterful. The clarity and definition of the elegant paint patterns elevate his decoys to being competitive with important oil paintings, moving them away from their created use as sport bird lures.

In the 1920s and 1930s, Joel Barber worked in New York City with John Blair, Jr. In his 1934 book *Wild Fowl Decoys*, Joel Barber sketched the classic Blair mallards, dated them 1866,

ABOVE: *Mallard hens by William Quinn (below) and Joe King (above). Both carvers were active as hunting partners during the 1930s and 1940s off Money Island in the Delaware River, and both were self-taught and skillful craftsmen.*

132

and recorded that after seventy years the original paint was still perfect. Blair had explained that his father had such affection for his decoys that individual canvas bags had been made to protect them and were in use to that day—the early 1930s.

With such stylistic adroitness achieved by John Blair, Sr., being considered as the ultimate in design along the lower Delaware, it is not surprising to find many features of his work incorporated into efforts by other carvers over the years. This has led collectors (including myself) to hope that cherished decoys might be recognized as Blair's handiwork and be accepted into the prestigious circle of Blair accomplishment. However, if a decoy does not strictly conform to the necessary characteristics, it must be identified as "Blair school," which seems an appropriate designation for historic classification.

John English (1852–1915) of Florence, New Jersey, was (along with John Blair) one of the earliest major carvers along the Delaware. He was a master carver with a high consistency of quality work and is credited with development of the "Delaware River style" followed by most of the carvers along the river in later years. This is characterized by lowheads (some resting on the chest) in a complacent, relaxed posture, carved and raised wingtips for puddle ducks (black, mallard, pintail, wigeon), and precisely incised tail and back feathers, with subtle and realistic feather painting. John English decoys have narrow heads, tack eyes, carved nostrils, exceptionally refined and studied carving toward the rear, and were generally thin-skinned and lightweight, despite a rectangular, multinailed lead pad weight.

Historically, there has been some confusion over the identification of decoys by John English because he stopped carving as early as 1900, and perhaps as many as one hundred of his decoys were spectacularly repainted by John Dawson between 1910 and 1920. Adding to the confusion, his son Dan (1883–1962) initially used his father's carving patterns before devel-

oping his own. Dan English's later decoys are more generous in size, have glass eyes, and usually have lowheads in a contented position. His other son, Jack English (1878–1944), remains a mystery but has been credited with making a few decoys using a pattern roughly similar to that of his father but with square, nicely carved tails. The paint on many Jack English decoys looks older than that on those by Dan English and could well be from John's era.

The unique carving style established by John English around 1870 to 1880 attracted other fine carvers in Florence and nearby. Firmly in the John English school to the south were Thomas Fitzpatrick (1887–1958) from Delanco, Jess Heisler (1891–1943), and Ridgway Marter (1893–1977) from Burlington.

Tom Fitzpatrick was a true river rat, living on the Dela-

ware in a mobile houseboat. "Fitzie" lived off the water, foraged, hunted, fished, and carved over one thousand black ducks. His earlier round-bottomed black ducks and mallards from the 1920s are most desirable—large, heavy-duty, deep feather carving. In the 1940s, he converted to flat-bottomed decoys, somewhat smaller in size, which were thought to ride the water with greater stability.

Jess Heisler was known as a skilled craftsman, a builder of quality boats and decoys, some of the finest on the Delaware River. His early round-bottomed canvasback decoys from the 1920s were as well-carved and painted as can be found. His appealing, flattish, oversize black ducks (17 inches in length) are known as his "rocking-horse" style, used on rough waters; the complex feather painting is an artistic achievement. A one-of-a-kind, turned-head black duck is special, clearly his best

Pre-1900 pintails: "W. Kuhn" is scratched on the weight of the decoy at top left; top right is branded "Saunders"; bottom left is a Blair branded "A. Tull, 1856"; bottom right is branded "G. Fox" and is ca. 1885.

134

work. There is an efficient simplicity of shape in his decoys, with deeply incised feathers. The precision painted plumage on his decoys is comparable to that created by the masters of the trade.

Ridge Marter also made fine duck boats and decoys, including a wide variety of species painted in great detail and in a spectacular manner. The large cheek jowls and the bright paint on his mallards demonstrate his flair for imaginative color.

Across the river from Florence were other followers of the John English school of carving. Several "old-timers" of high note lived in and around Bristol, Pennsylvania, including William Quinn (1915–69) and Joe King (b. 1909). Bill Quinn was an avid hunter from 1930 for over thirty years and may have made 100 or so decoys for his own use. It has been said that Bill Quinn rowed across the Delaware River to visit Dan English and brought back a basket of finely carved English heads. Quinn and his hunting partner, Joe King, then flawlessly carved wigeon bodies with upward-lifting large rumps and small, pointed tails. Quinn painted them in an elegant manner.

Joe King was an active hunter with Bill Quinn in the 1930s and 1940s. He carved fewer than fifty decoys, and his work was consistently excellent. His decoys have a soft, round,

flowing appearance and have great visual appeal. His weights are thick and bear the stamp "J.S. King."

Upriver, in Bordentown, New Jersey, was a large group of carvers influenced by the early work of Charles Black (1882–1956), including his son Chester Black, Charles Allen, Harry Fennimore, and John McLoughlin. The Black family made hundreds of decoys, mostly for family use—even the ladies were active hunters. Decoys of Charles Black had flat bottoms, limited carving detail, weights far to the rear, and the tails frequently carved from the bottom of the two body boards. He hunted actively into his seventies and had the reputation of being one of the best shots on the river.

Early Bordentown decoys had a minimalist look. Despite this generalization, John McLoughlin made some of the best carved heads ever—and before he reached the age of 20. McLoughlin and Charles Allen improved considerably over the years, and their product kept getting better. Harry Fennimore, in contrast, completed his best work when young, during the 1920s.

John McLoughlin (1911–85) was a favorite source among those seeking decoys for their rigs because he always completed them well and made many fresh stylistic changes over the years.

Wigeon drakes by William Quinn. Quinn shaped the bodies and painted the decoys, but the heads are believed to have been carved by Dan English. These decoys were among Quinn's very first carving efforts.

He had a restless knife and created unusual products through such extra effort as turned heads or high heads, or his cross-winged black ducks or the maple-leaf wing design on his early canvasbacks.

Sam Archer (b. 1894), also of Bordentown, specialized in carving boat oars (over 1,000), killing foxes (over 500), and shooting deer (two each year), but he also carved about 50 decoys. His American merganser ice ducks are marvelous examples of early folk art. Sam Archer claimed to have made only seven mergansers, but at age 90, when presented with several other pretty mergansers with folksy heads, he thought it might be nice to claim them, too.

John Dawson (1889–1959) lived in Trenton, New Jersey, and hunted from his cabin on Duck Island in the Delaware River. At about 20 years of age, Dawson carved decoys, which had a squarish but studied appearance; his redheads and canvasbacks had pointed triangular tails with paint applied in a patient manner with precise tiny feathers (and branded "JD"). The Dawson-carved American merganser flat-bottomed ice duck with its racy head is his best work. It is a marvelous piece of sculpture painted with a very modernistic flavor with draftsmanlike precision—way back in 1910!

Around 1910 to 1915, Dawson embraced the work of John English, buying perhaps as many as one hundred John English carvings and repainting them in a magical manner. Dawson created precision patterns like modernist paintings that are so unusual they act as signatures for the author's work. Dawson was an accomplished stylistic artist. The English-carved, Dawson-painted decoys are painted with unusual artistic merit and must be considered a masterful combination of decoy sculpture and painting.

Seasoned collectors cherish their decoys for the pleasure they render. They also have a nagging feeling that they could not be replaced if ever lost. The trend of increased values in the marketplace for decoys restricts new purchases by those who have favored decoys the longest and withdraws valued decoys from collections for resale by the people who have loved them the most.

Decoys from old hunting rigs represent many things: they are superb folk art, beautiful floating sculpture full of history, fun, good friends, a remembrance of less-complex times, a matching of wits with nature. Like the ducks themselves, decoys are in increasingly diminished supply. Accordingly, those fortunate enough to own them hold on tight.

135

CHAPTER 11:

MARYLAND

by Jeff Williams

The graceful skipjacks that once ruled the mighty Chesapeake Bay have all but disappeared, and the watermen who plied the bay harvesting its bounty of oysters, clams, and crabs have diminished too. Both are victims of changing times and the environmental havoc wreaked upon the bay for years. Conservation measures are now being taken, but it will take many years to reverse what has been done, and the bay will never approach the levels of productivity that enriched the lives of so many people over the centuries.

The Chesapeake Bay is America's largest estuary and encompasses a magnificent 4,000 miles of shoreline along Maryland and Virginia. For centuries the men and women of the Chesapeake Bay have counted upon the bay for their livelihoods. Fishing, crabbing, and clamming were the mainstays of every small port town. Hardy watermen not only provided their own families with food from the bay, but also hunted the abundant waterfowl that populated the bay and tidal marshes that surround the area. Market hunting became a lucrative business and led to the crafting of decoys to lure the waterfowl. Indeed, some of the finest decoys ever produced were made for use on the Chesapeake Bay.

The bay is divided into three distinct areas, and each produced carvers who developed their own, easily recognizable style. Upper Bay and Middle Bay decoys were made for use in the open waters. Lower Bay decoys were primarily made for use in the small estuaries and tidal marshes that dot the Lower Bay. While there are many famous carvers, there are just as many anonymous ones who produced decoys for their own hunting rigs and have descended into obscurity. Even though

their names are no longer known, their wonderful carvings and legacy will live on forever.

The Upper Chesapeake Bay encompasses the area where the Susquehanna River flows out of Pennsylvania into the bay and includes the town of Havre de Grace, where decoy carving has been a tradition for over one hundred years. Decoys were also carved in the towns of Elkton and Charlestown and around the Northeast River. Virtually all of the carvers in this region made decoys for their own rigs as well as guiding hunting parties and gunning for the commercial markets. Decoys were valued for their utilitarian function and were never considered for their artistic merits, as they are today.

While there are many carvers in the Upper Bay area, the most prolific came from the town of Havre de Grace, which sits at the mouth of the bay where the Susquehanna meets the Chesapeake. Havre de Grace is renowned for its hunting and fishing and has been a mecca for both sports since before the turn of the century. Many men made their living guiding hunting and fishing parties, and the center for much of this activity was the old Bayou Hotel, which is located near the city dock and is a residential condominium today. Wealthy sportsmen came from all over the country to partake of Havre de Grace's natural resources, and the hotel served as their headquarters. This was in the days when the river and bay would be black with canvasbacks and redheads. Aside from the sportsmen, Havre de Grace supported a large number of market hunters. One of the market gunners' favorite tools was the sinkbox. This device was nothing more than a large box with a space in the middle for hunters to sit in. The box was floated

OPPOSITE: Setting up a sinkbox out in the bay.

ABOVE: This remarkable pair of Upper Chesapeake Bay canvasbacks was made by John "Daddy" Holly. In original paint, they are among the finest Upper Chesapeake decoys known.

138

out on the Susquehanna Flats and counterbalanced with heavy cast-iron decoys. When the ducks came in, the market gunners had them. Havre de Grace carvers are famous for these sinkbox decoys, which were primarily cast at the old Principio Furnace, located above Havre de Grace near Northeast. Many of these were made from a pattern created by one of Havre de Grace's earliest carvers, John "Daddy" Holly.

Born in 1819, "Daddy" Holly was a waterman and hunter all his life in Havre de Grace. Like many others, he made decoys for his personal use and for sale to other gunners and guides. His decoys are in the classic Upper Bay style and have rounded bottoms, lead weights, and anchors, as do all Upper Bay carvings. The round bottom and weight allow the decoy to be used in the rough, open waters of the bay and river. This style has become the trademark of Upper Bay carvings. Holly carved canvasbacks, the quintessential Susquehanna Flats decoy, redheads, and blackheads. Holly had three sons, William,

OPPOSITE TOP: *Teal by Charles Wilson of the Upper Chesapeake Bay.*

OPPOSITE BOTTOM: *Wing ducks made by Ben Dye and John Graham in the late 1800s.*

John, Jr., and James, who also carved decoys. "Daddy" Holly died in 1892.

Sam Barnes (1857–1926) was another Havre de Grace carver who made decoys for his own use and for the guiding and market hunting he did for a living. He is particularly well known for his swan decoys, but also carved canvasbacks, red-heads, and black ducks like most of the other Upper Bay carvers. Barnes taught R. Madison Mitchell, a decoy maker of the old school, how to make and paint decoys.

Charles Barnard (1876–1958) was born in Havre de Grace and worked, until his retirement, for the old B&O Rail-road as a signalman. He made decoys for his own personal use and for use as a guide and market hunter. Many collectors consider his canvasback decoy to be the finest example of an Upper Bay carving. It exhibits all of the classic Upper Bay characteristics and has simplistic but serviceable paint.

Robert "Bob" McGaw (1879–1958) carved decoys for

ABOVE: *No one knows who made this magnificent swan: some collectors attribute it to Sam Barnes, some to the Holly family of Havre De Grace. The removable head is stamped with the Roman number II.*

140

ABOVE: Bob McGraw.

RIGHT: Bob McGraw is credited with making this pintail. He owned the first decoy-making machine in Havre de Grace.

himself and for other hunters while he worked on the Pennsylvania Railroad. He owned the first decoy-producing machine in Havre de Grace and later sold it to Madison Mitchell. The machine is now on display at the Havre de Grace Decoy Museum, which is devoted to the decoy legacy that abounds in Havre de Grace. McGaw carved canvasbacks, redheads, black ducks, bluebills, and some mallards. Later in life he also made geese as well as pintails and wigeons. Prior to acquiring the decoy machine, McGaw hand chopped his decoys and made many miniatures after the gunning season was over.

Jim Currier (1886–1969) also made decoys in Havre de Grace from the 1920s to the 1940s. He was the postmaster in Havre de Grace for many years and started carving decoys for his own use. His decoys were hand chopped and made from white pine and, later, cedar. He painted all the decoys himself, working in a small shop behind his house on Market Street. His main production was canvasbacks and redheads, although he made other species, including a few geese later in his life. His high-head decoys are much sought after by collectors. Although it is not documented, Currier may have learned how to carve from Sam Barnes. Currier died two weeks after his wife in 1969.

Many other carvers lived and worked in the Upper Bay area from the late 1800s until the 1930s and warrant acknowledgment. They include Ben Dye, Dick Howell, William Heverin, John Graham, Leonard Pryor, Henry and George Lockard, and Scott Jackson. These men were all fishermen and hunters who made varying numbers of decoys for their own use and for other hunters and guides. All of their carvings are in the classic Chesapeake Bay style. Today, numerous carvers in the Havre de Grace area carry on the old traditions. Perhaps the last of the great Upper Bay master carvers is R. Madison Mitchell who turned 88 in 1989. Mitchell was an undertaker by profession and made decoys in his shop behind the funeral home. Mitchell had Bob McGaw's original decoy machine in his shop prior to building one of his own. He made canvasbacks, redheads, mallards, black ducks, geese, and swan decoys for

use by hunters all over the country. Mitchell helped many young Havre de Grace carvers get their start by hiring them to work in his shop. Among the more talented and famous carvers who gained experience under Mitchell's tutelage are Charlie "Speed" Joiner, Jim Pierce, and Harry R. Jobes. Jobes is a prolific carver who produces all species in the traditional Upper Chesapeake Bay style. His three sons, Bobby, Charles, and Joey, all carve decoys and miniatures, making them Havre de Grace's unofficial decoy-making family dynasty.

Another important Havre de Grace carver was Paul Gibson (1902–84). Gibson was a fireman who carved in his spare time in a shop behind his house. He hand chopped his decoys until he purchased the decoy lathe that came out of Madison Mitchell's shop. Gibson carved all species and is particularly well known for his swans.

Down the bay from Havre de Grace is the Middle Bay area, probably the best-known part of the Chesapeake Bay

ABOVE: This regal Canada goose, with inletted head and two-piece neck construction, was found in Bucks County, Pennsylvania.

OPPOSITE: Pair of wood ducks by R. Madison Mitchell. The painting on these two decoys shows the heights attained by Mitchell's great skill.

LEFT: Steve and Lem Wood.

OPPOSITE: Standing bluebill made by the Ward brothers in 1918. Lem said this was the first standing decorative carving he ever made.

144

thanks to James Michener and his sweeping saga *Chesapeake*. Places like Tilghman's Island, Rock Hall, Kent Island, Easton, and Cambridge all have a long seafaring and hunting tradition that has produced many memorable carvers. Market gunning was a huge and serious business here. The use of night lights and big guns that could net the hunters thousands of waterfowl in a few, short hours were among the favored tools of these market gunners. When the government outlawed market hunting in 1918, there were some serious altercations between game wardens and hunters.

Ed Phillips (1901–64) was a decoy maker who lived near Cambridge. All of the decoys he made were for his own use and follow the typical Upper and Middle bay pattern of rounded bottoms, straight necks, and weights attached with lead ballast on the bottom. Phillips made canvasbacks, redheads, bluebills, black ducks, pintails, and wigeons. Collectors consider his wigeon his finest carving, and many also favor his bluebills, which have oversize heads and are of hollow construction. Compared with other Chesapeake Bay carvers, Phillips's production was low. He also carved miniatures in many different species.

John Glen carved decoys in Kent County, Maryland, during the early 1930s. Amos Waterfield, a hunting guide and later a well-known collector, bought many Glen decoys for the famous Cedar Point Gunning Club. Since Glen had a fear of power tools, all of his decoys were hand chopped. His wife would sand and putty them and often paint them too. Glen made canvasbacks, redheads, bluebills, wigeon, black ducks, mallards, and geese, although many collectors feel his pintails are his finest carvings. Later, Glen moved next door to Captain Jess Urie, a professional waterman who piloted his own charter boat on the bay. Urie made many decoys with Glen before Glen's death in 1952. Urie was a fine decoy maker in his own right, making most of the species common to the bay. Captain Urie is perhaps best known for the thousands of miniature decoys he carved with the help of his son, Roger.

Other important decoy makers from the Middle Bay area include August Hennefield, Ed Parsons, the Elliott brothers, and Josiah Travers.

Of the carvers still making decoys in the Middle Bay area, the most interesting and important is Charlie "Speed" Joiner. An alumnus of Madison Mitchell's shop, Joiner makes decoys

that are particularly noted for the artistic attention to detail and the excellent paint patterns. Mitchell once commented that Joiner was the best painter in the Chesapeake Bay area. Joiner's decoys reflect the majority of species that fly the bay area, and examples of his work are highly prized by collectors.

Farther down the bay is an area that maintains a special mystique for decoy collectors, Crisfield, Maryland. While the lower eastern shore of Virginia was noted for the wonderful decoys of the Cobbs, the lower eastern shore of Maryland holds special esteem as the home of the Ward brothers, Lem and Steve. Many collectors believe the Wards were among the most talented and prolific decoy makers of all time.

Crisfield, Maryland, is typical of other waterfront towns along the Lower Bay. The majority of the population worked on the water for a living, and the hunting of ducks came as a natural complement in providing a livelihood for their families. One of the first decoy makers in Crisfield was Travis Ward, the father of Lem and Steve. Travis was also a boatbuilder and, along with Noah Sterling, pioneered the Crisfield style—wide bodies and flat bottoms. These decoys differed in design and construction from those of the rest of the bay area, which employed rounded bodies that rode well in the rough bay waters. This difference in design may have resulted from the fact that some of their hunting was done along the marshes and creeks that surround Crisfield. Their decoys were very utilitarian, with rather primitive carving and sufficient paint to attract the ducks. Because of their historical importance, they are very collectible.

The Ward brothers got their start in decoys by working in their father's shop. Much of the paint on Travis and Noah's decoys were the earliest experiments by Lem and Steve. They began carving as a team in 1918, and most of their early decoys were for their personal hunting rigs. Soon, however, their reputation spread through Crisfield and the surrounding areas, and decoy making became a profession. Steve proved to be the better carver, while Lem excelled in the painting of the decoys. Lem probably painted just about all the decoys during their carving career. Although the Ward brothers' reputation grew because of the workmanship and lifelike appeal of their working decoys, the thought of shooting over one of them today is unthinkable to any collector.

146

Canvasbacks made by the Ward brothers.

The Wards were barbers by trade, and their barbershop in Crisfield became a gathering place for hunters and local townsfolk. Both of the Wards were poets who loved to write; many of Lem's birds included a poem written on the bottom. They also sang in a barbershop quartet, with Steve traveling far and wide for recitals. Steve was also a noted storyteller, sharing hunting tales and old folklore about their beloved town of Crisfield. Noted collector Bill Purnell recalled Steve's fondness for music: "The last time I saw Steve alive, he was sitting in his barbershop, obviously in a great deal of pain, listening to an old Victrola recording of 'Danny Boy.' I left that afternoon, and the next day Steve was gone."

Lem never had a formal art lesson, but through his willingness to experiment, he pioneered many innovative painting techniques that are still used by decoy makers. The oil paints he used were blended with a mixture of kerosene and gum turpentine. The result was rather slow drying, but the paint proved to hold up well under the weather and salt water. He would also prime the bodies by dipping them in hot linseed oil, which he would wipe off with a rag and let the decoy dry. This proved to be an efficient base to paint upon. Lem was also famous for bringing his palette right to the duck blind in the

marshes to mix the paint. After shooting a duck, he would straighten the feathers, study the bird, and mix his colors right there on the spot. Lem felt that the colors of the bills of many ducks, especially pintails and wigeons, changed shortly after they were killed and removed from the water. He went to these measures to insure authenticity in his decoys.

Most of the Wards' decoys tended to be oversize, and most were carved out of cedar. However, after World War II, balsa became available because of the abundance of balsa rafts; consequently, some balsa decoys were made. The Wards liked working with the material because it was generally soft and easy to carve. However, to accommodate the need for a hardier working decoy, the Wards found some balsa from Honduras, which was nearly as hard as pine.

The Wards made many species, including canvasbacks, black ducks, mallards, pintails, wigeon, green- and blue-winged teal, bluebills, goldeneyes, redheads, and Canada geese. Lem's favorite bird was the pintail, while Steve favored canvasbacks. Early working examples of the 1930s are very sought after by collectors.

By the 1950s, more collectors were seeking Ward decoys than hunters, and Lem began to make mantel birds, decoys

The Ward brothers made this pair of pintails for Glen L. Martin. With their pinched breasts, they are considered the most stylized pair of Ward pintails.

148

Canada goose by the Ward brothers; 1939. It has flat lead weights on the bottom and is the most stylized of their goose decoys.

ABOVE: Pair of bufflehead decoys made by Lloyd Tyler. These are considered rare since this species was not common to the Chesapeake Bay region.

destined for use over a fireplace rather than at work in water. Lem spent more time and gave greater attention to every detail to insure authenticity in his reproduction of the birds. He began to enter some of the national carving competitions and won many a ribbon. Many of the carvings look so real you want to reach out and see if the feathers will move. Although Steve never made decoratives, he did make a number of miniature decoys. As their reputation grew, they eventually earned the title "Counterfeiters in Wood." Steve passed away in 1975, and Lem died in 1984. They became legends in decoy-making history and shared their talents with many of the young carvers who passed through their doors. The Ward Foundation Museum in Salisbury, Maryland, opened in 1971 and is dedicated to the tradition and talents of these two great decoy makers and the folk art in which they shared.

A contemporary of the Wards from Crisfield was Lloyd Tyler. Tyler often referred to himself as the "poor man's decoy maker" because his decoys were so much cheaper than those of his neighbors, the Wards. Although his carvings were rather crude, they were finely painted and fairly efficient. He never painted the bottoms of his decoys, claiming, "Painting bottoms is a waste of paint and time." Tyler passed away in 1971.

OPPOSITE TOP: These wigeon decoys were made by Ed Phillips of Cambridge, Maryland, for his own rig.

Next to those made by the Wards, the most collectible decoys from the Crisfield area were made by Lloyd Sterling. Collectors consider his pintails, wigeons, and blue-winged teal the most desirable. Occasionally, Sterling would get the Wards to cut out his bodies on their band saw.

Another maker from Crisfield was Gunner "Will" Sterling. It's not known whether he was related to Lloyd, but a number of canvasbacks and bluebills have been attributed to him.

As the last skipjack sails into an autumn sunset on the Chesapeake Bay, the call of geese and canvasbacks can still be softly heard on the wind. This sound may serve to inspire future generations, just as it inspired the decoy makers who established a tradition along its shores.

RIGHT: Pair of blue-winged teal by Noah Sterling. These were probably made for an early fall shooting rig, the season blue-winged teal were in the area.

CHAPTER 12:

VIRGINIA

by Jeff Williams with William Henry Purnell, Jr.

A visit to Virginia's eastern shore today is much like stepping into the past. A way of life exists there that has continued for centuries, relatively unchanged and unaffected by modern times. It is a way of life bound to the ocean and bays that traverse the landscape and dependent upon nature for sustenance. The watermen plying the bay for oysters, crabs, and fish make their livelihood much like their great grandfathers before them.

Naturally, it is an area rich with seafaring tradition and culture, and the art of decoy making holds its own special place, born out of necessity and evolving into a uniquely American art form.

From the earliest days, when decoys were hand chopped and made from the masts of wrecked ships, to the refined and collectible art that they are today, decoy making has occupied a cherished place in Virginia's history and culture. Some of the finest examples of decoy carving were produced on this small ribbon of peninsula. Decoy legends, like Ira Hudson and the Cobb family, called this area home and pioneered the way for the rich legacy of carvers to follow.

The majority of Virginia carvers are primarily found in two Virginia counties, Accomac to the north and Northampton, which extends to the tip of the peninsula where the Atlantic and Chesapeake meet. Both areas are inextricably linked to the waterways that surround them, and decoy making came as second nature to the men who lived and worked here.

Chincoteague Island, a barrier island in Accomac County, has a long tradition of seafaring. It is famous for Chincoteague oysters and the annual pony penning, an event in July during which wild ponies, descended from ponies shipwrecked with Spanish sailors in the 1600s, are herded across the channel from neighboring Assateague Island and auctioned off by the Chincoteague volunteer fire department to raise funds. Chincoteague was also immortalized in the famous children's book *Misty of Chincoteague,* by Marguerite Henry. The decoy-carving tradition in Chincoteague dates back to the days of market gunning, when many men made their living by the mass shooting of waterfowl for sale to hotels and restaurants all over the East Coast. World famous for oysters, its fishing, clamming, and crabbing were also mainstays of the Chincoteague economy. Guiding hunting and fishing parties for wealthy mainlanders provided many Chincoteaguers with a reasonable living.

Among the Chincoteague carvers are many whose names have become synonymous with carving. Ira Hudson (1876–1949) was perhaps the most innovative and prolific carver in all

BELOW: Pair of Ira Hudson hooded mergansers. Only three other pairs are known to exist.

OPPOSITE: Shorebirds by Charles Clark. Left to right: A black-breasted plover, curlew, and yellowlegs. Their knobby heads make these decoys unique.

of Accomac County. During his lifetime he carved very lifelike decoys and built boats that gained him fame far and wide. Hudson's carvings are characterized by round weighted bottoms and simplistic paint. As was the case with many carvers of that era, Hudson found that wood was scarce and so made many of his decoys from old ship masts and other sources of wood that were readily available. The availability and size of the masts dictated the kind of decoys he could produce from that cut of wood. Most of Hudson's decoys are made from white pine and cedar, and a few were carved out of balsa. Besides his full-size decoys, Hudson also carved miniatures and a few flying birds and fish for which he is particularly well known. Most of his birds are solid, but on occasion he made a few hollow ones. The species that he carved included shorebirds, black ducks, mallards, pintails, brant, geese, bluebills, canvasbacks, buffleheads, goldeneyes, and red-breasted and hooded mergansers.

Hudson, like many carvers who were also watermen, used common marine paint, which was tough and durable, for his colors. After the decoys were painted they were set outside wet, and the dew flattened the colors.

Hudson lived most of his life in Chincoteague, producing decoys and boats for hunters. He himself was never much of a

hunter and was rarely, if ever, seen with a gun. The decoys produced by Ira Hudson showed a great deal of artistic foresight even though this was probably the farthest thought from his mind when he was carving them. He died in 1949 of a blood clot, having received very few accolades in his day, since decoy carving was a new and unrecognized art form.

Dave "Umbrella" Watson (1851–1938) was born in Fenwick Island, Delaware. He lived in Willis Wharf, Virginia, and in Chincoteague. He preceded both Ira Hudson and Miles Hancock as a carver, but Hudson and Hancock undoubtedly both knew Watson. His nickname was derived from the fact that he always carried an umbrella, rain or shine. Watson's carving skills came out of necessity, as he was a market hunter who made decoys at first for his own use. He carved perhaps one or two decoys a week, and many of these went to the famous Gooseville Hunting Club in Hatteras, North Carolina, which is now a federal wildlife refuge. From the late 1800s until the early 1900s, Watson hunted for the market and carved decoys as he needed them. When he began to carve commercially his stools were characterized by hollow carvings made out of white pine and a few balsa decoys. He made brant, geese, and black ducks primarily with a few canvasbacks, redheads, pintails, and bluebills and a limited number of shorebirds. The painstaking

154

ABOVE: Since they came from a rig he owned, these shorebirds are attributed to William Matthews. Their heads and wings give them a special look.

OPPOSITE: Ira Hudson made this flying mallard, which was originally part of a family group that included six miniature ducklings.

care that his carvings show is evidence of the time it took to carve them. He was a slow carver, and most of his decoys were too expensive for the average hunter.

Miles Hancock (1888–1974) was considered by everyone knowledgeable in these matters to be the best shot on Chincoteague. He made brant, geese, black ducks, bluebills, canvasbacks, buffleheads, goldeneyes, red-breasted and hooded mergansers, and pintail decoys as well as some decorative carvings and a lot of miniatures later in his life. His decoys were inexpensive and not very stylish but extremely serviceable, and they looked good on the water. Hancock's decoys tended to be oversize, and many were made of cottonwood, which would lighten up like balsa and float well. In the summertime you could see piles of decoy bodies in Hancock's yard.

He was undoubtedly influenced by Ira Hudson and for many years helped Hudson fill his decoy orders by carving the decoys and selling them to Hudson unpainted. Today, there are several baldpates carved by Hancock and painted by Hudson that are documented. Hancock died just as he was starting to see some measure of fame come his way, as decoy carving and collecting was just beginning to attract mainstream appeal.

Two members of Chincoteague's Jester family are also renowned as carvers. Charles Edward Jester (1876–1952) and Samuel "Doug" Jester (1876–1961) were first cousins and contemporaries of Ira Hudson. Charlie Jester was a market hunter and then a guide after market hunting was outlawed in 1918. He then did an about-face and became a game warden for thirty years. He used his considerable knowledge of the area to enforce the law, but never abandoned his love of the water. The decoys he produced were primarily for his own use and were hollow. He made black ducks, a few brant and broadbills, redheads and buffleheads.

LEFT: Ira Hudson restricted his production of shorebird carvings to greater and lesser yellowlegs. Because of their extremely thin necks, their heads often break off.

BELOW: Setting out stickup shorebird decoys.

Doug Jester was a more prolific carver than his cousin, and his decoys are very simplistic and unstylized. He carved all species but concentrated on bluebills, buffleheads, black ducks, brant, geese, and a few pintails. The most collectible Doug Jester decoys are the hooded and red-breasted mergansers.

Another Chincoteague carver known for his shorebird decoys is Charlie Clark. His shorebirds are notable for their distinctive skinny necks and knobby heads. After World War II many of Clark's shorebirds were used as lawn ornaments in gardens.

William Matthews also carved decoys for hunting guides in Chincoteague. His birds were generally of the utilitarian type favored by hunters. However, there are some Matthews decoys that show very distinctive features and were possibly made for his own use. Many of the shorebirds display small nuances that set them apart, such as a turned head or neck.

Many carvers on the island of Chincoteague still make decoys, but the one who probably best represents the old school of carving is Delbert "Cigar" Daisey. A duck trapper, waterman, and "certified character," "Cigar" can sometimes be found at the Chincoteague Decoy Museum, where he is the resident carver.

Down the coast is Northampton County and the town of Willis Wharf, home of Charlie Birch. Birch was a commercial decoy maker who was born in Maryland in 1867 and moved to Willis Wharf in 1906. He was a waterman who sold oysters and clams, and he made decoys that included black ducks, brant, geese, redheads, pintails, and buffleheads. Birch is better known for his carvings than his paint, which tended to be simplistic but serviceable. He made one known rig of swan decoys especially for a Talbot County, Maryland, rig. His swan and geese were also known for the oak bill that was made

158

Pair of pintails made by Dave "Umbrella" Watson. These were found in 1938 in a shed about to be demolished on Virginia's Assateague Island.

separately and inserted through the head with a slit and an oak spline to wedge it into place. His best decoys were hollow, and the solid ones he made later in life have little aesthetic appeal.

Moving farther down the coast into Northampton County is an area spoken of reverently by many decoy collectors, since it is the home of the Cobb family, who inhabited Cobb Island from 1839 to 1896. The Cobbs carved perhaps the boldest and most innovative decoys in all of Virginia. The Cobb family story has a legendlike quality and has been retold many times by various chroniclers. Cobb Island is a desolate spit of sand located off the coast near Oyster, Virginia. The island is flat with very few high places, and unlike other barrier islands it has no trees or forest for protection. Today, Cobb Island is a wild, uninhabited place much like it was in 1839 when Nathan Cobb, Sr., arrived there with his ailing wife, Nancy, and three young sons.

Cobb was a shipbuilder with his family on Cape Cod, Massachusetts, when it was discovered that Nancy had tuberculosis. They were advised that a move to warmer weather would be beneficial to her health. The Cobbs sold their share of the shipbuilding business and set sail in a schooner for more

temperate climes, with no particular destination in mind. They were forced into an inlet near the town of Oyster by a storm. Warmly received, the young family decided to stay, Virginia being warmer than Cape Cod. Nathan, Sr., soon opened a small general store, and the family built a house. The three Cobb boys, Nathan, Jr., Warren, and Albert, soon became proficient at hunting and fishing in the nearby bays and creeks.

Soon, however, Nathan, Sr., tired of keeping shop and dreamed of moving to the wild, sandy beaches of the barrier islands off the coast. Always a shrewd businessman, Cobb knew that there was a profit to be made from salvaging the cargoes of the ships that inevitably foundered off the coast. He decided that if he had a base of operations offshore he could successfully and profitably salvage these wrecks.

Grand Sand Shoal Island was owned by the descendants of Andrew Fabin, who had owned the island with William Satchel since 1734, when the provincial governor of Virginia gave them the deed to it. Nathan Cobb, Sr., bought the island for $150 and soon after the Cobb family built a small house. It became known as Cobb Island.

Nathan Cobb's Yankee ingenuity and shrewdness soon

Canada goose by Walter Brady. This decoy was formerly in the collection of William J. Mackey.

ABOVE: Red-breasted merganser drake by Doug Jester. This decoy is notable because it is made of cedar and not the cottonwood Jester usually used.

RIGHT: Swan decoy by Charlie Birch; early 1930s. This decoy, hollow with all original paint, was one of a dozen made for a Talbot County rig.

made the salvage business a success, and written accounts show that he drove a hard bargain when it came to negotiating settlements. At the same time, the Cobb family rescued many a ship's crew from the treacherous Atlantic. The first of two Coast Guard stations opened on Cobb Island in the 1870s. The "new" station opened in 1900 and still stands today, although abandoned.

Nancy Cobb died the year after the move to the island, and Nathan, Sr., remarried a few years later. In time, the three boys also married and brought their young brides to the island.

Along with their salvage business, the Cobbs soon became market hunters, tapping into the vast amounts of shorebirds and waterfowl that were in ready supply. After the game was cleaned it was shipped out on passing vessels to markets in Baltimore and New York. When hunters learned of the excellent gunning on Cobb Island they began requesting trips and expeditions to the island, which led the way for the Cobb Island Hotel. In its heyday the hotel could accommodate 100 guests as well as the attending help and the growing Cobb family. Hunters came from all over the East Coast, undertaking an arduous journey by train, horse and buggy, and sailboat to the island. They would stay about one week and hunt the entire time.

Northeastern storms are the bane of the Atlantic coast, and Cobb Island was no exception. Nathan Cobb, Sr., died in 1890 at the age of 92. Soon after, a "nor'easter" hit the island and destroyed almost everything. Everyone, except Nathan, Jr., and his family, had departed the island. In October 1896, another storm came and destroyed everything left on the island. The Coast Guard evacuated the remaining Cobbs just as the storm unleashed its devastating fury.

The decoys made by the Cobbs are extraordinary for their lifelike poses and innovative style, especially the brant and geese. No two are alike, and their appeal to gunners was and is overwhelming. Cobb decoys are earmarked by small nuances—the curve of a neck, turn of a bill, or carving on a shoulder—that set them apart from other decoy carvings. The Cobbs used the masts from wrecked ships for their decoys as well as copper nails salvaged from boats in the construction of their decoys.

OPPOSITE TOP: Oversize black-duck decoy by Nathan Cobb, Jr., the largest known.

BELOW: Turned-head brant by Nathan Cobb, Jr., that shows his ability to instill life.

RIGHT: A group of sportsmen prepares for a hunt at one of the many sporting clubs along Virginia's eastern shore.

In all likelihood, and as best can be documented, Nathan Cobb, Jr., carved and painted all the decoys. His attention to detail was meticulous, and the carvings have many small features that set them apart. He used glass eyes, generally black, imported from Germany, and the lead weights were attached to the bottom with brass screws, not nails. The bodies were primarily hollow, the tails notched, and most of the heads were inset into the body.

The Cobb decoys are all carved with either an "N" for Nathan, "E" for Elkenah, or "A" for Albert. This did not signify that those individuals carved the decoys. Most likely, it was used to signify and identify which decoys belonged to whom.

To meet the growing needs of the island, Nathan, Jr., and his "shootingest" brother, Elkenah, traveled to another famous decoy maker in search of more decoys. That maker was Harry Shourds of Tuckerton, New Jersey, and many hundreds of Shourd's decoys lived out their usefulness on Cobb Island.

Nathan Cobb, Jr., of Cobb Island, is best known for his carvings of geese and brant and for the personality conveyed by each one—such as this.

166

ABOVE: Rare Cobb bufflehead, probably included in a sport hunter's rig to give it a lifelike look. In the days of market gunning, bufflehead were not considered worth eating.

OPPOSITE: Cobb Island shorebird decoys. Left to right are a curlew, knot, and curlew.

The Cobbs also used decoys made by Joe King that were branded "E.B. Cobb." The Cobb decoys that remain today are the remnants of what left Cobb Island with Elkenah. The rest were, unfortunately, left to the tide and wind on Cobb Island.

Another Northampton carver who was probably influenced by the Cobbs is Walter Brady. Very little is known about Brady, and there are few known examples of his work. He may have been a guide on Cobb Island, and he may have lived in Oyster, Virginia. His goose decoys are considered to be among the finest examples of Virginia carving.

Decoys were also carved on Virginia's Hog Island, but there are no documented Hog Island decoys. The town of Broadwater had a population of around 400, and decoys were undoubtedly carved and used by local hunters. The carvings attributed to Hog Island are generally not distinctive and are most often somewhat primitive.

No discussion of Virginia and its decoy tradition would be complete without mention of some of the other famous gunning clubs that dotted the coast and provided one of the single biggest outlets for many of the decoys. Most of these clubs no longer exist, but some are still operating. However, when the retention rights that these clubs have had for years expire around 1999, they will cease to operate, and the rights will revert to the government for use as refuges and wetlands.

Among the more famous clubs are the Green Run Association, Bunting's Club, and Bob-O-Dell, on the island of Assateague. Bob-O-Dell was founded at the turn of the century by New York financiers who wanted to escape the crowds hunting on Long Island. It was originally known as the General Motors Club. Another famous hunting club was owned by Sam Riddle, who owned the famous race horse Man-o-War. This club, now known as Highwinds and owned by the federal government, encompassed vast acreage and was also once owned by Thomas B. McCabe of the Scott Paper Company. The powerful and wealthy would come from all over the country to hunt at these clubs, and many business and political deals were struck on the marshlands of Virginia.

The decoy legacy in Virginia is rich in many respects. Not only is the body of work produced by the Virginia carvers impressive, but the people whose lives and history were inextricably bound to these carvings are also represented and will be remembered by generations to come.

CHAPTER 13:

NORTH CAROLINA

by D. C. North, Jr.

Very little information about our Carolina decoys can be established before the mid 1800s. The one hundred years between 1850 and 1950 were the golden years for the handmade decoy. Few were needed before 1850 because fowl and game were not shipped due to transportation and refrigeration limitations. However, with the population growth in the mid 1800s, hunting fowl for food and sale to markets and restaurants began, along with sport hunting. During the post–Civil War period some of our finest decoys were made, those that collectors consider part of our American heritage. Starting with the mid 19th century, sportsmen came to gun our vast waters from Knotts Island south to Onslow Bay. Pressures on the market hunter to supply food for the table precipitated the need for more and better decoys, important and necessary tools to lure fowl.

Regional characteristics soon developed in the same way that our ancestors developed characteristics for furniture, pottery, boats, and many other functional necessities. The knowledgeable collector is aware of these variations. Wood has long been the favorite material for carving decoys: cedar, pine, and balsa were the woods most often used. However, some decoys were made of a wooden bottom board, a wire frame or body with canvas stretched over it, and a carved wooden neck and attached head. Such nondescript lures were made by the thousands. The only real advantage to this type of lure was its true-to-life size with a minimum weight, but they were easily damaged because of their fragile nature.

The opposite of the canvas decoys were the wing ducks used for battery shooting. Most were made of cast iron. Battery shooting was in wide use in North Carolina until 1935, when this savage means of hunting was outlawed. As many as fifty battery rigs were used in Currituck County and more than twenty in Dare County. These blinds were towed by tender boat to the fowling grounds and anchored. After securing the battery box, two hundred to three hundred wooden decoys would be rigged out in the water around this floating blind. Canvasback, geese, brant, redhead, and scaup were the common species used for this type of hunting. The decoys were generally oversize with simple paint patterns and usually were repainted each year for optimal visibility for big water shooting. A battery decoy with its original paint is an important addition to a collection.

Cast-iron wing ducks. The equipment and manpower needed to operate a battery shooting rig were justified only by the large kills for the market.

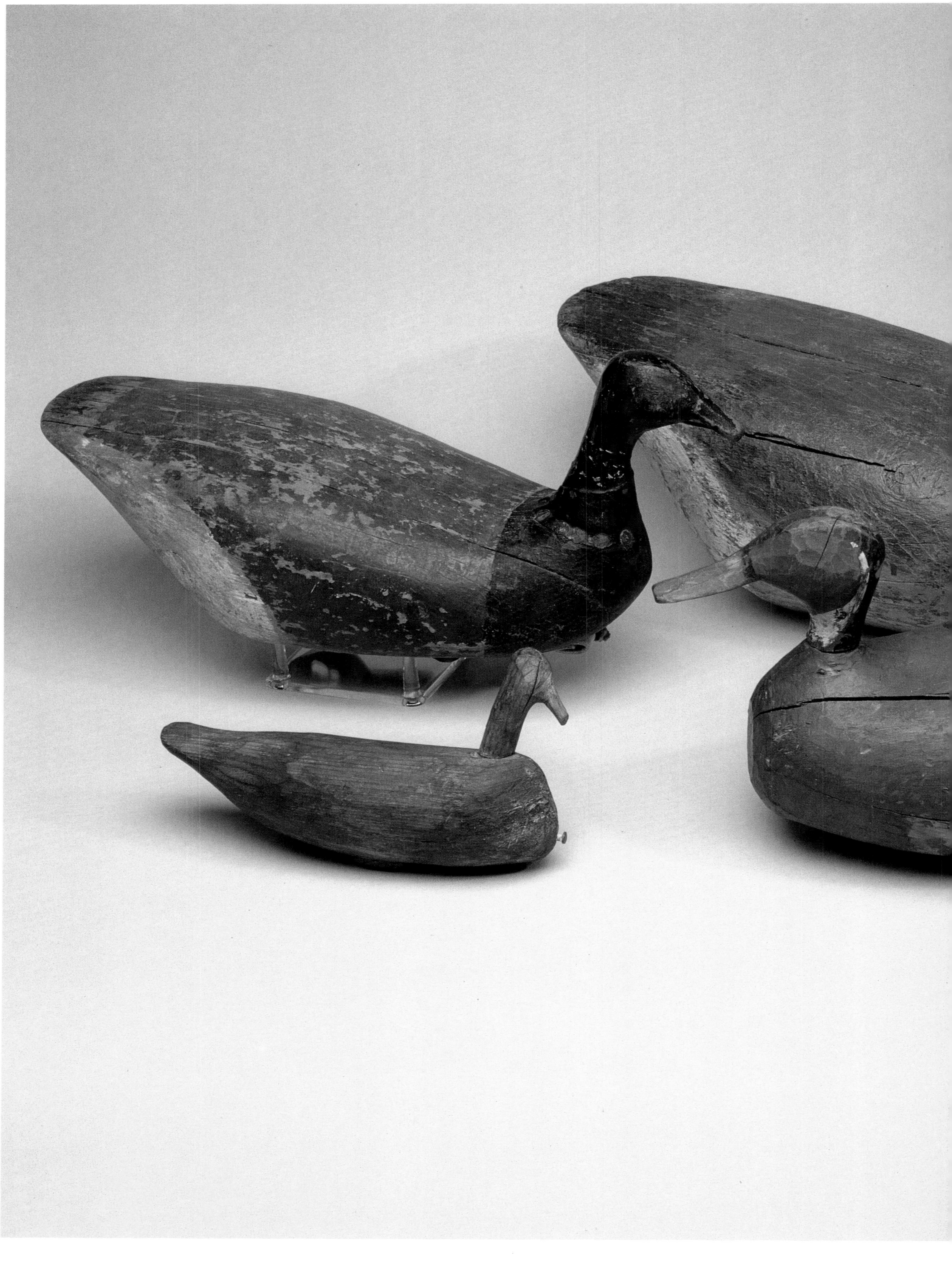

Roothead decoys. The long-forgotten makers of these rugged, primitive decoys showed more than a little imagination.

Cast-iron decoys served as a memorable part of battery decoy history in Carolina. These unique iron sculptures were used in conjunction with the battery shooting rigs. These battery, or sinkbox, rigs could best be described as water coffins. The gunner's watertight box was literally below the water, supported by hinged wings extending from the front and two sides of the box or battery. Some boxes were made for a single gunner, others for a pair of gunners who shot side by side. After extending the wings of the battery on the surface of the water, the gunner or gunners would sit or lie prone in the box. The iron wing decoys or an occasional wooden bird would be placed on the wings for stability, also helping the battery remain as inconspicuous as possible on the water. A foundry in Elizabeth City, North Carolina, made thousands of iron decoys for battery shooting, and some of the original castings that were lost overboard half a century ago are still being dug up by oystermen and clammers. Geese, brant, redhead, scaup, canvasback, and a rare ruddy decoy were cast for this purpose. History has recorded that over five hundred birds were killed by a single battery gunner in one day. The kills in these contraptions were barbaric, with thousands of fowl killed each day.

The punt gun or big-bore gun was also used in Carolina for night shooting. With a lantern on the bow and a large fowling gun loaded with shot mounted on the boat, the hunter would sneak up on the fowl with his blinding light, killing fifty to one hundred fowl with one shot. Sometimes such guns malfunctioned, seriously injuring the hunters. A law was enacted in 1918 outlawing this type of hunt. Thus ended the slaughter of migratory fowl in this manner.

Some individuals produced hundreds, even thousands, of decoys, while others only a dozen or so. Body and head style may be a thing of beauty, while the painting may be simple. One collector may regard a specific decoy as truly an object of beauty while another would condemn it as a crude block, but this variation in construction and paint has brought about a lasting appreciation of our decoys. What constitutes a good decoy is open for debate—there are no generally accepted rules.

Decoys made for use in the Carolinas include tiny ruddies, large canvasbacks, redheads, and scaup, purposely oversize for visibility on our open waters. Also included are our stately swan decoys that show such a purity of form and grace that surely their makers used angels as patterns for these monumental birds.

North Carolina carvers rate with the finest carvers of American waterfowl decoys. Anyone who has held a tiny ruddy decoy made by the skilled hands of Lee or Lem Dudley, John Williams, Ivey Stevens, or Ned Burgess can certainly understand that these little ruddies literally speak and add a certain dimension to a collector's shelf. Nowhere were any finer ruddy decoys carved than in Carolina.

North Carolina's most famous decoy carvers are the twin brothers Lee and Lem Dudley of Knotts Island, North Carolina. They were born January 21, 1861. They made canvasback, black duck, mallard, redhead, scaup, a few pintail, geese, wigeon, and ruddies.

Identifying a Dudley is easy. Find the "L.D." branded on the dead rise, the bottom part of the decoy, and it is certain that one of the brothers carved it. However, not all species were

172

ABOVE: Green-winged teal by Lee and Lem Dudley. This little teal was originally collected by William Mackey.

OPPOSITE: Ruddy-duck decoy by Lee and Lem Dudley. The crown jewel of North Carolina decoys, Joel Barber collected this.

branded. It is speculated that the "L.D."-branded decoys were used for the Dudleys' personal rig. The heads on Dudley canvasbacks, ruddies, and wigeon are outstanding. All Dudley bodies were carved to represent actual species.

In 1981, a team of sixteen knowledgeable collectors from different parts of the country assembled to discuss and evaluate the Shelburne Museum collection at Shelburne, Vermont. This important collection was assembled by Mr. and Mrs. T. Watson Webb, who founded the Shelburne Museum in 1947. The nucleus of the collection was the collection of Joel Barber of Wilton, Connecticut. This fabulous collection had been bought by the sons of Mr. and Mrs. Webb and presented to them as a gift. After judging the merits of over fifteen hundred decoys, a Dudley ruddy decoy was chosen as the top decoy in this prestigious collection.

In his book *Wild Fowl Decoys*, published in 1934, Barber writes,

> *On a visit to Knotts Island, for example, I add to my collection a group of old-time ruddy duck. They were very old and of singular perfection. As a collector I was elated for ruddies are among the rarest decoys on the whole Atlantic Seaboard. But that does not complete the story.*
>
> *In the very act of opening the door of the old boathouse where I found them, I recognized historical ground—my kind of history. The ruddies, six or eight of them, lay forgotten in a corner with miscellaneous gear. Some were broken beyond repair, all were scarred by service and bleached by exposure. Only traces of the original painting remained, but on the bottom of each decoy, burned deep on the dead rise, bore the initials—L.D.*

174

Carolina shorebirds: although made in most species for hunting the birds that frequented coastal waters, such decoys are relatively rare.

Discussion as to the finest carver our state produced can be debated by collectors and historians, but my favorite is James Best. Best was born at Kitty Hawk, North Carolina, on May 26, 1866, and died February 4, 1933. History records that for a rig of swan, geese, and other decoys, he used the mast from the schooner *William H. Davidson,* which wrecked near Paul Gamiels Hill Life Saving Station on December 12, 1910. A stately redhead decoy was found adrift in Kitty Hawk Bay in the 1930s by Allen Tillett. It lay in his boatshed until 1968, when it was bought for the sum of $5 by the late Vernon Berg. Berg was the first North Carolina collector to research the carvers and decoy history of our state, and I was privileged to spend many pleasant hours swapping and trading decoys and stories with him. I feel that Berg wanted me to care for this special decoy. My friend passed away six months after our trade—it is indeed my favorite decoy, full of special memories.

Ned Burgess (1863–1956), from Churches Island, was North Carolina's most prolific carver. A Burgess specialty was his canvas-over-wire-frame decoys. His wooden-bodied decoys were carved from the quarter of a log. He then used a wood

LEFT: Redhead decoy by James Best. History records that this decoy was carved from the mast of a schooner wrecked in the "graveyard of the Atlantic" on December 12, 1910.

175

rasp to simulate feathers on the body. His heads can be described as dainty and always erect. Although his paint patterns were usually simple, I have seen ornate painting on his wigeon and pintails. Collectors will gladly pay the price for one of old Ned's ruddies. They are fat, sassy fellows and are rated among the top ruddies in Carolina.

Burgess coots can actually take on a comical appearance when rigged out, the heads having been carved in many naturalistic positions. He also carved most species of divers and puddle ducks. In original condition, a Burgess decoy is a welcome addition to any collection. His style is unique to North Carolina.

John Williams (1857–1937) of Cedar Island, Back Bay, made many species of decoys. However, he will be remembered for his monumental swans along with his fat, pert ruddy decoys. Williams carved in a style similar to others around Knotts Island. His decoys were proud and sassy. As a professional guide, Williams truly was a student of nature, spending hours hunting the Carolina waters. Ivey Stevens and members of the legendary Waterfield family carved with Williams, and sometimes even the most knowledgeable collector has difficulty trying to assign the real maker. They were all talented; to attain a decoy by any one of them would be a delight.

I'll never forget a story told me by Steve Barnes, a local

RIGHT: Ruddy-duck decoy by Ned Burgess. With thousands of decoys of various species, Burgess was North Carolina's most prolific carver, but no more than three dozen ruddy decoys have survived.

waterman and decoy collector. One fall afternoon in 1981, he was poking around in a deserted, cobweb-infested barn on a farm near Knotts Island. Reaching into an old wooden flour barrel, he pulled out not one, but three tiny ruddy-duck decoys. Since the carver remains a mystery, they are known as the Mary James Farm Ruddies. Mary James's husband, Milton, guided for the Piney Point Club and was killed by lightning in 1942. Shortly after Steve's discovery, another local collector found rig mates on the same site. So far, eight have surfaced—perhaps more are waiting to be discovered. History has already recorded them as North Carolina classics. These superb little fellows "speak to the collector."

Dare County produced one of the finest carvers of decoys in Carolina, Alvirah Wright. He lived most of his life at Duck, North Carolina, on the Outer Banks. Wright decoys are sought after by collectors throughout the country. His total lifetime output of ruddies, canvasbacks, a few blackheads, and redheads numbers fewer than twelve dozen. His carvings have a bold, simplistic look of their own. As a boatbuilder, he developed a style of decoy that was influenced by this skill. Wright was born in Camden, North Carolina, in 1869 and died in 1951 at the age of 82. In my early days of collecting, I was offered a

rig of *six* Wright canvasbacks for $75 each. How I wish I had known then what I know now. I still do not own one of his majestic canvasbacks.

Within the past five years a rig of six swan decoys has been positively identified. These magnificent birds, five hollow, one solid, were made by William Henry Basnight of Manteo, North Carolina, circa 1890. Mr. Basnight served as caretaker of the Durant's Island Club in Dare County. All six of these decoys have been accounted for; five in private collections, and one at the Shelburne Museum. They are authentic gunning swans, having been made prior to the early 1900s, when a law outlawing the harvesting of swans was enacted. Swan decoys made after 1918 were supposed to be used only as confidence decoys, luring ducks, brant, and geese to the hunter's gun. An authentic gunning swan is really a prize possession. In the early 1980s, swan hunting was again allowed in North Carolina on a limited basis.

Also made in Dare County, a few miles from the Durant's Island Club at Mashoes, North Carolina, was a rig of five swans, circa 1840–60. These are the oldest documented decoys I have found. They were carved by the knowing hands of Tom Midgette. One of the swans is in its original coat of light gray paint that depicts a cygnet or young swan. Tom Midgette must

OPPOSITE: Decoys by John Williams. From left to right, a canvasback, swan, and ruddy duck. These show the classic style Williams made for use on the waters near Knotts Island.

ABOVE: Ruddy-duck decoys by Alvirah Wright. These hand-chopped birds must have inspired confidence when rigged out in natural surroundings.

LEFT: Mary James Farm ruddies. These superb ruddies—so small they can be held in the palm of a hand—lay forgotten in an old barrel on the farm.

178

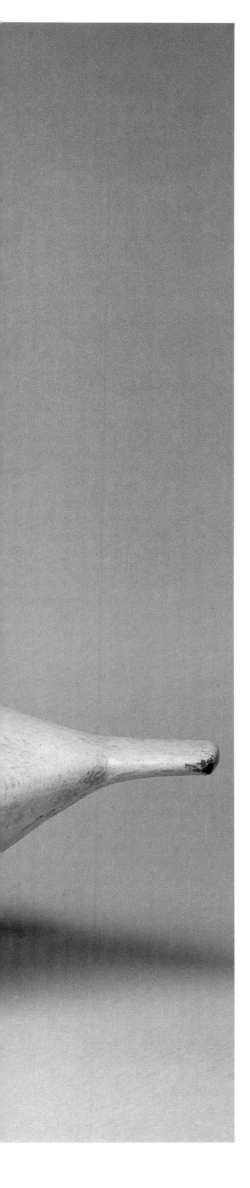

179

be given extra credit for this unique touch. I rank the head and neck carving as fine as any Carolina swan ever produced—a bold statement. The style and grace of these swans are second to none.

Ocracoke and Portsmouth islands were home to the O'Neal family—"Big Ike," Walter, and George—and the legendary Captain Gary Bragg and Stanley Wahab. These men carved geese, brant, and duck decoys using a design that incorporates a wide hip body with forward-tilting root heads. The decoys from these islands reflect these makers' rugged environment and the use of available materials, such as ships' spars found adrift on lonely beaches.

When talk turns to decoy carvers in Carteret County, the name Mitchell Fulcher stands alone. Using his familiar Rodgers pocketknife, hatchet, and sandpaper, and with little formal education, he literally carved his name at the top of the class. As a young man Mitchell served as a professional hunting guide for the Cedar Banks Hunting Club, but he made a living catching terrapin, trapping otter and mink, and fishing Core Sound.

The carved "M.F." initials have been found on geese, brant, swan, pintail, redhead, blackhead, black duck, merganser, and even one confidence decoy, an American egret. In the same area, many decoys have turned up that Mitchell reheaded. Decoy historians feel that many James Holly decoys found their way south from Maryland as several Hollys have been discovered with Mitchell heads and paint pattern, complete with Mitchell's initials. Mitchell made heads for another talented carver from the area, Robert Pigott, but the heads are the only similarity, as Pigott bodies did not have the style and grace of Mitchell's decoys.

Many a tale has been told about this special Carteret County character, and one was told by his friend and hunting companion, Julian Hamilton, of Beaufort, North Carolina:

> One day Mitchell was out checking his otter and mink traps when who should he meet but "Mr. Polecat." Neither had any intention of getting out of the way, both standing firm in the path. Mitchell, determined to pass Mr. Cat, reached for a long net stake that lay nearby to bust the cat over the head. Mitchell missed, and the cat released a liquid that blinded him and left him gasping for breath. Realizing he had been defeated, Mitchell went off for home in search of whatever comfort and relief he could find.

ABOVE: Canvasback by Alvirah Wright. This splendid Wright decoy was carved around the turn of the century on the Carolina coast.

LEFT: Swan by William Basnight, carved before 1900 and one of the few remaining examples of a true gunning swan.

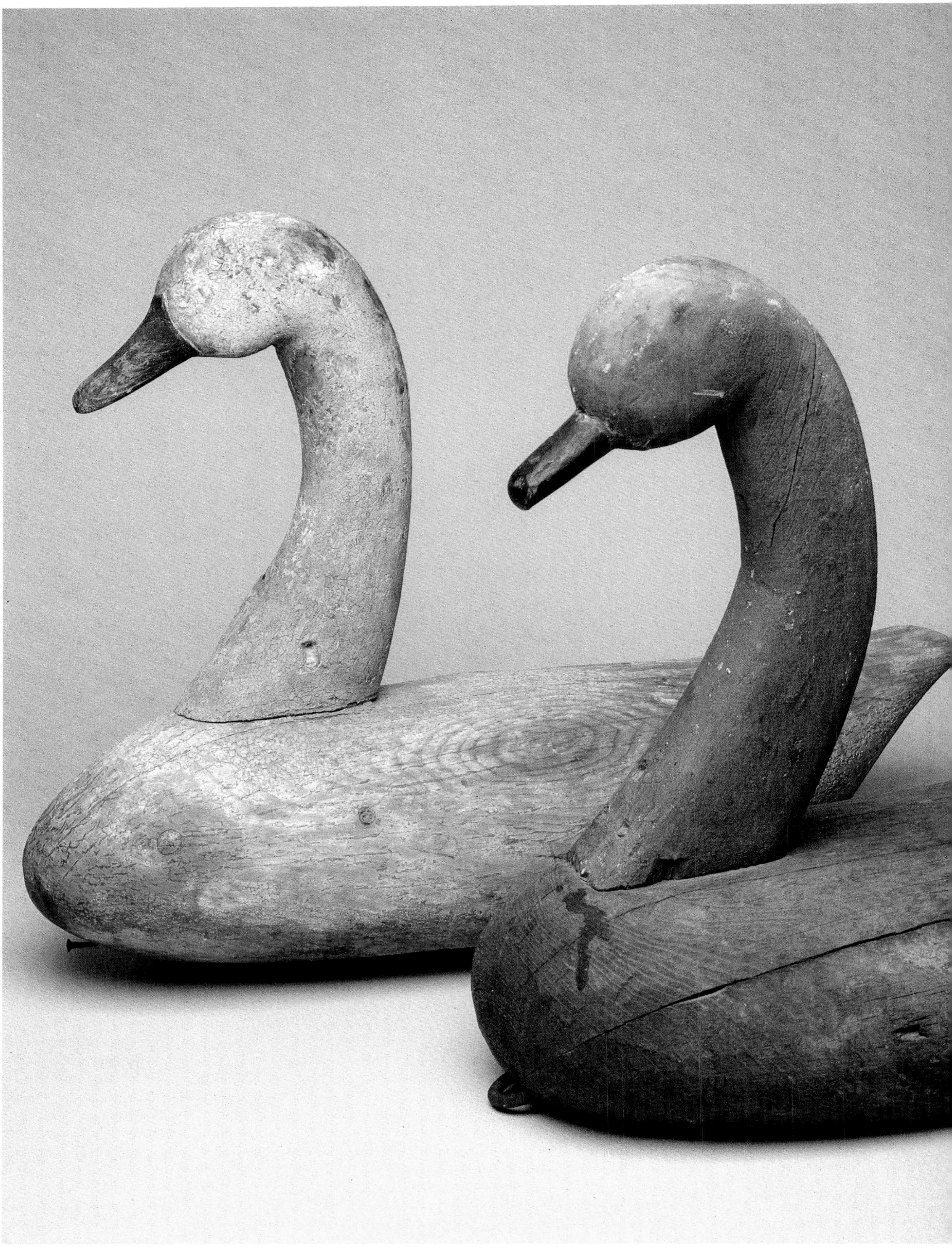

Swans by Tom Midgette. North Carolina's oldest documented decoys, these swans are considered among the finest hunting decoys ever discovered.

181

Mitchell Fulcher certainly left his mark as one of the most talented carvers Carteret County ever produced. He was born in the community of Stacy, North Carolina, February 10, 1869, and died at the age of 81, August 8, 1950. This closed the chapter on one of Carteret County's most unique characters.

Some of my fondest memories of ducking are the trips to the community of Davis, in Carteret County, with my two young sons. We would pack our gear for the two-and-a-half-hour trip up the coast. Arriving about sundown, anticipating a great shoot the next day, we would be welcomed by our host and guide, Clement "Chill" Willis, and his wife, Miss Norma. Their home was located on Core Sound, and in the evenings we could watch the movement of literally thousands of redheads and blackheads flying over Core Sound. Miss Norma's suppers consisted of ham, collards, and dumplings, and of course sweet-potato pie, around which we swapped duck stories. Up at five the next morning, we would awake to the smell of the strongest brewed coffee on the Banks. After eating a huge breakfast of country ham, eggs, grits, and biscuits, we would gather our gear and walk down to Chill's boat for a fifteen- or twenty-minute ride to one of his famous stake blinds, which rose majestically from the water some twenty or so feet. There, bobbing in the water around the blind, would be some twelve dozen hand-chopped decoys made by the legendary decoy-carving team of Eldon Willis and Elmer Salter—names that are synonymous with decoy history in Carteret County. What a sight as redheads and blackheads set their wings over the decoys on a cold, gray blustery morning. Usually we had our limit by noon and would be on our way home with fond memories and several braces of duck for the table.

More recently I had the pleasure of hunting with Roy Willis, Eldon's son, near his home at Stacy. After his dad's death, Roy inherited some of the finest Carteret County decoys known. Roy is an experienced waterman and guide and, to say the least, is "a great shot." He can see a flight of ducks thirty seconds before the normal eye can spot a flock.

Time was turned back on a recent hunt as Roy set out a stool of buffleheads his dad had carved some fifty years ago. These little gems worked miracles as, time and time again, buffleheads would light into the dozen or so of "Mr. Eldon's" tiny works of art. At day's end, Roy would pluck each one from the water and tuck it in a gunny sack with loving care.

Green-winged teal are also a joy to the collector. They remind me of the story the late Bill Mackey told of his trips to Knotts Island, and of how he tried on many occasions to pluck a little Dudley teal from his guide's rig without his usual success. Finally, after many visits, Mr. Mackey succeeded in placing a facsimile in the rig, and, as we know, the Dudley teal was collected. However, the story of the little teal does not end here. After Bill Mackey's death, the decoy was bought by a California collector, Eldon Smith. The little teal returned to North Carolina in 1986, having been acquired by one of Carolina's more persistent and knowledgeable collectors, Ed Johnston of Charlotte.

An interesting group of Carolina shorebirds include a cork-bodied roothead curlew and snipe found in an old net house on Harker's Island. These decoys may possibly be two of

182

LEFT: Yellowlegs decoy by an unknown maker. This North Carolina sculpture presents the ultimate in style and grace.

OPPOSITE: Pintail decoy by Mitchell Fulcher. This decoy bears Mitchell's carved initials and was made for his personal gunning rig.

the earliest shorebird decoys ever discovered, as fowling on this lonely island has been recorded for over one hundred twenty-five years. The maker will remain a mystery, but his simple decoys are folk art at its best.

A small roothead snipe was made by Charles Fulcher of Stacy around the turn of the century. This decoy was carved from available native material and has real character.

A plump dowitcher is certainly one of the finest shorebird decoys as to form and paint. It was carved by Calvin Gaskill of Stacy, circa 1880–90. Holding this decoy in your hands, you get a feeling that it will somehow come alive.

One egret, or scoggins, is from a rig of five made by Alphonso "Fonnie" Tillett from Kitty Hawk, circa 1900, and is made from a native cypress root. The Tilletts shot egrets for food for the table. Clay Tillett says that when he was a young boy he would go with his father and two older brothers, Avery and Allen, to shoot these egrets and act as the bird dog, retrieving the fallen game.

One of the most graceful Carolina shorebirds ever carved is a yellowlegs, or yellow shaft, as it was known locally. Seeing this decoy in its natural habitat, one feels that the decoy is actually in motion. Shorebird decoys by this anonymous maker from Knotts Island have also been featured in *American Decoys*, by Quintina Colio, published in 1972. A shorebird of the character and grace that this carving displays would thrill any collector, for one could not ask for a better example of Carolina

shorebird carving. This little fellow was carved before 1900.

Shooting clubs throughout the coastal regions of our state have played host to hunters from all walks of life. As the sportsmen came to gun our vast Carolina waters, local economy prospered. There was always a need for guides, caretakers, and decoy makers. Hundreds of clubs dotted our coastline and marshes, and for a few bucks, a man could hire a professional guide who would pole him to a blind, set out decoys, and retrieve the fowl.

Some of the more fashionable clubs included the Currituck Shooting Club, founded in 1857 by a group of gentlemen from New York. In recent years the Hanes and Chatham families from North Carolina, names that are synonymous with the textile industry, have owned the property. In 1894 President Grover Cleveland was a guest of the Swan Island Club, which was begun in 1870. Early members were the Endicotts from Rhode Island, the Palmers and the Forbes from Boston. Decoys now known as Swan Island decoys were used in great numbers and probably were carved on Long Island instead of in Carolina. These birds are found with the Forbes and Endicott brands.

The Monkey Island Club, founded 1866, was used by the executives of the American Tobacco Company. The Whalehead Club, built by Mr. E. C. Knight, Jr., of Philadelphia, was the most lavishly furnished club in Carolina. The three-story club featured piped-in salt and fresh water and had nine main

bedrooms and eight baths. Tiffany chandeliers, corduroy wall coverings, and cork inlay for the floors were used for decorating this beautiful lodge. Mr. and Mrs. Knight entertained often in these sumptuous surroundings.

Ogden Reed, owner of the *New York Herald Tribune*, built the Flyway Club in 1920, where he and his guests experienced some of the finest gunning in Currituck. The publisher of the *Ladies' Home Journal*, Joseph P. Knapp, built a fine hunting lodge in Currituck County in 1916 known as Knapp's Lodge. Knapp also contributed his financial assistance to build a school for the children of the county. The island he owned on Knotts is known today as the Mackay's Island National Wildlife Refuge. Just south is Bell's Island Club, founded in the 1920s by Hobert Bell, principal of General Mills.

Dare County clubs include the Bodie Island Club, Off Island Club, Duck Island Club, and the Jack Shoals Club. The Durant Island Club is famous for the rig of six swans carved by William Basnight before the turn of the century. The Gooseville Gun Club was founded in 1914 by Albert Lyons of Detroit, inventor of the automobile bumper. Van Campen Heilner, author and sportsman, was a frequent visitor here. The Jack Shoals Club was founded by the Kohler family, noted bathroom-fixture manufacturers.

Over in Hyde County, many came to gun the waters of Lake Mattamaskeet, and the local economy flourished during the gunning season with locals providing food and lodging.

Also in Hyde County were the Green Island Club, the Beach-combers Lodge Club, and the Beacon Island Club.

Carteret County's clubs include the Davis Island Club, Harbor Island, Salters Lodge, Hercules Club, Cedar Banks Club, and Great Island Club, to name a few. Lesser known than some of the larger clubs, these were used primarily by native Carolina sportsmen.

Down in Craven County the Camp Bryan Rod and Gun Club was founded in 1896. Ellis Simon served as general manager for many years until his death in 1984. Club guests here included "Babe" Ruth of baseball fame; Frank Stevens of New York, the inventor of the hot dog; and Bud Fisher, creator of the "Mutt and Jeff" comic strip. The decoys that were made for these clubs were carved by well-known carvers as well as others who will forever remain anonymous. These men carved their place in history as well as our hearts. Their decoys are the part of our Carolina waterfowl legacy that today is recognized as true American folk art.

I believe a collector can hold a decoy in his hands and communicate with the carvers, smelling the sweet cedar chips as they carved late into the night and weathered a cold nor'-easter as it blew the salt fragrance from the marsh through the cracks of their hunting shacks. Today, the collector is preserving a part of our past that history will never repeat. I trust that future generations will be able to experience and enjoy a part of our waterfowl heritage.

CHAPTER 14:

SOUTH CAROLINA:

DECOYS BY THE CAINES BROTHERS

by Joe Engers with Dick McIntyre

Until the 1980s, most collectors accepted the notion that there were no examples of handmade decoys from South Carolina. Joel Barber, the dean of decoy collectors, lamented in his book *Wild Fowl Decoys,* "The southern gunner, while a user, has never been a maker of decoys, or if so, none of them remain. At the same time, rules of this kind are subject to exception, and exceptions are frequently of great distinction. So it would not surprise me at all some day to add to my collection an outstanding example of decoy making from this romantic region."

While Mr. Barber never garnered one for his collection, eventually a number of southerners became aware of a small group of elegantly carved, sculpturally refined decoys discovered around the coastal waterways of Georgetown, South Carolina. As decoy collectors noted their existence, theories circulated as to their origin. Some initially guessed that the decoys could be traced to Louisiana because of the elaborate style and wing carving. However, continued research has indicated that they were made by a group of brothers who were raised in the marshes north of Georgetown—"Hucks," "Sawney," "Pluty," "Ball," and Bob—the Caines brothers.

The Caines brothers were commercial fishermen and gunners from the mid 1800s to the early 1900s. They lived at a settlement called Caines Village, an area fronting on Muddy Bay, facing Pumpkinseed Island, not far from Georgetown. The village had originally been settled by their grandparents, and like their forebears, they initially worked on the rice plantations that surrounded their homes. Shortly after the Civil War, the Caines brothers turned primarily to the surrounding waters for their livelihood. This included commercial fishing and gunning, which led eventually to the making of decoys. No one knows which of the brothers actually made the decoys, although Hucks and Ball undoubtedly worked together, and all

of them at one time or another may have been involved. In 1905, the coastal plantations, which included Caines Village, were purchased by the well-known American statesman Bernard M. Baruch, and Caines Village became part of his famous estate, Hobcaw Barony. As was the custom in the south, when Baruch purchased the plantations, the tenants and their settlements were included with the purchase. For years, the Caines brothers had shot ducks and rail on the surrounding rice fields and marshes for sale at the market. During the fall and winter months, this was their primary source of income. The sudden fact that the land was now privately owned and posted against trespassing perplexed them. In rebellion, their hunting activity (poaching, in Baruch's opinion) on Hobcaw increased. In his autobiography, Baruch recalls apprehending Hucks Caines one morning with 166 black ducks and mallards in his possession. Following the ensuing confrontation, Hucks was promptly employed to do what he had always done every November, hunt ducks. Only now he was required to take Baruch's guests out hunting with him. Eventually, Hucks became Baruch's favorite guide. All the Caines brothers were eventually employed by Baruch with the exception of Ball, who never accepted his offer.

Approximately fifty examples of Caines decoys still exist today. From the wonderfully elegant "snakey-necks" to the primitive split-tail mallards, each decoy shows a continuity that exhibits a stylistic progression in their carving careers. The slope of the breast, the rounded neck seats, and the shallow behind the neck—which helped hold the anchor line—are all shared characteristics of Caines decoys. The majority of the decoys have some form of raised-wing carving, varying from approximately 1/8 inch to almost 3/4 inch on the large, oversize birds. These larger decoys are referred to as "raised-wing" mallards. Some of the decoys also are constructed with a peg under the bill that was apparently added by the Caines to

OPPOSITE: Hen mallard by the Caines brothers carved in their turn-of-the-century "snakey-neck" style.

ABOVE: Black duck with pegged bill by the Caines brothers. Such pegs repaired broken bills and prevented further breakage.

prevent the bills from being damaged during usage.

Species now in collections include mallards, black ducks, and one pintail. However, all of the black ducks were originally mallards later repainted as black ducks. Many believe that all of the original Caines decoys were mallards.

A few hollow decoys are also in collections, all branded "B.M.B." for Bernard Mannes Baruch, and these are considered to be from his own personal rig of decoys, which were reportedly made by Hucks. In comparing the carving details and construction, there is little doubt that these hollow birds were made by the same skillful hand that fashioned the great "snakey-neck" mallards.

The Caines brothers probably made a few hundred decoys. The original Hobcaw mansion burned to the ground in 1930, and the boatshed, where most of the decoys were stored, burned in 1951. Neglect, termites, and powder-post beetles further reduced the survivors.

The South Carolina decoy is not as readily available as those from other geographic regions; for fifty years they were completely unknown to most collectors. As their existence has become public, they have finally been appreciated as among the most sculpturally refined examples of decoy art.

CHAPTER 15:

LOUISIANA

by Charles Frank

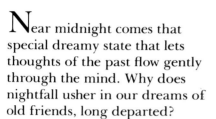

Near midnight comes that special dreamy state that lets thoughts of the past flow gently through the mind. Why does nightfall usher in our dreams of old friends, long departed?

My wife gently reminds me that I've been working too long and chides me that I've been retired almost six years. No matter, the dreams of old decoy carvers awaken the memories that keep collectors of memorabilia in a most pleasurable frame of mind. Black Cajun coffee and chicory and country roads, ofttimes shadowed by stately oaks and tall cypress trees festooned with Spanish moss; thousands of miles traveled over dusty roads with tracks that followed meandering bayous; hyacinth in purple splendor covering the marsh in spring and summer, red and gold swamp maple brightening the land in fall, and winter graced with hosts of waterfowl migrating to Louisiana—no wonder my endless search to document Louisiana carvers has been so pleasant.

I think of sitting on a worn porch step on an autumn afternoon with my old friend Mitchel Lafrance. Charles Hutchison, a very talented disciple and I had been reminiscing with Mitchel, age 90 but with a memory for detail I still envy. I asked him about a New York publisher who had come to Louisiana each year to hunt. "Tell me, Mr. Mitchel, did Mr. Pulitzer shoot well?"

With a twinkle in his eyes, he said in that soft Creole accent, "Well, Mr. Frank, let me tell you about him. He was a very nice man. I remember one afternoon, putting him in a blind back of Davant where we hunted. I recollect the winds was out of the northwest. Blowing pretty good, it was. Out in front I saw a pair of pintails start to flare. I gave a little whistle, and they turned and cupped toward our 'coys. I whispered to him, 'I'll tell you when.' Now those birds came in just fine. I was a pretty good caller, you know. When they was in range, I touched his arm and said, 'Now.' He stood up and emptied his gun. Never touched a feather. I said, 'Watch me.' I caught those birds crossing and brought them both down with one shot. You asked me how he shot? He shot real good, just couldn't hit much."

I remember the evening I sat at Mitchel's wake, thinking that once again an old carver I had learned to love and respect had gone to his reward. Just as leaves are brightest in the fall, so men, frequently, can be most colorful at the instant they too fall and are picked up by the Almighty.

The memory of this and a hundred other moments just as vivid are the legends of the marsh. Men like Nicole Vidocavitch, Mark McCool Whipple and his brood, Reme Ange Roussel, Jr., James Curtis Roussel, the Viziers (Odee and Clovis), the Comardelles, Tonasia de St. Germain, Victor Al-fonso, Domingo Campo, and Dewy and Theodule "Tatie" Pertuit all are a part of the tapestry of lives, touched often with tragedy, but never daunted by adversity. Their strength was rooted in a deep-seated faith in a supreme being who guided their destiny and whom they never doubted or questioned.

Why are Louisiana decoys unique? Certainly every area has its idiosyncrasies. The difference lies in the conditions under which the carvers lived and is reflected in the style of their blocks. They are lighter and longer, consist of smaller stools, are more concentrated in the areas in which they were produced, and are more widespread in their distribution. All of these things are a fascinating part of Louisiana folklore.

An oft-told tale is that if you drew a line down the length of Bayou Lafourche, from Donaldsonville to Grand Isle, you'd find that a good percentage of the decoys of Louisiana were carved within fifty miles north or south of that meandering line. The reason could be traced to the antediluvian age of slipped tectonic plates. This has caused the area to be referred to by geologists as the tilted triangle. The earth's surface is formed on "plates" that rest on one another. The shifting of these plates can cause an earthquake or a change in the surface that creates great plains, depressions, or swamps. Our tilted triangle, where these plates shifted eons ago, has created a vast marshland, in which soft, rotted vegetation has sunk and covered the plates. A layer of water several feet deep covers this, and a matted layer of new aquatic plants has furnished another cover that can support construction in some sections but will hardly support a man's weight in others.

The unique lightweight of Louisiana decoys is a result of this fragile surface. If a hunter had to walk the marsh, he darn sure wanted lightweight decoys that wouldn't cause him to break through this swamp. Another reason for the concentration of carvers in this area was that it was an area where the hunter needed to bring the birds to his blind. In north Louisiana, rice, bean fields, and grain were the lures that brought in great flocks of mallards and huge bands of blues, snows, and speckled bellied geese. Here hunters could watch the flight pattern and walk to another hide. The ground was firm and cover was plentiful. No real need for decoys.

The wood was available. Cypress root and tupelo gum were both plentiful and lightweight. Forests of bald cypress and tupelo were in every swamp for the taking. Today, tupelo gum has been recognized by world-class carvers as the finest material for decorative wildfowl art, as early Cajun carvers knew well. Dense grained, lightweight, even textured, rot resistant, and with the excellent cross-grain characteristics so important to the artist, tupelo has become the choice of world-class carvers.

OPPOSITE: Mallard drake by Mitchel LaFrance. This bird is typical of those turned out by LaFrance, Joefrau, and Fredericks in LaFrance's shed.

TOP: Gadwall by Domingo Campo (1887–1957), a hunter, trapper, and fisherman whose creations exemplify the work of the early Spanish emigrants to Louisiana.

ABOVE: Turned-head mallard hen by Antonasia de St. Germain. Pinned with cypress pegs, this decoy has survived many years of use in Mississippi potholes.

RIGHT: Two canvasbacks by Dewey Pertuit, one of Louisiana's most prolific carvers. His patterns of mallard, teal, ring-necked duck, canvasback, and pintail stayed the same, but his paint pattern changed.

Mark McCool Whipple carved and painted this canvasback drake just after World War II. Even were its paint removed, this decoy's head and body style would make its identity clear.

The number of decoys in a stool was not nearly as important as in more northern latitudes. This left the craftsman a smaller task when carving his rig. I think this accounts, in part, for the wonderful quality of so many small stools. An exception to this rule are the large rigs of ringnecked and scaup decoys used on our larger bays and lakes. I've seen as many as several hundred ringnecked decoys in use by my old hunting buddy Joe Bishop, in the halcyon days when Simoneaux ponds was a mecca for New Orleans sportsmen. A former rice plantation, the ponds were still divided by levees. Willows had grown tall along each pond, and hunters' blinds were isolated, so that birds shot over in one area would circle briefly and cup into another stool not too far away. Ducks were so plentiful (circa 1946–50), that a limit of twenty-five birds could be taken in the early morning and the "sport" back in his New Orleans office by 10:00 A.M.

Louisiana hunting was famous, both for its great numbers of waterfowl and the hospitality of its people. The great depression had left its mark, and guides got $3 a day; birds were picked and cleaned for another dollar. The hunter frequently used decoys carved by his guide, and in fact many of our best-known carvers were guides to the affluent visitor, who returned home with a stool of decoys he'd fancied on a visit "down south." You'll find many Louisiana decoys in collections all over the country and frequently hear the remark, "This is one of my favorites, but I've no idea who carved it." With the publication of many regional books, and this overview, that situation will vanish and provenance will be more readily established.

Since many of our carvers lacked formal schooling, recording and cataloguing of their art has been a very confusing and challenging chore. Frequently, we have been mislead by the mistaken premise, "My grandfather carved these birds." Since grand-dad hunted and carved a few decoys, anything left in a sack was thought to be carved by dear old grand-dad. You'd find the work of half a dozen identifiable carvers mixed in a rig,

BELOW: Warren A. Seebt used the balsa life rafts from merchant vessels sunk by German U-boats at the mouth of the Mississippi River during World War II to make many of his decoys, including this wigeon drake.

190

and what was left required cross-referencing to establish authorship. We're still trying to pin down a number of loose ends, one of the most tantalizing being John Bruce of Bruce's Island in the Rigolets, a tributary of Bayou Barataria.

Now the facts are clear on several points. John Bruce was a most remarkable man. I've traced his roots as well as the tangled skein will allow and have never heard a single derogatory statement about his abilities or character. He was born in Larose in 1857, and some of his cousins still live there. I've interviewed a nephew there, who remembered only kindly incidents. Bruce moved to the Lafitte area, about twenty-five miles due south of New Orleans, as a young man. Fishing and trapping were his original means of livelihood, but his skill as a guide and decoy carver gradually led to his appointment as head guide and off-season watchman and caretaker of the famous Little Lake Hunting Club. This little island, now under several feet of water due to saltwater intrusion, is still a well-known spot to many of Lafitte's older residents.

I interviewed sisters, a daughter, sons, grand-children, and other relatives. One daughter, Augusta ("Augie"), a fisherwoman and lifelong dweller on the banks of Bayou Barataria, was most helpful. She showed me John Bruce's gravesite in the Flemming cemetery. It is a lovely spot under the shade of several gnarled oaks, with heavy cover of Spanish moss. The atmosphere lends another note of reverence to this man's history. A carefully whitewashed headstone and artificial flowers were there when I visited on All Saints' Day. On one edge of the cemetery is a small hillock, topped by a stately, moss-draped live-oak tree. It's an Indian mound, with an ancient gravestone on top. This Indian mound, site of a village of Houmas Indians, is gradually being absorbed by waves from the wake of oil-field service craft. Bayou Barataria gets wider each passing year, and in time the gravesite and Indian mound will vanish, as Bruce's Island did, into the mist of time.

Bruce's other daughter, Agnes, told me her father had a cow and a flock of chickens and some live decoys he kept in memory of the old days when they were legal. A small truck farm completed his independence from the urban world.

BELOW: Victor Alfonso carved and painted this turned-head mallard drake as a wedding gift for his wife sometime around 1929. Many collectors consider it among the best Louisiana decoys ever made.

ABOVE: *Pintail drake by Adam Ansardi. Well-to-do, Ansardi carved and painted decoys for his own use; the feather pattern is sophisticated.*

RIGHT: *Gadwall (below) and scaup (above) by Reme Ange "June" Roussel, Jr., who shared his patterns with so many others that identification is sometimes difficult.*

192

When his wife was ready to deliver a child, he'd go out on the end of a small pier in front of the island and fire three blasts of his shotgun to summon the midwife. After the birth, he'd return to the pier, announcing to the world the birth of a daughter with a single blast, two shots for a son.

An old tavern, Babe Chaferra's Place in Lafitte, had his decoys on its shelves. The tavern burned down several years ago. Another bar and dancehall, which looks like a haunted house from a late-night movie, seemed like the place to find a treasure. I drove to Lafitte a dozen times before the reclusive owners would let me in. This had to be the place! There was old furniture and a bar that had seen many a Saturday night *fait do-do* (country dance), all covered in a blanket of dust and falling plaster. I rooted around as much as propriety would allow, but not a sign of a decoy. The owners remembered some old decoys that had been in back of the bar, but someone had swiped them many years ago.

Then Agnes found a faded picture that one of Bruce's sisters had kept. I now possessed the first photograph of this mystery man, standing in a pirogue with decoys in front of him. I had the photo copied and enlarged as much as possible. The heads of the decoys seem to bear a striking resemblance to those of Nicole Vidocavitch. A young friend from Lafitte who had helped me in my search found two decoys that the owner claimed were from Bruce's knife. Again a remarkable similarity to Vidocavitch. The decoys had been in a fire and were somewhat burned, but in good overall condition. The Little Lake Hunting Club burned down a number of years ago. Were these decoys from the John Bruce stool, carved for some New Orleans sportsman?

The last treasure received from Agnes was the pattern of a small teal duck head. I traced the cardboard cutout and returned the original to John Bruce's daughter. The tracing again has the Vidocavitch look. What is the connection, or is there any?

Recently, a collector friend purchased a decoy that was traceable to the owner some twenty-eight years ago. Found in an attic where it had laid these past decades, it is also reputed to be a Bruce decoy, with a ducklike bill and paint and carving like nothing I've ever seen on a Louisiana decoy. He asked me, "Could it be a snow goose decoy carved by Bruce?" I hate to puncture balloons, but after careful investigation, I think not.

"I found it in an old attic, where my grandfather lived. He hunted with John Bruce. So this is a John Bruce decoy." That just won't do for me.

Then the luck that persistence brings came into play. Morgan Perrin found a miniature mallard that his grandfather had kept for many years. Not much larger than a pocketknife, it also

194

ABOVE: Canvasback by Arthur de Jean. Bayous Gauche and des Allemands were noted for large beds of wild celery; thus, a great number of canvasback decoys were carved there.

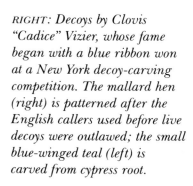

RIGHT: Decoys by Clovis "Cadice" Vizier, whose fame began with a blue ribbon won at a New York decoy-carving competition. The mallard hen (right) is patterned after the English callers used before live decoys were outlawed; the small blue-winged teal (left) is carved from cypress root.

was unlike any decoy I've ever examined from our bayou carvers. I decided to take the owner of the "goose" and Morgan Perrin with the miniature to see what the Bruce sons and daughter could do to throw any light on the mystery. By God, we did it! All three, John's daughter Augusta and his sons John and Adam, took one look and said, "That's my Daddy's decoy." The goose, they adamantly insisted, was not their father's decoy.

This is but one example of the research future generations will have to face. I'm sure somewhere, someone will find the answers that will flesh out the story of other equally remarkable Louisiana carvers. When their story is unfolded, it will be from a cache of decoys, in an old burlap sack, in a town named for some long-forgotten event—with a Cajun name with a French, German, or Spanish-Illeano ring to it. That's what makes the search so romantic.

Another remarkable character was Nicole Vidocavitch. Nicole, a Yugoslavian (a "Taco" in the local vernacular), was the youngest son of John and Charlotte Vidocavitch. Their roots in Europe were to a closely-knit clan that sought escape from the poverty of the Old World of the 1800s. Legend has it that John Vidocavitch was a seaman who jumped ship and swam ashore at a small town near Empire, Louisiana. We do know that he was born in Castlenuovo (Herzog Novi), a small village in Dalmatia, Yugoslavia, and arrived in the New World in the early 1840s. A slave owner, he was master of a small plantation with six slaves and also worked the oyster beds of Bay Adams and Grand Bayou. Parish records show that he purchased his first male slave in 1850. It was a rough life in this remote little settlement, and John died of tetanus, contracted from an injury he sustained on his boat in the oyster beds in 1885 or 1886.

A photograph of the little frame cottage John built in Sunrise, a few miles from Empire, shows the house to look quite European. Neat flowerbeds and a picket fence attest to the orderly life-style of this family.

Nicole was the youngest of John and Charlotte's seven children. In the strict and conservative atmosphere of the time, the children were all expected to earn their daily bread. He was attracted to the outdoors from early youth and frequented the marsh that surrounded the passes at the mouth of the Mississippi River. He was recognized as an exceptional hunter, with an intimate knowledge of the latticework of shallow ponds and passes that bordered the river, and was selected as one of the first guides of the then fledgling Delta Duck Club.

He worked there from 1890 until 1915, guiding prominent New Orleanians who frequented the area. It was an unbelievable land of bounty. Ducks, geese, deer, oysters, and fish

LEFT: Nicole Vidocavitch, guide, market gunner, faith healer, and—beginning at the age of 62—master carver of cypress-root decoys.

OPPOSITE: Black ducks and miniature by Laurent Verdin, Sr. Verdin used no sandpaper on his decoys, smoothing his blocks with broken oyster shells. He bought his paints at a hardware store on Bayou Lafourche.

Henry remembered going in a model-T Ford with his grandfather and a friend to cut tupelo and cypress root for his decoys in the swamps that surrounded New Orleans. A picnic lunch and a day on the Mississippi River made days John would never forget. Nicole was a kindly hero to all who knew him, part of the legacy of tenacity that marks the character of men who never bow to adversity.

The legends of Louisiana carvers are replete with others who left indelible marks on the pages of our history. Mark McCool Whipple was another of these great bayou carvers. Born in Bourg, July 21, 1884, he has been an inspiration and a role model for generations of decoy carvers along Bayou Terrebonne.

There is a syndrome I like to call the master-carver effect. Louisiana was a largely rural state in the days and years that followed the Civil War. Small communities were isolated from one another, connected only by roads that were impassable in all but the best weather. Until the massive road improvement program of the Huey Long era in the thirties and the later interstate projects of the fifties and sixties, the degree of isolation kept communities tightly enclosed ethnic and cultural units. Thus decoy styles developed in many small towns that mirrored the technique and pattern of a master carver. Money was scarce and frequently a pattern was shared for a bushel of greens or a quart of honey. Men like Reme Ange Roussel gave patterns to dozens of men in the Houma area. I've been fooled several times, mistaking the work of Willie Badeaux, who cut tupelo gum for Reme, and Curtis Chauvin, Reme's nephew, for work of this master craftsman. Many skills were developed in these isolated communities. Men bartered services and depended on one another. They lived in an age when men knew their survival and comfort depended on this exchange, freely given. They were builders, builders of boats, of homes, of friendships, and of decoys.

In the Bourg-Monteguet area the master carver was Mark McCool Whipple. It is still said that when someone blows a duck call on Bayou Terrebonne a Whipple is bound to answer. And so a distinctive style developed. Knowledgeable collectors can tell at a glance: Bourg/Monteguet, meaning of course, "In the style of Mark Whipple." His brothers, sons, and nephews all carved from patterns similar to the master. Even the paint patterns are similar. Roderick "Duck" Whipple, Walter, Max, and Houston were all carvers in his style.

As a young man, Mark was employed on the boats that worked the head of the passes of the Mississippi. The huge congregations of waterfowl imprinted a love of the out of doors that was never to leave him. He became a tugboat captain but spent every leisure hour carving decoys and improving his skills as a carver, hunter, and finally as a guide. Increasing deafness forced Mark to leave the river and move to Bourg. Here he began taking hunters into the marsh beside Lake Long. He teamed up with brother Walter, and they developed an excellent rapport with the sportsmen they were guiding. The trip to the lake was a tough, cold, ten-mile round-trip in the winter months. So Walter bought a small boat named the *Rover*, built a protected shelter for the sportsmen, and towed the guides and pirogues to Lake Long.

Max told me that the fee for guide services was $1 for the

graced the table, and sportsmen who hunted there frequently referred to "a four-pound week," a reference to weight gained at the camp. Clouds of waterfowl descended on the beds of wild celery, delta duck potatoes, wild rice, and arrowroot that covered vast sections of the tidal flats. About this time Nicole began to be recognized for the magnificent decoys he was creating. Many a northern visitor went home with a dozen blocks, a gift from local steamship magnate John Waterman. Since many sportsmen belonged to more than one hunting club, stools of Nicole's birds were also purchased for use at the Litier Club, on lower Bayou Lafourche, and the Avoca Island Club, near Morgan City.

For several years after the passage of the Migratory Bird Act, Nicole continued to be a market hunter. No one during this era looked down on the profession. Ducks were so plentiful, and law enforcement so haphazard, that no one bothered about the barrels of waterfowl shipped daily to the marketplace in New Orleans. My grandfather posed in his store beside a mound of mallard and teal. This was in the restaurant supply house he founded in 1892. The firm recorded purchase prices of 25 cents a pair for mallards and 10 cents a pair for teal.

In 1915, one of those terrible hurricanes that hit the Louisiana coast with regularity wiped out the town of Sunrise. Nothing remained. With little left but the clothes on his back, Nicole moved to New Orleans to seek more profitable employment. He was 62 years old. It was a tough time to start a new life. Undaunted, he set to work, chopping out his cypress-root beauties. He was able to command $18 to $24 a dozen, a top price in those days. Frugal, and a dedicated family man, he was remembered fondly by his grandson, the late Henry Collin. Henry told me that Nicole was known as a "traiteur," a faith healer. His ability to give relief from such maladies as migraine headaches was freely offered. However, he considered this gift from God sacred and never accepted money for his treatment.

boat ride and $5 a day for the guide. The guide was expected to pole the hunter from the *Rover* to the blind and back, call and retrieve downed birds, and gut the kill. Remember, too, that in those happy days a morning's shoot seldom was fewer than fifty ducks and "poule deau" (coot). In 1946 things had changed but little. I paid my guide at Simoneaux ponds $6 for a morning hunt. The limit was ten ducks and fifteen coot. You were also expected to shoot an extra limit for the guide.

In 1923 Mark purchased "Ole Doube," a 12-gauge Winchester pump shotgun, nickel steel with a 32-inch full-choke barrel. He quickly developed a reputation as one of the best marksmen in an area where men were expected to make every shot count. Tales of his marksmanship are still part of the lore of the bayou.

Mark was then asked to be the head guide at the prestigious Avoca Island Duck Club, located in the Atchafalaya Basin near Morgan City. Mark earned the "princely" sum of $100 dollars a month, plus room and board. Hunting season was only three months long, with an extra month of preparation to cane the blinds and refurbish the decoys from the preceding season. To earn his keep the rest of the year and take care of his growing family, he and his son, Max, carved and painted as a team. Whipple decoys are among the most plentiful of quality birds because of this man's prodigious energy. He used tupelo gum, cut from the bottomlands of the basin. I've never seen a Whipple decoy that wasn't carved from the best of blocks. They never show shakes (hidden flaws) or splits, attesting to the care in drying and painting each decoy. Worth hundreds of dollars today, some old hunters point with pride to Whipple decoys their families have used for generations. Hundreds of paddles and duck calls of elderberry with tongues scraped from old pocket combs are still turning up, all part of the legend that is Mark McCool Whipple.

I've been recording the story of Louisiana decoys and the history of their makers for many years. In 1970, I was asked to list my choices for the twelve most historically significant carvers in our state. In 1986, I was asked again, and when I look at the list now the only changes I'd make would be to expand the list. Names like Vizier, Seebt, Roussel, Pertuit, Lafrance, Fredericks, Whipple, de St. Germaine, Campo, Joefrau, Vidocavitch, Comardelle, Ansardi, Alfonso, Armstrong, and Dugas are all part of that glorious era in which the craftsmen shared their knowledge and their art with their neighbors and friends.

Another family that has left its mark on our cultural heritage is the Vizier family. Odee and Clovis were the progenitors of decades of carvers who followed in their footsteps and copied their patterns and their style.

LEFT: Pintail drake by Sidney Duplessis, a guide and carver for generations of New Orleans sportsmen. He made his decoys sturdy to stand the rigors of marsh hunting, but his painting was fine and delicate.

OPPOSITE TOP: Bayou Gauche decoys have never been known for artistic execution, so this chip-carved pintail drake by Duncan "Papa-Dunc" Savoie is even more exceptional.

198

One characteristic of the Bayou Lafourche master carver is the use of "English callers" as models. For a number of years I was puzzled by the rather short bills on Clovis ("Cadice") Vizier's mallards. One day I was knocking on doors along Bayou Lafourche when a small band of mallards swam into view. I knew at once that what had been bothering me was solved. Many of the Cajun families who live along the bayous of south Louisiana keep a small flock of the little mallards known as "English callers." In the days when live decoys were legal, Louisiana guides would keep these little three-quarter-size birds in pens. When hunting season started, a guide took several of these bayou songsters to be tethered on small platforms amid a rig of decoys, or to swim about with a short piece of line attached to the foot. Calling each time a band of ducks passed overhead, they'd lure mallards to the stool better than the finest duck call. Now, Cadice had these little birds before him constantly. Watching them, it was only natural that he carved their feather detail and shape—hence his rather small, short-billed decoys. I'm always pleased and surprised when I find bands of these little birds in a bayou pond, kept as an ornamental reminder of days long gone.

Clovis and Odee are two of the ten children sired by Beauregard Vizier. The Viziers' origin lies in the maritime provinces of Canada. Migrating to the south, they settled in what was then known as Caminada Village, near the community of Grand Isle. The heroism of Beauregard Vizier in the hurricane of 1893 is recounted in *Chenier Caminada*, a small booklet published by Dale P. Rogers of Thibodaux. When this killer storm hit the Chenier Caminada, Beauregard rescued many of his less fortunate neighbors, bringing them to the safety of the small knoll on which his home had been built.

The early carvers of the lower end of Bayou Lafourche revered Cadice. He was a grand old gentleman. I spoke with him one afternoon in the twilight of his years. He was wrapped in a quilt and sat half asleep until we started talking decoys. Suddenly, the old fire lit his eyes and he started to talk of the blue ribbon he'd taken in the New York Sportsmen's Show of 1921. Proud as a peacock and animated beyond his years, he talked of his love of the marsh, love of family, and the pride his carving gave him. He had used God's gift to the best of his abilities.

The Viziers are a very close-knit family interrelated with the Benoits, the LaBauves, and the Legendres. Many of these names reoccur in the tapestry of Louisiana folk art and the carving of working decoys, the artifact that has become an object of art. Look closely at these cypress-root beauties. They were carved to be hunted over. Lighter in weight than their tupelo brothers, they were meant to be carried in a sack, slung loosely over the hunter's shoulder, and then thrown, to self

right, in the potholes of Pt. au Cheine. No wonder Tan Brunet, a kin of the Viziers and a five-time world champion decoy carver, held a Cadice blue-winged teal in his hands while visiting my studio and whispered softly, "He was the best."

Then there was Reme Ange Roussel. A clerk and delivery boy in his youth, a house painter and carpenter for some thirty years, he found the recognition he so richly deserved in the last few years of his life. Shortly before World War II, Reme complained to his friend and hunting partner Dr. Ayo of feeling poorly. He was diagnosed as suffering from lead poisoning, a common ailment of house painters, who in those days used lead-based paints. Volatile solvents and no face-mask protection had affected his lungs. Dr. Ayo told him to give up painting.

This was a blessing in disguise to Reme and to decoy collectors. He turned to gunsmithing and decoy carving as one of our first full-time professional carvers. His work from the start was beautiful. No other carver had his innate sensitivity for form. An unpainted Roussel decoy can be identified by species at a glance. As he progressed, he spent more and more time on each bird, never being satisfied until he had fulfilled his personal best. Almost apologetically he began to charge $10 and $25 dollars for his "decoratives." Each cardboard pattern was so true to species that no color was necessary to identify each bird.

I remember my last decoy purchased from him. In the afternoon before he passed away, I was scheduled to participate in a small local skeet shoot. Reme had been in the hospital for a heart problem and had suffered a cardiac arrest. Dr. Wilson Erochis, his friend and physician, had told him, "If you get by the next six weeks, you're out of the woods." He had been convalescing at home for exactly that time when I called. I had ordered a gadwall from him several months before and on an impulse decided to give him a ring, more to inquire on his health than with any expectation that he'd done any carving. He allowed as to feeling "Right well, and ready to do a little carving." Well, we chatted a while and he said, "Did you ever make me the knife I asked you for?" I replied, "Yes, you old coot, when are you going to start on my gray duck?" I was elated to hear him say the gray duck was finished and I could get it as soon as I brought him his new knife.

Well, I called off my squad position in the skeet shoot, picked up the carving knife I'd made from an old "Double Duck" straight razor, and drove the fifty-odd miles to Raceland. I'd just finished a drake shoveler, and his compliments on that bird meant more to me than any "cordon bleu." I presented him with the knife, and he fondled that darn thing for a few moments and then told me he was going to start carving in the morning. We then had the only argument I ever had with Reme. He didn't want to accept any payment for the gray duck!

We chatted a while over a cup of black coffee and chicory, which his wife, Eula, had freshly dripped, and I left, little dreaming I'd never see him again. Next morning, his son Warren called at 6:00 A.M. to tell me his Dad had passed away during the night.

Reme was a man who understood the medium he worked in. His workshop was well organized, and his patterns neatly stored. I see in my mind's eye the shelves of neatly cut blocks of gum, runners under each row to insure slow and uniform drying. His saws and the tools of the gunsmith's trade were old, and many were handed down from his father, but each had been sharpened and oiled. They were the tools of a finished craftsman, standing in mute testimony to the memory of one of Louisiana's greatest folk artists.

Let's reminisce again for a moment about this man's character. He was one who should be recorded in the Book of Life as "one who loved his fellow man." I knew Reme but a few short years. I learned to consider him one of nature's noblemen. He was the master carver of the Houma-Thibodaux area. I still see his influence on the working decoys coming from this section of the great wandering main street that is Bayou Lafourche.

I suppose it was his innate kindness that bound me to him. He was a teacher to many, and his generosity led him to bestow patterns on any who couldn't afford his work. When I first met him, he was selling his ringnecked ducks and teal for $10 and his big ducks, mallards, and pintails for $25. He was the first of the old carvers to move from strictly working birds to the semidecorative. He could have carved a heck of a lot more birds, but his pride in the decoys he carved and painted took time. He was always behind on orders, but the gunsmithing work he did on shotguns claimed more of his time, and he always said, "I just have to get these guns ready for the hunting season."

These men were the pathfinders of our wetland heritage. The magnificent work they created has established their place in the folklore of Louisiana history, and I'm proud of the legacy they left. Decorative carvers from our state have made their mark in competitions the length and breadth of these United States, but we are all in the debt of these early artists who showed us the way. Our bayou artists of an era now passed have given us a legacy of folk art without equal. The graceful lines of decoys carved to float in a pothole are now mantelpiece art. Museums and collectors vie with one another to possess the cypress and tupelo decoys that have made a place for themselves in the minds and hearts of all who have come in contact with their unique beauty.

Tucked-head blue-winged teal by James Curtis Roussel, brother of Reme Ange Roussel.

CHAPTER 16

OHIO

by Joe Engers with Gene and Linda Kangas

Although Ohio's hunting grounds have never really received the popular acclaim they are due, the state has a rich decoy history, and it begins early in the 19th century. Ohio was an important gunning area, for it is located along the eastern zone of the Mississippi flyway and is thus a major stopover for migrating ducks and geese. The identities of only a few major 19th-century decoy carvers are known, something that is true of many other North American hunting areas.

Although documents attest to market gunning in the Ohio region as early as 1820—to serve such growing cities as Cleveland, Detroit, and Toledo—the majority of the duck hunting in Ohio was for sport. The heaviest gunning was centered along the southwestern shore of Lake Erie, from Cleveland to Toledo, including the Sandusky Bay area. Hunting took place along the lake's shores as well as on the marshes and waterways that fed it. Lake Erie's south shore was home to some of America's earliest gunning clubs, the Winous Point Shooting Club, established in 1856, being the first. By the end of the Civil War, more than fifty private hunting clubs were in operation in the area.

As was common in hunting clubs throughout the young republic, those in Ohio employed guides, and among the responsibilities given those guides was supplying decoys to shoot over. The names that appear on such decoys do not, however, indicate specific carvers. Club members' brands on the bottom of decoys indicate only when the decoy was used in Ohio. Thus, the initials "G.A.S."—for George A. Stanley, a Winous Point member from 1857 to 1864—appear on several Ohio decoys from the hands of several different early carvers.

Decoys usually display characteristics that readily identify them with a geographic region. Unfortunately, the features of mid-19th-century Ohio decoys are reminiscent of several East Coast regions. Some early Ohio decoys were hollow, two-piece designs with rectangular lead bottom weights, a style also typical of New Jersey decoys. A few Ohio decoys have inletted necks, a sturdy construction technique commonly used in Maine and a trademark of 19th-century Michigan decoy maker Nate Quillen. The beautifully painted patterns and body styling found on many Ohio decoys are similar to the wonderfully painted Blair school decoys of the Delaware River.

Blair school decoys and some from Ohio exhibit paint patterns not too different from those on decoys made by the Peterson (1873–84) and Dodge (1884–94) decoy factories of Detroit. The mystery of the identities of early Ohio makers and their styles is probably linked to the movements of wealthy sportsmen. Stylistic developments and influences in the early to mid 1800s may well have traveled either from east to west or west to east—or may have occurred simultaneously.

Decoys may well have been brought to Ohio from other states by the wealthy sportsmen who gunned at the state's many clubs. Many sportsmen traveled with their favorite shotguns and hunting dogs, and they may also have carried along with them some of their own decoys. Decoys from various regions have turned up in the gunning clubs along the coasts of Virginia and the Carolinas, lending support to this theory. Among the non-Ohio decoys used in local clubs are examples made by Elmer Crowell of Massachusetts, Nate Quillen of Michigan, as well as some by the three Detroit factories of Peterson, Dodge, and Mason. Members of such Ohio clubs as Winous Point and the Ottawa included a mix of local and out-of-state railroad executives and bankers. It was very common for such well-to-do gentlemen to travel around the country in search of good sport.

Northwestern Ohio was settled in large part by people from Connecticut, and the early settlers may have brought with them either a few decoys of their own—made in Connecticut, or at least in the East—or "eastern" ideas on making decoys. The development of the Ohio-style decoy may be tied to this early immigration from the East Coast.

Early guides and decoy makers probably discovered early on that hollow-constructed decoys worked well in the protected marshes along the lake shores, and a few appreciated the fact that inletted necks helped eliminate breakage. This suggests that the observant decoy carvers were able to combine the best of these regional traits by crafting delicate, well-painted decoys that performed well in the region's conditions.

Most of the early decoys used in Ohio were probably made there. This conclusion is supported by evidence from early Ohio gunning clubs, the existence of club members' brands, the variety of related decoy styles found in the state,

OPPOSITE: Bluebill drake by William Pepper; ca. 1930.

and the identification of several carvers. These decoys are a proud heritage of the Ohio gunning clubs.

The earliest and most important Ohio decoy carver was Ned John Hauser (1826–1900), who emigrated to America from Germany and made his home in Sandusky, at that time the heart of Ohio's waterfowl hunting. A man with many talents, he was employed as a painter by the Ohio railroads. His decoys date from 1850 to 1880. Because his hollow decoys predate most so-called club decoys, Hauser should be considered the father of the Ohio school. Surviving examples of his work include hollow canvasbacks and mallards and one example of a small solid-carved bufflehead hen.

Another 19th-century Ohio maker was Adam Hartung (1860–1909), also from Sandusky. The captain of the local fire department, Hartung may well have made his decoys during his waiting hours at the fire department. He made about one hundred during his life, a mixture of both hollow and solid birds, including canvasbacks, bluebills, redheads, mallards, and pintails.

Since the 19th-century gun clubs hunted in the protected marshes, bays, and rivers, the decoys they used tended to be lighter and more rounded. Most 20th-century Ohio decoys, on the other hand, were designed for use on the open lake waters. For that reason, they are larger, and the majority are solid and have flat bottoms. The works of three carvers are typical of this

ABOVE: Redhead drake used at the Winous Point Shooting Club in the 1800s bearing the brand of club member W. H. Harris.

202

Canvasback drake by Ned John Hauser; ca. 1850–80. Hollow, this decoy has carved eyes and its original weight.

period: John Rider, William Enright, and William Pepper. Pepper's decoys are nicely made, with rounded lines, flattened bottoms, and a pleasant folksy attraction. His decoys employ inletted, removable bills, a unique feature that simplified repairs.

John Frederick Rider (1881–1967) of Port Clinton made hundreds of solid-bodied duck and goose decoys. Identifying characteristics of Rider decoys are the painted and sometimes relief-carved wingtips on his solid, hump-backed, wide-bodied, flat-bottomed decoys. Species he is known to have made include black ducks, bluebills, crows, canvasbacks, coots, mallards, pintails, redheads, and geese. He is also known to have carved a wonderful owl and to have fashioned many brightly painted miniatures.

William T. Enright (1913–79) of Toledo was one of Ohio's most prolific 20th-century decoy makers. His commercial production spanned the 1930s to the 1960s, though he is known to have made decoys almost until he died. The majority of his decoys were made with cork bodies finished with pine heads; only a few are of wood. These cork decoys were credited with being sturdy, working birds and served many years in the water. Known species include black ducks, mallards, pintails, redheads, bluebills, canvasbacks, and geese. Enright also varied head positions, with content, lowhead, high-head, and turned-head postures. He also made miniatures.

Enright gained local and national fame when he competed in the National Decoy Makers Contest in New York City in 1948 and walked away with a number of ribbons. What was even more significant was that Enright picked his entries off his shelf of working birds, and these randomly selected birds bested Shang Wheeler, the noted Connecticut champion. But Enright, a true duck hunter at heart, did not bother to compete again, for he felt such competitions distracted him from his first love, duck hunting.

The work of John Sharon (b. 1921), also from Toledo, shows the influence of Enright. His decoys are, in fact, very similar to those of Enright, except that they have a more rounded appearance. During the 1950s and 1960s, Sharon made several sleepers, and these have become the favorites of collectors.

Josef Wooster (b. 1934) grew up in Ashley in central Ohio and was carving decoys when he was ten. In the beginning, his output was also of cork, but he took to using wood when he began entering competitions. "Buckeye Joe," as he is known to many, was very successful in competitions and was honored with many awards and ribbons. Many collectors favor his decorative decoys because of his strong background in making working decoys. Wooster made mostly coots, black ducks, bluebills, redheads, and ringnecks, but his decorative wood ducks and mergansers are considered his highest achievement.

Green- and blue-winged teal drakes used at the Ottawa Shooting Club by member Rollin C. White. The painted rings around tack eyes were a common feature of early Ohio decoys.

CHAPTER 17:

MICHIGAN

by Bernard W. Crandell

In 1701, Antoine de la Mothe Cadillac, a captain in the French army en route to his command at Fort Michilimackinac, sailed a boat northward up the Detroit River to Lake St. Clair and then crossed the lake to the delta of the St. Clair River, where many channels entered the lake. Cadillac was amazed at how many ducks he saw and noted this in his journal: "Ducks covered the water so that they drew up in lines to let boats pass through."

This entry, only an incidental footnote to Michigan history, may be the first recorded observation of the overwhelming abundance of waterfowl in the area now known to duck hunters and decoy collectors as the St. Clair Flats.

The vast marsh of the St. Clair Flats, lying on the northern edge of Lake St. Clair, extends across both Michigan and Ontario, for the U.S.A.-Canadian boundary runs down the very channel Cadillac was traversing. It has been a lush breed-

ing and feeding ground for myriad ducks, geese, swans, and other waterfowl for at least 4,000 years, after the north-south water highway connecting lakes Huron and Erie took its present geological form.

Duck hunters began exploiting this waterfowl bonanza in the 1850s—perhaps a little earlier—coming from nearby Detroit, the villages spotted around the lake, and, of course, from Ontario, traveling distances from Toronto and London in a day when only rail, buggy, and boat got you there.

Hunters brought with them the usual paraphernalia—warm, waterproof clothes, boats, guns and ammunition, and, most important to this account, a rig of decoys to lure the game in close enough to shoot. The larger the rig of decoys the more attractive it became, so hunters took with them all the decoys the boat could hold. To keep decoy weight down, the makers hollowed them out from the bottom, then nailed or screwed on a thin bottom board, sealing it occasionally on the inside with glue and the outside with paint.

OPPOSITE: Black ducks by Charles and Frederick Unger. The Ungers, father and son, were among the earliest Michigan carvers. These have hollow bodies with square-cut nails on the bottom boards.

ABOVE: Goldeneye hen (below) and canvasback (above) by John Schweikart of Detroit; early 1900s. Both of these classic decoys have wide, hollow bodies, and the canvasback has wingtips made of aluminum.

Hollowed decoys have been made and used by hunters across the continent, and we will leave to historians any debate over who started that particular form of carpentry. The St. Clair Flats was characterized by at least two styles: large, oversize decoys for the high visibility of their bulk; and small, thin-shelled lightweights of about one pound that achieved visibility by sheer numbers. The most popular wood used by the carvers was cedar for the bodies and either white pine or basswood for the heads. Bottom boards were most often from discarded shipping boxes.

LEFT: Canvasback (below) and black duck (above) by Zeke McDonald, who lived on an island in the St. Clair Flats in the early 1900s. Both decoys have hollow bodies.

BELOW: Canvasback decoy made by an unknown carver. This unusual decoy, with its thin neck and wedge-shaped head, is known among collectors as the "pinch-neck" canvasback.

The carvers of Mt. Clemens also utilized balsa after World War II when the wood became available at low cost. It was very weight-effective but prone to dents and wear when exposed to the rough treatment of hunting use.

We offer here the names and carving styles of some of Michigan's great decoy makers, all but one or two of whom have passed on to that great marsh in the sky. Names like Schweikart, Bach, Unger, Schroeder, Quillen, Kelson, Schmidt, and Reghi have made their impressions in the collectors' world. We also take a look at William J. Mason, who founded the Mason Factory of Detroit. Mason collectors are in countless legions, certainly a body politic if ever they had to vote on a favorite. We also will involve Jasper Dodge and George Peterson in their commercial enterprises in Detroit, since they followed each other with little overlapping, and see if each had any influence on the other's decoy designs.

Let's first approach the Flats carvers, then travel south through Lake St. Clair and the Detroit River to Lake Erie. This is the heartland of Michigan decoy carvers.

Although there is emphasis here on the St. Clair Flats, duck hunting in Michigan was by no means limited to that area or to the southeastern segment of the state. Michigan borders on four of the Great Lakes and has smaller lakes, ponds, and marshes by the thousands throughout both its upper and lower peninsulas. Thus it has a tremendous resource of waterfowl habitat.

So much for the geography relating to the need by thousands of duck hunters for tens of thousands of decoys.

Of all the decoys made to supply the needs of this market, only a relatively few are desired by collectors, who revere beauty of line, shape, and paint in these wooden relics. These particular few were artists as well as artisans, instinctively combining sculpture and paint to create a portrait in wood.

Tom Schroeder, a Detroiter of German ancestry, felt extremely competitive in his ability to fashion the perfect decoy, both utilitarian and beautiful. Born in 1886, he started making decoys in his teens and continued doing so until two years before his death in 1976 at age 90, a 70-year carving span. His decoys had a feature he called "hydro-dynamics." In his earlier years he placed on the bottom of his decoys a galvanized tin box to act both as keel and container for the anchor and line. The box was rectangular and open at both ends so it acted like a sea anchor with water flowing through and stabilizing the lure. That was the "hydro-dynamics."

Canvasback drakes by Ferdinand Bach. These sculptural decoys show style variations by Bach from 1920 to 1926.

This unique feature also was used on a hollowed body with a bottom board but also with an extension, like a skirt, down from the sides of the body for convenience in wrapping the anchor line around it. On this extension Schroeder placed another bottom board with large holes fore and aft to permit water to flow through.

A well-known advertising executive, with New Era potato chips as his big account, Schroeder in the early 1940s had heard of the International Decoy Makers Contest in the National Sportsmen's Show at Grand Central Palace, New York City. But only when Joel Barber, noted decoy historian, told him the best decoys ever made came from the shop of Connecticut's Charles E. "Shang" Wheeler did his competitive instinct flare up. This made him mad enough in 1948 to carve four decoys and ship them off to the contest. But they were broken in transit. In 1949 he shipped 21 decoys in special boxes, and these arrived safely and took four firsts and Best Amateur decoy, a canvasback sleeper. Schroeder was on a roll. The next year he took 19 ribbons, including several firsts, and came to the attention of Raymond Camp, outdoor editor of the *New York Times*, who wrote:

> *When it came to turning out a Judas duck, Tom Schroeder of Detroit made the eastern amateur decoy makers look like a group of rainy day whittlers for his entry not only took first place in the amateur class but was also judged Best of Show. As more than 650 decoys were entered Schroeder had a lot of competition. His winning entry, a canvasback, was one of the most unusual ever seen. Any wildfowler who attends the show should make an inspection of Schroeder's design a 'must' for he has stumbled on something new in a craft that is a couple of thousand years old.*

Camp was impressed with "hydro-dynamics." Schroeder continued entering the contests through 1956, but a head-to-head match with Wheeler never came off as the great Stratford carver died just before Schroeder's campaign.

Schroeder dearly loved hunting the St. Clair Flats and to more fully appreciate the atmosphere of the environment lived for many years in a hotel in Fair Haven, nestled on the edge of Anchor Bay of the lake.

Another Michigan carver who entered the New York contests was Charles Pozzini of Birmingham, who followed the carving patterns and painting style of Wheeler. In the 1947 Sportsmen's Show he placed with his entries and in 1948 scored firsts with a pintail, canvasback, and redhead. Pozzini made approximately one hundred decoys, including geese, blacks, mallards and bluebills, never selling any but giving some away.

Examples of work by both Pozzini and Schroeder are in the Shelburne Museum, Shelburne, Vermont.

Two other names, both of German ancestry, are known to collectors for the unusual quality of their work in the pre-1900 period. They were the Ungers—Charles J. and his son Frederick C.—and John Schweikart. All lived and worked in Detroit but had cottages for hunting, fishing, and sailing on islands in the St. Clair Flats.

It is not yet known whether only one, or both, of the Ungers are responsible for the delightful folk art bearing their "Unger" brand on the bottom boards. Some of their decoys

210

are not branded, yet their beginnings are circa 1865–80. For 23 years, beginning in 1858, Charles was a ship's carpenter, a profession highly efficient in woodworking, while Fred, born in 1851, learned his father's crafts as well as making a living in cigar manufacturing.

Among the earliest of Flats carvers, the Ungers made canvasbacks, redheads, and blacks whose bottom boards were nailed to the hollow bodies with square-cut nails. In the interests of lighter weight, they hollowed the heads of some of their decoys by boring a hole horizontally in under the bill, then stopping it up with a plug. A collector can get fussy with one Unger detail, however: the very small glass eyes are out of proportion to the rest of the beautiful bird.

The Schweikart clan was large and successful, father Walter, a stonecutter and woodworker, starting it all by emigrating from Germany to Detroit in 1859. John, born in 1870, was the third son among five children. During the period the family lived and ran a commercial fishery on Belle Isle in the Detroit River, the children had to row across to Detroit and back to attend school. The city purchased the island for a park in 1879, and the Schweikarts moved back to the mainland. In the 1880s, still feeling a strong attraction to water, Walter built a retreat on Strawberry Island in the Flats, where hunting and fishing were recreational compensation for his hard work.

John's skill at woodworking in boats was readily carried over to his decoys, which he made for his own use. At least some collectors, viewing a Schweikart canvasback for the first time, have been transfixed by the experience.

Schweikart cans, with their bull-size necks and authoritative stare, have the commanding presence of a top sergeant about to dress down a platoon of rookies at boot camp. They are oversize and are not only highly visible from above but, with their strong, wide bodies, appear in charge of their domain.

John came up with unusual innovations for some of the decoys. To solve the problem of showing the wingtips, rather than carve in wing relief or simply paint the effect, he cut triangles and crescent-shaped pieces out of sheet aluminum and nailed them to the body of the decoy. He then painted the bird, aluminum pieces and all.

Another innovation was his use on some decoys of thin brass sheeting for keels. Each bird had two such keels, which were hinged so that they hung down in the water when floating and could be folded up flush with the bottom board and held in place by a wing nut when being stored.

Although exact dates of his decoy-making career are not available, it may be assumed that he was most active in the period 1900 to 1920. He made canvasbacks, redheads, whistlers, and coots, the first three species in various head poses. His lowheads have special appeal to collectors.

John was well-known as a boatbuilder who, in partnership with brother Carl, constructed the fastest racing yachts on the Detroit waterfront. He sailed his own speedster, *The Huntress*, to victory in many races and, when in need of relaxation, could also cross Lake St. Clair to Strawberry, where he moored it at the cottage. He used both the boat and decoys until his death in 1954.

Another maker who styled decoys with a forceful and challenging appearance was Zeke McDonald, who lived at the turn of the century on a small island in the Flats known as McDonald's. His redheads and canvasbacks appear ready to dominate any kind of water and wind, while his blacks are overbearing masters of the marsh.

One collector has described the strong head and jutting bill of the McDonald canvasback as a "snowplow blade," but I liken it to a big-nosed, avuncular professor aggressively laying the facts of history on a class of uninterested students. Only the spectacles (perhaps a *pince nez*) are absent.

The bull-neck, arrogant pose of the lordly canvasback also was caught in the carving of Carl Wallach of Detroit, who, coming along at a later time, undoubtedly was influenced by those powerful designs.

Did the maker impart to these decoys personalities of their own? Indeed he did. Not only to impress ducks flying overhead, which will turn to look at even blackened Chlorox bottles, but to please the maker himself. The appreciation of artistic decoys, then, began long before collectors arrived on the scene. It began at the moment the decoys came off the workbench. Carvers, above all, could confirm that their creative expressions pleased their eyes, scratched their egos, and stirred their competitive plasma as their rigs were compared to others.

One might expect that Detroit, the automobile-manufacturing capital, would produce a carver with a background in that industry. We look no farther than Ferdinand Bach, a designer and draftsman with Studebaker, Dodge, Rick-

OPPOSITE: Pintail drake with hollow body by Christopher Columbus Smith; ca. 1910. Smith made this for his own use as a market hunter on the St. Clair Flats before founding the Chris-Craft Boat Company.

ABOVE: High-head canvasback with hollow body by an unknown maker of the St. Clair Flats. A favorite among collectors because of its unusual pose.

enbacker, and Chrysler. A native of Switzerland, Bach emigrated to America in 1916 and soon was located in Detroit. He lived in a log home on a canal leading into the Detroit River and kept a houseboat on the Clinton River at Mt. Clemens, close to the Lake St. Clair duck hunting.

Bach made beautiful oversize solid-body canvasbacks, redheads, and bluebills of cedar converted from old telephone poles. He used sugar pine for the heads. They are almost oval-shaped, with carved wing relief and feathering in the wings. The painting was a blend of color that was true to the plumage pattern of the living bird.

Bach's first big rig of 72 decoys was destroyed in a fire that consumed his boathouse in 1925, but a year later, on a new houseboat, he carved another rig. He kept very good care of those decoys, cleaning and storing them in bags at the end of every season. Thus collectors today can enjoy works of art that are virtually unblemished. Bach died in 1967 in a drowning accident in his own canal.

Pair of mallards by Jim Kelson, famed fishing and duck-hunting guide on Lake St. Clair. These decoys show excellent carving detail and paint.

213

Of the carvers who lived near Lake St. Clair and hunted for their own, or market, consumption, Michigan collectors have found several whose products are worthy of display.

One of those market hunters was Christopher Columbus Smith, born near Marine City in 1858, later moving downriver a few miles to Algonac. Chris Smith is better known nationally for his boats. While a young man, he tinkered with gasoline engines and, with older brother Henry, built small boats for sale. Their boatmaking graduated to sailboats, then small motorboats, and eventually the great *Miss America* speedboats that Gar Wood drove to victory in the Gold Cup classics on the Detroit River. Their company was Chris-Craft, still a great name in boating.

The decoys made by Chris and Henry were small, hollow, and light so they could pack 200 of them into their boat out to the hunting area where the north channel of the St. Clair empties into Anchor Bay. They made their decoys, and some boats as well, from logs supplied by ship captains transporting cargoes of wood past Algonac. The Smiths were popular with the captains, who threw off logs that could be salvaged.

The boat they used for duck hunting was like a sinkbox, rectangular and boxlike, with a boat in the center. A canvas skirt with wood floats around the box stopped some of the waves, and a coaming at the top of the box also helped keep the water out. Thirty-pound iron decoys weighed down the box to keep it in low silhouette.

With a family to support, Smith figured he needed to shoot and sell from 700 to 800 ducks a week to keep things going, and these had to be canvasback, redheads, or bluebills. Mallards and blacks were not saleable, so Mrs. Smith put those on the table when her husband, blown off the big water by a storm, had to go into the marsh and shoot puddlers.

Smith made both lowheads and upright birds, the latter with the neck coming up from the body about an inch before joining with the head. On some, he placed a strip lead keel with "C.C. Smith" stamped in. The bills were not delineated from the head, and there were no mandible cuts. Only on canvasbacks did he make an exception to this. His total output was between 700 and 1,000 decoys, including canvasbacks, redheads, bluebills, whistlers, blacks, and pintails.

By the time Smith died in 1937 his four sons had taken over the boat business. He had encouraged them to put up homes near his on Water Street. Some Smith history flashed through my mind as I was returning from a duck-hunting foray several years ago and stopped at the home of a locksmith in Algonac. Waiting for him in his living room I noted a beautiful bar made of mahogany. When the locksmith arrived he explained the background of the bar. "One of the Smiths lived here," he said. "The boat company supplied both the wood and the carpenters." On the way out I also noted—you may already have guessed—that the home was on Water Street.

Other carvers in the Algonac area are recognized for special artistic features. Nearby Marine City gave us Walter Struebing, who in the 1920s made oversize canvasbacks and redheads with unusual paint and unique keels. In painting the drakes, Struebing used paint that had dried out in the can to a point of thickness before it was put on the body. He then stippled the heavy coat with a brush until the feather texture stood up in wavelets, giving it a rough but realistic effect.

214

The Struebing keels are four inches deep, set between two strips of wood, and are removable. Lead in the shape of a new moon is incised into the keel. Further, on the canvasback keels he attached a six-inch metal swinging keel to improve stability for the 16-inch-long decoys, for they were used most often in rough water.

One of Struebing's friends in Marine City, Fred Zimmerman, copied his basic keel with incised lead when he turned out big divers for sneak shooting. However, his paint technique was different. He let the paint thicken before applying it, and then used a graining comb to put tight swirls simulating feathers across the entire body, a unique texture feature.

Other makers of note who lived along the St. Clair River in the 1920s were John Finch of Port Huron and William Finkel of Algonac. Their black-duck decoys were well proportioned with high, stylish heads and hollow bodies.

Budgen Sampier lived at Pearl Beach along the north channel of the St. Clair and turned out canvasbacks, whistlers,

redheads, and bluebills that had a common, but unusual feature: the top of the bills ran virtually to the top of the heads and were sharp on the top side, making the bills almost wedge-shaped.

The Meldrum clan of Fair Haven, located on the north edge of Anchor Bay, produced decoys in two size extremes. Tobin Meldrum carved flat-bodied redheads, canvasbacks, and blacks with high heads and hollow bodies, rather small for the usual rough water of the bay. His uncle, Alexander "Yock" Meldrum, believed in oversize cans and redheads with bulky, yet hollow bodies, explaining: "When I make a sneak down on a flock of cans, my decoys are so big they block the ducks' view of my boat!"

We have mentioned Mt. Clemens and the Clinton River as important parts of Lake St. Clair geography. For collectors, they evoke such names as Jim Kelson, Ralph Reghi, Alfred Dreschel, Pecore Fox, and Nick Purdo.

Kelson, born in Woodstock, Ontario, in 1888, lived his

adult years in Detroit and at the mouth of the Clinton River where it empties into Lake St. Clair. He was an excellent fishing and duck-hunting guide, knowing where the small-mouth bass were in the summer and how to decoy the migrating flocks of ducks in the fall. He made hundreds of decoys, selling rigs that he had used. His early products in the 1920s were solid-body mallards, blacks, canvasbacks, and bluebills with stamped-in feathering. The keels were made shallow at the front end, tapering to three inches deep at the rear. This feature gave a rudder effect for better stability.

Kelson's carving and shooting companion in later years was Ralph Reghi of Detroit who, as a boy, was attracted to the older Kelson by their mutual love of the outdoors. In the 1930s Reghi produced the distinguished bull-neck canvasbacks that have become a collector's prize and in 1939, with Kelson, experimented with balsa for decoy bodies. Together, they overcame the lightness problem with balsa by making a low-profile, oval-shaped body using the keel developed earlier by Kelson. They

helped keep the center of balance as low as possible—thus controlling pitching in rough water—by making many of the decoys in the turned-head sleeper pose. The sleeper pose was extremely effective as ducks passing by saw a contented flock on the water, resting peacefully.

That particular style was soon copied by others in the area, helped along by the abundance and cheapness of war-surplus balsa. These carvers were known as the Mt. Clemens school of carving, and Jim Kelson was the acknowledged "dean."

Of all the noted Michigan carvers who lived in the Detroit area, Benjamin S. Schmidt (1884–1968) was by far the best-known. He made literally thousands of decoys for his own use and for sale, and it was the late William J. Mackey, Jr., noted decoy authority, who described his product as "just about the all-American working decoy."

Schmidt made his first decoys in 1914 when he needed some for hunting, then gradually built up production to a commercial volume. His older brother Frank joined him for a

216

period of several years, using old telephone poles for the cedar they needed. The poles were cut to length for a decoy body, then split into two halves. Schmidt went to a friend for a bandsaw to rough out the shape of the body and then used a hand axe to take off more wood. When chopping with a hand axe and lather's hatchet, he rested the block on a log raised to waist level on three two-by-four legs. Schmidt finished off the sculpture with spokeshave, smoothing plane, and rasp.

217

A distinctive feature of Schmidt's carving was the feathering, which was stamped in with a special tool he had made. He placed the metal tool against the decoy and rapped it with a hammer to make the indentation. Several feather sizes were available for various areas of the body.

Schmidt's workshop was in Centerline, a community on the northern edge of the Detroit metropolitan area. Many of his friends, other carvers, and customers came to this workshop. Dozens of ambitious carvers would purchase a Schmidt decoy to use as a model, resulting in a lot of rigs that were not exactly Schmidt look-alikes but close enough to show Schmidt influence.

Schmidt sold decoys by the hundreds to sporting-goods stores, one of his primary outlets being the sports department of the big J. L. Hudson department store in Detroit. On some Schmidt decoys today one will see the Hudson price mark on the bottom: $4.60 for a mallard and $5.30 for a pintail.

When he got behind on his orders and needed help to make a deadline he would turn to either his brother Frank or Walter Snow, of Royal Oak, whose style had the Schmidt look. At one point, behind on head production, Ben asked Nick Purdo to supply several dozen canvasback heads. Purdo's canvasback heads are an art form second to none, and thus some Schmidt decoys today sport a very aristocratic look.

Most of Schmidt's work was done in the 1940s and 1950s and included all the species of ducks and geese that were hunted in the Midwest. Later on, he specialized in special-order decoratives, miniatures, and one-third sizes.

Frank Schmidt's carving ranged from excellent to mediocre, depending on how much time he wanted to invest. Most often he wanted mere volume to meet his orders and skipped the detail that would have made them more attractive. When he did occasionally stamp in feathers it was with a bent wire.

ABOVE: Lowhead redhead drake with hollow body and head by Nate Quillen; ca. 1885. Made for use at the Pointe Mouillee Shooting Club on Lake Erie.

LEFT: Decoys by Tom Schroeder. From left to right, a brant, green-winged teal, and mallard. Schroeder achieved fame in the International Decoy Makers contests in New York during the 1950s.

218

Another commercial maker during the Schmidt period was Ralph Johnston, a Detroit pattern maker who turned out approximately 7,000 decoys in species hunted in the area. His blacks and goose decoys are distinguished, but, overall, Johnston decoys never achieved the popularity among collectors of Ben Schmidt's. He owned a commercial-size band saw and did a lot of work on bodies for the Schmidts.

The Detroit River sweeps from Lake St. Clair 32 miles to Lake Erie, a very busy waterway both for shipping and for ducks. Many islands break up the river at its lower end, and marshes along the Lake Erie shoreline have made the area a duck hunter's paradise, both for those who like to sneak shoot over the big water and those who prefer the puddlers in the ponds. There were, of course, dozens of carvers among the hundreds of hunters in this general area. We will emphasize two whose decoys have become well known: Nate Quillen of Rockwood and Edward F. "One Arm" Kellie of Monroe.

Quillen (1839–1908) was self-employed as a cabinet-maker, locksmith, boatbuilder, and decoy maker and, during the duck-hunting season, worked as a punter for the Pointe Mouillee (Wet Point) Shooting Club in the marsh along western Lake Erie. Collectors proudly display his lowhead redheads, canvasbacks, bufflehead, blue-winged teal, pintails, mallards, blacks, and wigeon. These have the standard hollow bodies, with thin bottom board, and sold for $1 each. When knots in the wood prevented hollowing, he made solid-body decoys, these going to local gunners for 25 cents each. His era of carving was 1875 to 1900, with production of about 200 annually.

The Quillen lowhead is a masterpiece of carpentry. To achieve lightness, he hollowed the body to a thin shell and even hollowed the head. The head is inletted into the body as with his other decoys. Another Quillen decoy style was somewhat in the shape of a boat body. He bored a hole into the body under the tail at the rear to lighten it up, then closed the hole with a plug.

This meticulous carver fully achieved his weight objectives. Six lowheads went on my household scales at 14, 12, 12, 10½, 9, and 9 ounces, while his mallard drake and hen came in at exactly 16 ounces each. A wigeon hit 13½ ounces.

Another lowhead feature is the concave contour of its cheeks, making it easy for the hunter when bringing in the rig to grab the head with no slipping as the anchor line was wrapped.

One of Quillen's artistic tendencies was to carve very thin necks in his regular pose decoys to attain a graceful appearance. This did enhance their looks but weakened the head and neck to a point of breakage when handled roughly in the marsh. Many of the decoys today have cracked necks, held together only because Quillen used a metal screw up through the neck and head that prevented them from coming apart.

Some Quillen history was revealed by the late William T. Barbour of Bloomfield Hills, a Pointe Mouillee club member who wrote a history of the club in 1922 after 26 years of enjoying its sport.

"He was an artist as well as an artisan," Barbour recalled. "He took great pride in the work he did. As models for his

decoys he used birds that were shot in the marsh. He was very neat, and everything had to be in perfect order. Not only would he make the decoys, but he also painted them, and every bit of color was applied with great exactness and care. His appearance and temperament were those of an artist."

Quillen's basic paint colors were white, willow green, roseate, and tobacco brown, which he could combine to get the desired plumage. The decoys are of white cedar.

To the south of Pointe Mouillee is Monroe where, in 1883, Edward Kellie was born. He loved the outdoors, hunting and fishing in the area. He was working in a local factory when his right forearm was caught in a press, injuring it so badly it required amputation. His next job was as signalman for the railroad, sitting in a tower and working the signals for passing trains. He had spare time, so he started carving small things like medallions. This led to setting up a workshop at home and carving decoys.

Known as "One Arm" Kellie, he turned out canvasbacks, bluebills, mallards, and other species that he sold for from $25 to $30 per dozen. His cans put him on the collectors' map. They have well-carved, distinctive heads in many graceful poses and bodies with a stubby tail. Later, he made a bobtail style. Painting was simple but effective, with colors blended realistically. How did he manage to carve with only one arm? He used his stump to help hold the block in position as a handsaw, spokeshave, and budding knife got the job done with the good arm.

OPPOSITE: Pair of pintail decoys by Ben Schmidt of Centerline, one of Michigan's most prolific decoy makers.

ABOVE: Barrow's goldeneye drake by George Peterson of Detroit; ca. 1870. A rare example from one of the earliest commercial decoy manufacturers.

Other carvers in the area who are receiving attention from collectors are Danny Scriven, Bill Dahlka, and Ed Murphy. Scriven and Dahlka made fine heads and typical "downriver" style bobtail blocks. Murphy made graceful blacks with extended wing primaries that lend artistic effect.

Supplementing all the individual carving talents were the commercial enterprises with duplicating lathes to turn out several bodies at a time.

There were three decoy factories in Detroit, beginning in 1873 with George Peterson. He sold his business in 1884 to Jasper Dodge, who manufactured decoys and, later on, canoes and oars, until 1905.

William J. Mason came on the decoy-manufacturing scene in 1896 when he listed himself in the city directory as a decoy maker, address 961 Tuscola Street. Mason continued making decoys until his death in 1905 from rheumatic fever contracted from lying in a marsh, observing and sketching ducks for the many styles and species he sold. His son Herbert took over the business, which continued until 1924. At that point Herbert, who had gone into the paint business in 1919 to supply the booming auto industry, decided there was more potential profit in paint and closed the "duck shop," as it was known to the employees.

Credit must be given Peterson, who was a carpenter, machinist, sawmaker, and chairmaker before seeing an opportunity in decoys, for features copied by both Mason and Dodge. He originated the scalloped painting, sometimes called the bib, outlining the breast, as well as the bill carving seen years later on Mason Challenge–grade decoys.

Peterson decoys have good lines and balance with a pronounced breast contour. The bodies were narrower than the wide-shouldered Dodges but had about the same proportions as the Mason Challenge. The Peterson design has not been defined well enough to make it easy for collectors to differentiate between Peterson and Mason decoys. If a decoy is obviously lathe-made and has a jutting breast, but is not quite like a Dodge or a Mason, it quite often gets called a Peterson.

Helping Peterson in his last few years was Frank W. Lambert, a painter, and their partnership was listed in the city directory simply as "Peterson and Lambert." Some Peterson decoys have outstanding painting, and we may speculate that Lambert was responsible for this artistic feature.

Dodge decoys are easier to identify than Petersons but are in so many shapes and sizes that they are impossible to categorize. This probably is due to duck hunters taking advantage of Dodge offering in his advertising to make decoys "after any model furnished."

Dodge stopped advertising and cancelled his directory listing as a decoy manufacturer in 1894, appearing to leave the business. From 1905 to 1908 he was president of the Detroit Canoe and Oar Works. A Dodge ad in a sporting magazine in 1905 described his oar manufacturing and also asked for duck-decoy business. It is not clear whether he still was making decoys in the 1894 to 1905 period as there is no evidence of advertising. Perhaps it is not important. In any event, Dodge retired in 1908 and moved to Bay City, where he died of "debility" in 1909 at the age of 80.

It is doubtful that Dodge ever provided much competition for Mason's Decoy Factory, which had a better product lineup, sales catalogue, and consistent advertising from the early 1900s onward. When he needed to expand, Mason moved the operation to another location and did this often enough to suggest a rapidly growing business. Mason shipped his products all over the world, but the bulk of his products was distributed in the U.S.A. Decoy buyers could buy ducks, geese, or shorebirds from a catalogue, or go to a retail sporting-goods outlet like Sears, which handled the cheaper Mason grades, on up to the very expensive Von Lengercke and Antoine of Chicago, which carried the very best.

Joseph R. Mason, one of Herbert's three sons, was not a part of the decoy business but does remember it as a boy.

"As a young fellow I remember the overhead belt lines and banks of wood lathes," he recalls. "The decoy bodies were turned on the lathes, using a model to trace from. The heads

Pair of tiny blue-winged teal by Nate Quillen. These are the most charming of the many decoy species Quillen made.

222

Canada goose by the Dodge decoy factory; ca. 1880. This has a hollowed body, square-cut nails, and seven pieces of wood in its construction, including dowels from head to neck and from neck to body.

were hand made. All were hand painted with conventional paint. In spite of some opinion to the contrary, there was nothing special about the paint, and it was pure coincidence that my father got into the paint business. It was not because he needed it for the decoys."

It was the author's good fortune in 1974 to interview the only known living employee of the Mason factory. It came about when the *Detroit News* reviewed the book *Mason Decoys*, and one interested reader was 85-year-old William C. Kurkowske, an employee of the Mason factory from 1905 to 1906 who was living with his wife at the home of their daughter and son-in-law in Plymouth, Michigan. After a few telephone calls, Kurkowske was interviewed and gave a full description of the Mason operations when the factory was located on Brooklyn Avenue in Detroit.

Kurkowske said the factory had two stories, with woodworking lathes downstairs and the painting done upstairs. He and his brother John first were employed as puttiers, smoothing the head-neck junction with putty, then were graduated to apprentice painters. The apprentice sat beside the expert at three workbenches and gave the decoys a primer coat, which was a mixture of linseed oil, turpentine, and white lead. After drying, the decoy was taken by the senior painter, who held it by the head while painting the body the right plumage pattern. After the body dried, the head was painted. The eyes, which had to be painted on the inside surface, were inserted after all the painting was complete.

Kurkowske said the decoys were balanced by floating them in a washtub and then adding a lead weight on the bottom.

The many differences in head and body styles on Masons over a thirty-year span are easily explained, as many different head carvers, each with his own ideas, came and went through the factory doors. Body patterns were changed, too, but not as often, as Mason management attempted to meet market demand. The one Mason feature that did not change with the years was the swirls in the paint showing the brush marks. This apparently was a "must" instruction to all the painters.

Mason factory decoys still are found in many duck-hunting rigs today, most of them being the less-expensive Detroit grades. But good-quality Masons of all grades are finding permanent resting places on collectors' shelves. Decoy auctions generally sell more Masons than any other make, with prices accelerating nearly every year.

A record price for a Mason shorebird was the $13,200 paid in 1986 for a curlew, one of a rig made on a "special order" copying the style of William Bowman, a respected Eastern carver. The highest price so far for a Mason duck decoy was $12,100 in 1988 for a "special order" goldeneye hen, originally part of a rig made for George Bacon of Vermont, who provided his own decoy as a model.

William J. Mason would have been shocked beyond belief had a fortuneteller in 1902 told him that decoys he was selling for $5 per dozen would, eighty-some years later, achieve such dizzying financial success.

In the years after Mason folded the decoy business, many individuals, in addition to the successful Ben Schmidt, tried to make a living from decoys. But there just wasn't enough profit margin to do it. David Simandl of Caro tried marketing decoys under the "True North" stamp in the 1950s but had to give it up. The demand for such a product was, of course, seasonal, and the competition was smothering.

Although some makers today still are selling decoys on a part-time basis, most sportsmen who want to use wood instead of plastic make their own rigs. Restrictions in Michigan on duck and goose shooting, with small bag limits, have tended to discourage hunters if a lot of preparation and equipment are needed.

This account ends with a "side trip" to East Lansing, where Dr. Miles D. Pirnie taught waterfowl management at Michigan State University. A Cornell University graduate in ornithology, Dr. Pirnie not only was a student of birds but was at home in a marsh environment and loved duck hunting. He began making decoys in 1935 while managing the W. K. Kellogg Bird Sanctuary near Battle Creek and continued carving almost until his death in 1978. He made most of his decoys in the 1950s and 1960s while at Michigan State.

Collectors find Pirnie decoys very realistic and artistic. He made all the divers and marsh duck decoys in dozens of body shapes and head poses. The bodies were white cedar and the heads either white or sugar pine.

Dr. Pirnie advertised decoys for sale in *Ducks Unlimited* magazine and, to speed production, took rough-cut bodies to Grand Rapids Carvers in Grand Rapids to be turned out on a duplicator lathe. He then would assemble the decoys and paint them. Since the lathe work cost about $1.50 to $2.00 per body, and $1 per head, his retail price of $5 for a decoy left him with only a small profit.

The Pirnie diver decoys had solid bodies, while most of the dabblers were hollowed. At one point, he visited Ben Schmidt and purchased three dozen of his decoy heads. As a result, the unsuspecting decoy collector may be quite correct, as well as astonished, at occasionally perceiving a Schmidt-like appearance.

Most collectors agree that Pirnie, perhaps because of his professional eye in studying waterfowl in every detail, made decoys that are most lifelike, a tribute not easily earned even among the best carvers.

Pirnie and the other Michigan carvers over the past 130 years have made a notable contribution to an American folk art that already has achieved historical significance. Their decoys are being enjoyed throughout the land.

Even Captain Antoine de la Mothe Cadillac—if only today he could know what the harvest of all those ducks had left for posterity in the form of wooden waterfowl—would be impressed.

223

Wood duck by the Mason decoy factory; ca. 1920. This rare example was a salesman's sample and is only 10 inches long from tip of bill to tip of tail.

CHAPTER 18:

INDIANA

by Donna Tonelli

Today, the state of Indiana is not known for waterfowl hunting, but before humanity spread out from cities, places like the vast Calumet marsh in northern Indiana were alive with waterfowl. Unfortunately, little of these marsh areas remains. Most have been filled in to make more room for progress. Two noted carvers are all that reminds collectors of waterfowling in Indiana: Bernard Ohnmacht and Paul Lipke.

Born in Indiana in 1889, Ohnmacht moved to Itasca County, Minnesota, when he was in his early twenties to homestead land along the Mississippi River. Here he learned to live off the land and built a reputation as an excellent hunter working as a guide in northern Minnesota. Bernard returned to Indiana during the 1930s and settled in Lafayette, a rivertown on the Wabash River. Here he created a haven that brought the nature and wildfowl of Minnesota to the heart of Lafayette. He planted yews and mountain ash from Minnesota and cedars from Canada as well as cherry trees and junipers on an entire city block that he purchased for his homesite. Once the trees grew, he built an aviary that housed mallards, wood ducks, tree ducks, teal, pintail, snow geese, and Canada geese. He planted natural wild feed crops to feed his charges. Ohnmacht was so successful at monitoring and controlling disease among his flocks, which he strengthened by adding wild geese and ducks he captured, that he was able to sell birds and fertilized eggs nationally.

Some people will find it hard to understand why a man like Ohnmacht would hunt waterfowl, but a sportsman knows the challenge of the hunt. Ohnmacht was an excellent bird caller and decoy carver. He preferred to hunt on a small stream or pond using a spread of two or three dozen decoys. There is a thrill of having a flock respond to decoys, calling and swinging over again and again, ever closer until they are in shooting range—and this thrill is even greater if you made the decoys yourself. This was the ultimate test of one's carving ability: to fool a wild bird, not to impress one's fellow man.

Ohnmacht started carving during the 1930s, making decoys entirely out of cork. These decoys have a basic form and simple, pleasing paint pattern. Although the cork was reinforced with several layers of thick paint, the cork decoys chipped badly and were unsatisfactory. Ohnmacht set out to improve his product. He abandoned the idea of using cork heads, since the head was the first area likely to break. He carved wooden heads and mounted them on his cork bodies in a unique, patented way. A long rod was secured into a hole drilled in the neck and then passed through a copper sleeve that ran the length of the breast to connect to a metal tie line holder on the bottom of the decoy. Another feature of Ohnmacht decoys, patented in 1941, was a rudder-stabilizer. He would mount a stainless-steel triangular plate to the underside of the decoy with a "skin" of plastic wood that covered the entire cork body to reinforce and protect the cork, which he preferred for its buoyancy. This plate held a rudder that was a built-in stabilizer and could be moved to compensate for variances in water conditions. Combined with a head held in a fixed position by the weighted mounting rod, this rudder system allowed the decoy body to swing from side to side, creating the illusion of a swimming duck.

Because he carved just for his own use, Ohnmacht produced only about one hundred decoys: mallards, pintails, black ducks, and Canada geese. His paint pattern was very intricate and appears to have been copied directly from the birds in his aviary. Each decoy has distinct varying shades and hues of color. It seems he may have tried to recreate his own flock. Fine dots denote the fine vermiculation (barred lines) on his mallard and pintail drakes. Soft gray cupping graces the mallard drakes'

OPPOSITE: Ben Ohnmacht.

ABOVE: Bluebill decoy by Paul Lipke. Little is known of the maker of these decoys, which show the strong influence the Mason company had on carvers.

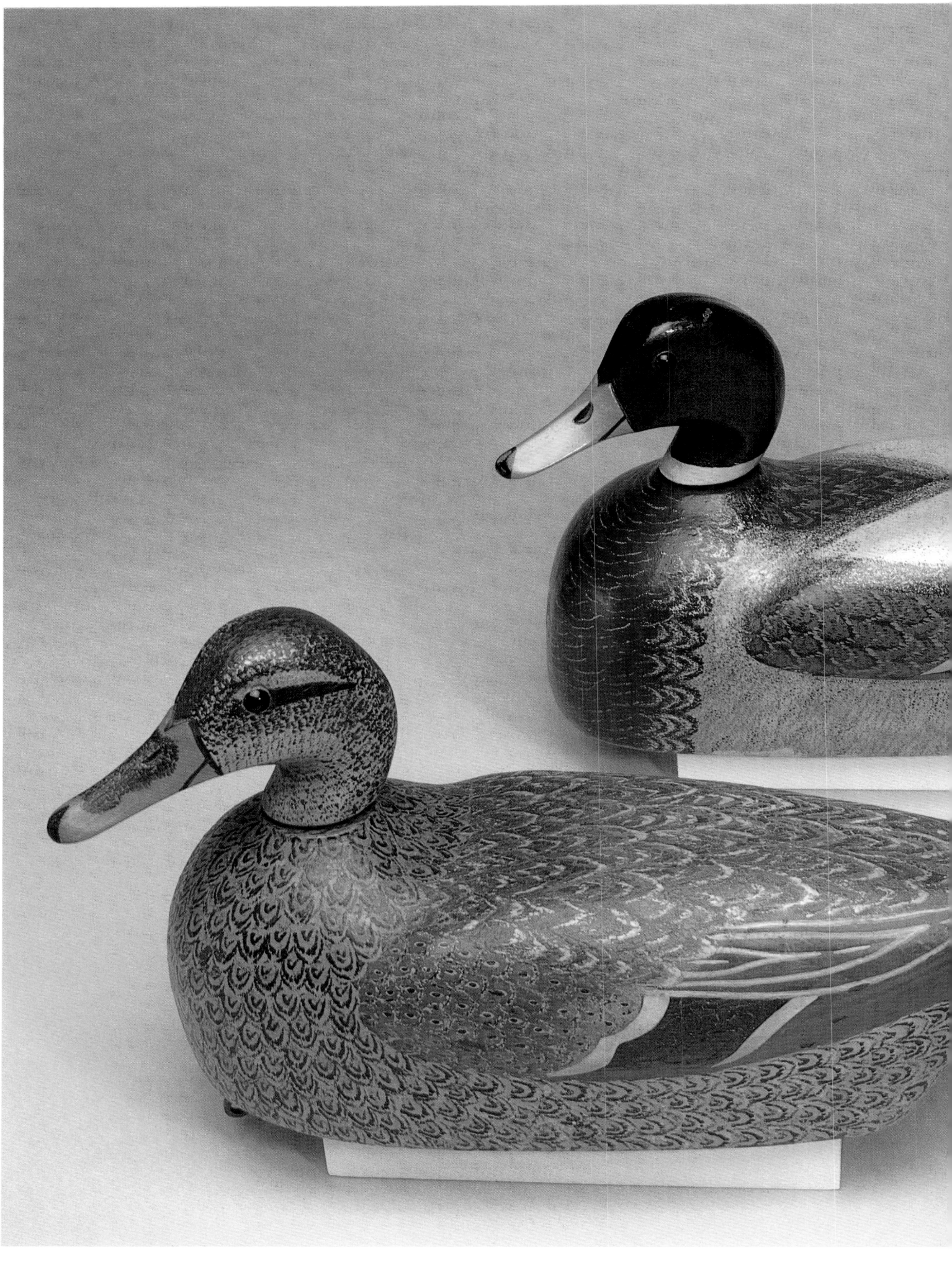

breast, and the feathering on his hens delineates small individual feathers across the entire body of the decoy.

Ohnmacht took special care to preserve his decoys. Each had its own hand-sewn woolen bag. When he took his decoys out to the water they were always arranged a certain way: some decoys were lead decoys, others were sentinels, and still others made up the heart of his flock. Ohnmacht was a dedicated man, and he moved his wildlife haven out of the city in 1950. He lived on the southern edge of Lafayette and loved and hunted waterfowl until 1973, when his property was sold. He died at the age of 86 on June 4, 1975, leaving a legacy that duck hunters and collectors can admire.

Very little is known about Paul Lipke. The picker who found Lipke's rig of decoys in the 1980s learned only Lipke's name and that the decoys came from the Whitting, Indiana, area. Whitting is a small town at the southern tip of Lake Michigan between Chicago and Gary. Some collectors question the existence of a Paul Lipke, although the initials "P. L." are found stamped into the round lead weights found on all Lipke decoys. Whether or not Paul Lipke ever existed, the decoys are obviously handmade and show strong influence of the Mason Decoy Company. There appears to have been only one rig of Lipke decoys, consisting of fewer than two dozen bluebill, redhead, blue-winged teal, canvasback and mallard decoys. The decoys are hollow with varying head styles. The teal have perky up-turned heads, and some bluebills have sleeper-style heads; some are lowheads like Mason Decoy Company sleepers and others are turned straight back like Illinois River–style sleepers. The heads all have a fat, cheeky appearance that is appealing. The birds have detailed bills with carved bill nails and glass eyes. The bodies are deep and flat-bottomed with a paint pattern that again strongly resembles the Mason decoy with stripling and loops denoting feathering.

Because of the lack of information about the maker of the Lipke decoys, it is impossible to date these decoys. Their near-mint condition and the lack of hunting in this growing area led collectors to guess that the decoys were made in the late forties or mid fifties. Together, Paul Lipke and Bernard Ohnmacht hold a place for Indiana in the history of waterfowling. Perhaps in the future more carvers will be discovered—maybe in a Gary, Indiana, attic.

227

Pair of mallards by Bernard Ohnmacht; 1940s. Ohnmacht took care to reproduce the soft feathering and used a patented feature to make decoys with reinforced cork bodies and heads that swung freely.

CHAPTER 19:

ILLINOIS RIVER

by Donna Tonelli

The Illinois River has been home to countless duck hunters, and boys here still grow up hunting and fishing. During the hunting season, they can be seen heading toward river bottoms with a shotgun thrown over their shoulders, off to learn the wonders of the river. Because ducks are nobler quarry than blackbirds or squirrels, the hunter must learn their habits to outsmart them. Young men learn early that trying to sneak up on wary waterfowl is rarely successful. The best way to shoot a duck is to get to its favorite waterhole before sunrise, set out some decoys, and hide. Most waterfowl are attracted to other birds rafted on the water. Thus, the decoy is so useful that Illinois River hunters consider it essential for a good hunt.

Something about decoys intrigues people, even those who have never hunted or have never seen a duck in the wild. What makes decoys unique are the men who created them, men who took a piece of wood and some paint and recreated birds cunning enough to lure live waterfowl to their hunting spots. What they created was a tool—the hunting decoy—but they also captured the attitudes and essence of the waterfowl, thereby creating a functional art form, a piece of folk art. Unlike today's anonymous plastic or foam decoys, which are formed in molds, each wooden decoy has a character and individual style that identifies its maker—and such makers rarely signed their work.

P. W. Parmalee and F. D. Loomis, commissioned by the state of Illinois to document all the decoys made in the state, recorded over two hundred carvers in *The Decoys and Decoy Carvers of Illinois*. As in any art form, some carvers were more talented than others. The most prolific and best-known carver on the Illinois River was Charles Perdew (1874–1963), who grew up in the river town of Henry, hunting ducks and harvesting wild rice for the Chicago market. While running a bicycle livery and repair shop, he made hunting decoys and repaired guns on the side. During his sixty-year carving career, Perdew produced thousands of hunting decoys using a drawknife, wood gouge, whittling knife, and a makeshift mechanical

OPPOSITE: Mallard by Charles Ruggles; late 1800s. Unlike most Illinois decoys, this is racy, with a wide, shallow, and elongated body and sleek head.

ABOVE: Pair of mallards by Charles Perdew. Both have deep, two-piece bodies with raised, carved wings; the hen's turned head has half-shut eyes that capture a pleasant pose.

sander fashioned out of an old treadle sewing machine.

Until 1941, his wife, Edna, painted most of his decoys. Although Charles and Edna used the same basic patterns and paints, their painting styles are very different. Edna's was softer because she used wet-on-wet blending and more "combing."

Combing was a technique used by many Illinois River carvers to emulate the duck's vermiculation (fine barred lines found on some feathers) by combing the thick wet paint with an English furniture graining comb. The graining comb was a flat piece of metal with notches cut into one end forming broad teeth. Perdew combed some of his birds, but he relied mostly on bold loops painted on dried base colors to detail his feathering. Early Perdew decoys have deep V-bottom bodies fashioned from three hollowed pine boards laminated together with a separate cheeky head with glass eyes. These decoys gradually became shallower with smaller heads.

Perdew carved mostly puddle ducks—mallard, pintail, green-winged teal, blue-winged teal, wood duck—and diver ducks—bluebill, canvasback, and geese—as hunting decoys. He also carved decoys for crow hunting. Bounties were once paid for dead crows in Illinois, and hunters used an owl decoy with several crow decoys to lure crows within shooting range. Charlie's crows were mounted on two heavy wire legs with fully rounded, flowing bodies. His best crows had smooth shiny heads and flocked bodies. He made a few mechanical owl decoys whose heads turned and emitted a rasping sound as a string was pulled. This turning mechanism was hidden by real

Mallard drake and pintail drake by Ignatius Stachowiak; 1940s. Although overshadowed by his teacher, Charles Perdew, Stachowiak made decoys now ranked among the best in Illinois.

231

feathers glued around the neck. He also made solid owl decoys, with simpler lines that were painted by Edna.

Perdew crafted wooden birdcalls to be used by duck and crow hunters. His common calls for duck and crow, made of red cedar, were turned on a lathe with decorative rings cut into the barrel of the calls. Both of these calls were reinforced with German silver bands. His "St. Frances" duck call had a checked-black walnut barrel with a small rectangle where he would carve in the owner's initials or V.L. & A. for Van Laflend & Antione, a well-known Chicago sporting-goods store that sold the calls. His special-order calls were impressive. Starting with a red cedar barrel, he would carve in relief a pair of mallards with an alighting drake and the owner's initials or name. The birds were painted and completed with tiny glass eyes. The barrel end was reinforced with colored celluloid rings. He also made a fancy crow call often depicting a mother crow in a tree with her nest of eggs. The finest example of his carved calls was a crow call with a hunting scene showing a hunter hiding beside a tree, pulling the string on one of Perdew's mechanical owl decoys. By 1930, Perdew was producing decorative pieces, like miniatures and songbirds. Since he liked the ladies who would visit with their husbands, it is not surprising that he sometimes

Mallards by Robert and Catherine Elliston; 1880s. The couple combined their artistic talents to create the earliest-known Illinois River decoys. Robert's turned-head sleeper style was copied by so many Illinois carvers that it is considered a characteristic of the Illinois River decoy.

presented them with a small carving of a duck or pheasant mounted as a broach or a pair of earrings.

Charles Ruggles (1864–1920) of Henry, Illinois, was a contemporary of Perdew. Perdew himself credited Ruggles with helping him learn the basics of decoy carving. Little is known about Ruggles other than that he was a professional painter, yet his decoys are excellent examples of Illinois folk art. His birds are light and racy, their bodies wide and shallow, with elongated heads. He used round-headed tacks for eyes, and his paint pattern matched the sleek lines of his decoys. Examples of mallard, redhead, and bluebill are in collections.

Just as Perdew was helped by Ruggles, Perdew influenced many Illinois carvers. Several he taught personally, such as Ignatius Stachowiak (1898–1964) of LaSalle, Illinois. Stachowiak's decoys are overshadowed by Perdew's because there are only minor differences in them. Stachowiak carved mallard, pintail, bluebill, and teal working decoys and a few miniatures, but because he was employed full time he completed only a few hundred decoys in his entire carving career. Even though he copied another carver's style, the quality of his decoys ranks him among the better decoy carvers.

Robert Elliston (1849–1915), acclaimed as the father of Illinois River decoy carvers, was the first-known commercial carver in the state and produced thousands of working decoys that were shipped throughout the Midwest. Born in Kentucky, Elliston learned the art of woodworking at the Studebaker shops of South Bend, Indiana. He started working there when he was 18, making wooden carriages and buggy bodies. By the time he was 30, his career as a buggy maker had led him to the Breton Buggy Shop in Lacon, Illinois. Once in the heart of the Midwest duck-hunting country, he started to make decoys. His birds were so well liked that when he moved to Bureau, Illinois, decoy carving was his full-time profession.

The mechanics of the Elliston decoy incorporated the skills he had mastered as a buggy maker. His decoys are wider and flatter than most Illinois River decoys, which eliminated the tendency of a decoy to roll in rough waters. (A few diver duck decoys have much deeper bodies than other Elliston decoys; these were probably made to the specifications of a customer.) The seamline on his hollow bodies was positioned well above the waterline to prevent leakage. These seamlines rarely show, even on a well-worn decoy, demonstrating Elliston's skill as a woodworker. His decoys have distinctive heads with rounded cheeks and finely detailed bills. Elliston set his enameled glass eyes high up in the bluntly pointed head, giving his decoys an almost froglike appearance. This eye placement is found on all Elliston species, including mallard, pintail, green-winged teal, blue-winged teal, bluebill, redhead, ringneck, canvasback, coot, and Canada geese. His style of depicting a sleeping duck, although inaccurate, was emulated by most Illinois carvers. The turned-head sleeper has an arched neck that rises over the decoy's body so just the tip of the bill rests midway

Canvasback decoys by Bert Graves painted by his wife, Millie; early 1920s. From left to right, a hen, drake, and immature drake. Graves hunted canvasback for the market.

on the decoy's back. His sleeper was very folksy and often copied by other Illinois carvers. Although Elliston made many decoys, they were well used, so few remain in their original condition despite his superior craftsmanship. Hunters usually discarded broken or leaking decoys and replaced them. Old hunting club caretakers often tell of hauling hundreds of discarded decoys off to be burned at the end of the hunting season.

All Elliston decoys were painted by his wife, Catherine. Her painting style was freeflowing and appealing, and her influence on the other ladies who painted decoys is easy to see. Edna Perdew used the same wet-on-wet feather blending, and

since Catherine was painting long before Edna, one can only assume Edna adopted the combing technique from her. In short, if Elliston was the father of Illinois River decoy carving, Catherine was the mother of Illinois River decoy painting. She also used a scratching technique on the backs of her mallard drake and hen decoys. After she indicated the feathers by brushing on dark loops over a lighter wet base color, she would scratch another loop around the dark loop with the end of her brush. This accentuated her feathering and suggested the light edging found on those feathers on a live duck.

Bert Graves (1887–1956) started the G. B. Graves Decoy Company in a small building behind his Peoria home during

Pair of blue-winged teal by Robert Elliston. Teal decoys are rare because teal don't respond to decoys; these examples are made rarer since Elliston made few teal.

the 1930s. The Graves decoys were products of this cottage industry in which Bert did most of the carving with part-time help from his younger brother, Orville. Bert painted some of his late mallard decoys, but most of his decoys were painted by Catherine Elliston, Robert's widow, and Bert's sister-in-law, Millie Graves. Both ladies used the paint patterns that Catherine used on her husband's decoys. The only difference was that Catherine painted the flanks an off-white and Millie painted them gray. One has only to glance at Graves's decoys to see the strong influence of Robert Elliston. They have the same quality construction and form, although Graves repositioned the eyes on his decoys. He also believed in using oversize decoys to

attract duck far off toward a normal-size decoy rig, so he made mammoth mallards, hens and drakes, that measure 22½ inches from tail to bill. Graves used Elliston's patterns for all of his species except his canvasback decoys. He was one of the few Illinois River carvers who made a canvasback decoy that looked like a diver duck. This is understandable because canvasback congregated in huge rafts on the wide waters of the Illinois River above Peoria where Graves often hunted. Graves produced mostly pairs of mallard, canvasback, and pintail, but examples of his black duck and even Pacific brant, believed to have been made after he retired, are in collections today.

Peoria was home to numerous decoy carvers. Some of the

235

most collectible decoys were made by an unidentified carver, and these were labeled Mr. X decoys by Joseph French, a well-known collector, during the late sixties. Mr. X made quality hollow birds. They have wide shallow bodies with perky little heads and bills carved of a hardwood and mitered into the head. He also weighted his decoys by tacking a lead strip inside the bottom half of their bodies before laminating the halves together. Both these practices were unique and may have been the reason "Patent Applied For 1889" has been found stamped on the bottom of his decoys. Nothing is known about the origins of the Mr. X decoys except that they were sold by the Portsman Sporting Goods store of Peoria.

237

LEFT: Wigeon made by the unknown Mr. X and sold in Portman's Hardware and Sporting Goods Store in Peoria during the late 1800s. These are part of a dozen found in the 1960s.

ABOVE: Heron by unknown maker. One of two such decoys used at the Grand Island Duck Club near Bath, this decoy's head is detachable and its legs and bill are walnut inserts.

Another decoy sold by the Portsman store was the work of Charles Schoenhieder, Sr. (1856–1924). Born in Poughkeepsie, New York, he moved to Peoria before the turn of the century. He was a professional carpenter who supplemented his income by hunting and fishing for the market. He also had thirteen children, including sons who loved to hunt and fish. One of his sons and two grandchildren carried on his decoy-carving tradition using his patterns. Schoenhieder decoys are long and slender hollow birds with round heads. He made pintail, mallard, canvasback, bluebill, redhead, blue-winged teal, geese, and American merganser, which he used as confidence decoys. He is best known among today's collectors for his standing "ice" ducks and geese. Using his basic decoy pattern,

he would totally round off the body and mount it onto a single metal foot cast in iron. The resulting decoys have a striking profile. One can really appreciate Schoenhieder's artistic ability by looking at a flock of Canada geese standing along the shore on the ice: from a distance they look just like Schoenhieder's standing geese. Schoenhieder did not paint any of his decoys, and many were painted by Jack Franks. Franks was a professional painter and very talented. He recreated the soft feathery character of an actual bird. His wet blended style was very realistic. At least one other person painted Schoenhieder decoys, but there is no documentation to substantiate any identification. His painting style was much simpler and lacked the quality of Franks's work.

A wonderful aspect of collecting Illinois River decoys is that many quality decoys were produced in the area by different individuals. Some of these carvers made decoys to earn a few extra dollars; others because they were living off the river; and still others just wanted to hunt over their own decoys. Hiram "Hy" Holtze (1886–1958) of Peoria, Illinois, is a good example of those who made decoys for their own use. He was a champion trap shooter and enjoyed hunting ducks over his own decoys. He made fewer than one hundred mallards and canvasback decoys, taking special care on every detail. He used only fine pattern wood and quality oil paints. His heads were patterned after Elliston's with the high-set eyes, but his body

style was his own. He even took the time to sign each of his decoys inside the body cavity.

Just south of Peoria, in Bartonville, lived a carver named Edward W. Keller (1888–1963) who produced a few hundred decoys for himself during the 1940s and 1950s. His decoys have very deep bodies with delicately contoured heads that he painted himself. His puddle ducks have highly detailed paint patterns, and the divers are much simpler, as they are in real life.

Another carver who hunted over his own decoys was Douglas Moseley (1860–1924). His first attempts at decoy carving were wooden pintail silhouettes with collapsible tin wings that he painted himself; these were followed by several folksy canvasback of his own design painted by his wife, Sara Louise (1861–1947), who studied at the Boston Art Conservatory. His mallards are wide with flat bottoms, unusual for Illinois decoys. Moseley had these mallards painted as hens and drakes by Henry Holmes. He also made redhead and bluebill decoys that possess classic Illinois River features—fully rounded, hollow bodies that are slightly V-bottom shaped and nicely formed heads with glass eyes and detailed bills. These divers were painted by Sara Louise.

Douglas Moseley was president of the Citizens Bank in the county seat of Bureau County, Princeton, and was a founding member of the prestigious Princeton Fish and Game Club: obviously, he could afford to buy the best hunting decoys. In

239

OPPOSITE: Mallard drake by Charles Schoenheider painted by Charles Franks; 1880s. This ice duck stands on a single cast-iron foot. Such ice decoys were used by heating the metal foot enough to melt the ice, which would refreeze and hold the decoy steady.

LEFT: Charles Schoenheider.

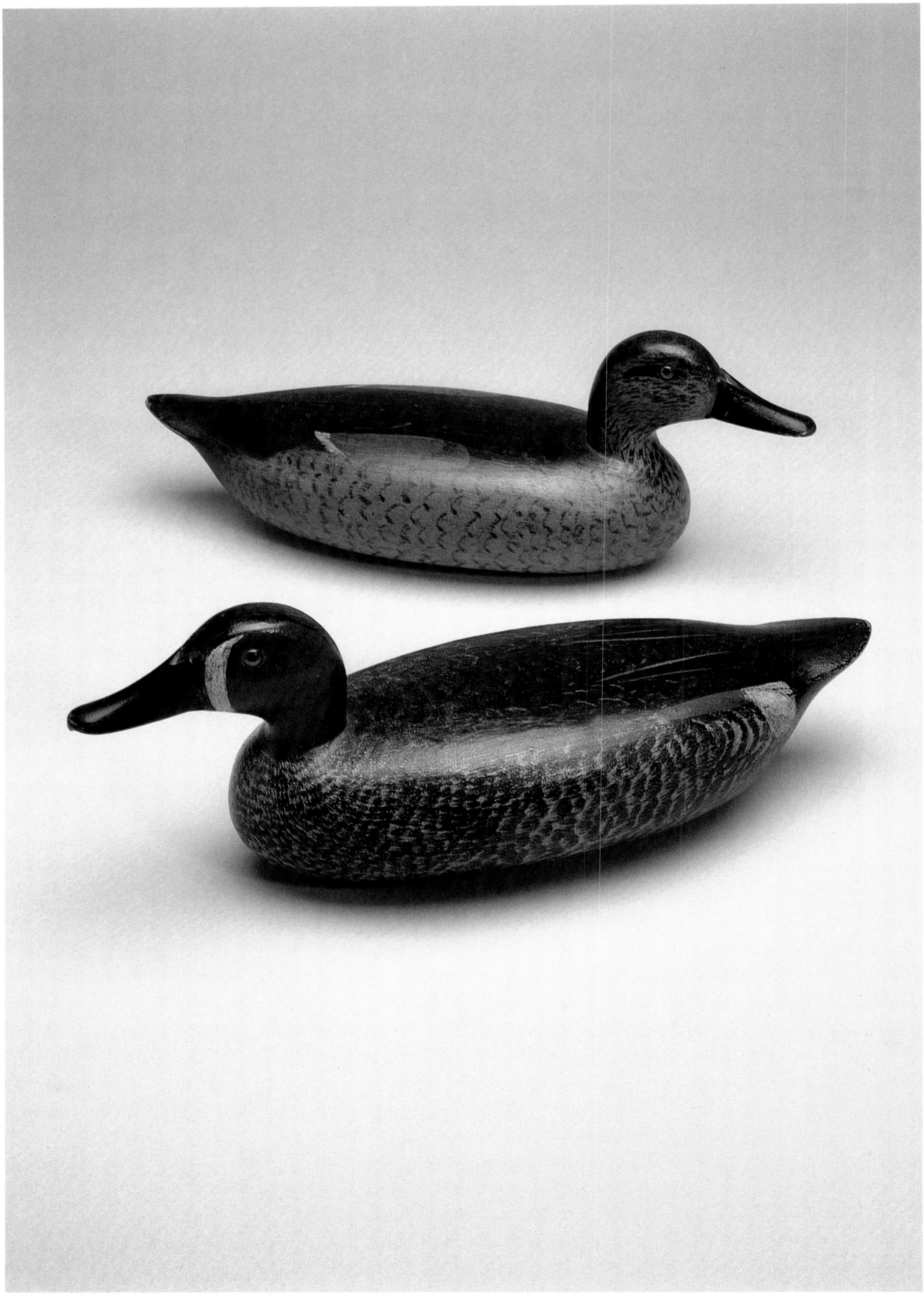

BELOW: Redhead by Douglas Moseley painted by his wife, Sara Louise; late 1800s. This has such classic Illinois River features as a rounded, hollow body; glass eyes; and detailed bill carving.

OPPOSITE: Blue-winged teal by Charles Schoenheider painted by Charles Franks; late 1800s. These small working decoys are lightweight and softly painted.

241

fact, all of his equipment was the best money could buy because he loved hunting. It is not surprising that the Moseley rig also included decoys made by Robert Elliston and Henry Holmes.

Holmes (1870–1926) was a carpenter by trade, building houses and making cabinets, but like many Illinoians, his passion was duck hunting. In his two-story workshop next to the railroad tracks in Bureau, Illinois, he produced several hundred decoys weighted with a lead strip inscribed "The Holmes Decoy." He made three sizes of decoy during his carving career. His earliest decoys were small, delicate birds like the pintails found in the Moseley rig. He also made bluebill and mallard decoys that he painted himself with heavy oil paints, blending and combing the paints while they were wet. His mallard hens have burnished brown breasts with a heavily feathered pattern utilizing rich browns and ochres. Only the limited number of his surviving decoys has prevented Holmes from being as well known as the major Illinois River carvers.

Robert Weeks (1898–1978) remembered watching Holmes as he carved decoys in his workshop in Bureau. Weeks became a decoy maker too. His birds are very similar to Holmes's, but retain a character of their own. He did not make many hunting decoys. Most were for his own use, but he was well known in Bureau County for his mantel birds. Until his death, he made mallards, pintail, green-winged teal and blue-winged teal, and canvasback birds full size and as standing or decoy-style miniatures that were sold exclusively under contract through the Ranch House, a local restaurant and motel frequented by local and out-of-town hunters.

Bob Weeks was also a member of the Princeton Fish and Game Club. Established by the social elite of Bureau County in 1884, this remains one of the most prestigious clubs on the Illinois River, and it has a strong heritage. One of the proudest traditions was to hunt over Charles Walker decoys. Although he was never a member of the club, Walker (1876–1954) carved his hunting decoys exclusively for its members. His decoys are considered by most collectors to be the classic Illinois River decoy. They have high heads and sleek bodies that capture the regal attitude of mallards swimming amid the wild reed grasses of the river backwaters. Each rig of decoys, usually made up of two or three dozen mallards—eight drakes to four hens—was carved differently, with subtle changes in the body pattern, such as having relief carving to delineate the wing area or flat bottoms as opposed to rounded bottoms. This may have been done to avoid any mix-ups in the members' rigs.

Walker carved a few pintail and canvasback decoys with the same regal appearance. He also carved several silhouette mallards and pintail. These birds were made from one-inch boards and mounted onto a notched wooden oval board. Wing nuts and bolts on the ends of eighteen-inch strips were used to join the silhouettes in an accordion fashion.

Walker painted his decoys himself using Parker and later Herter's decoy painting kits. By looking at the literature that came with the kits, one can see that Walker followed their patterns, adding refined feathering and some combing. Many heads that collectors believed to be repainted may have just been given two coats of slightly varying shades of green originally to highlight the cheeks and cover the base coat completely. Although he made only a few miniatures measuring ten inches as gifts for his family members, these birds are treasured, exact replicas of his hunting decoys. Made in pairs with sleepers, some sets included tiny five-inch ducklings. There are several pairs of mallards and one known pintail hen sleeper.

Charles Althoff (1859–1942) worked with Walker as a professional painter in Princeton. His artistic endeavors included painting complex church interiors and making carousel animals as well as hunting decoys. As one would expect, his decoys are finely carved, sometimes with raised carved wings, and they are nicely painted. His paint pattern was softly feathered and highly detailed. Some of his birds have been found with Walker's paint, but his style of painting and carving was entirely different from Walker's. Unfortunately, few of his decoys survive in their original condition, something that is true of too many good Illinois carvers.

Another carver few collectors have heard of is Charles Shelstrom (1866–1950). Little is known about Shelstrom: he was not even listed in *Decoys and Decoy Carvers of Illinois.* He lived in Tiskilwa and made decoys during the late 1800s. His birds were small, lightweight decoys with fine heads and solid construction. Since he did not paint, owners had to get his birds painted themselves. A few of his mallards painted by Sara Louise Moseley were found in her husband's rig. Despite this lack of fame, Shelstrom decoys are representative of the Illinois River. Another carver from this era was August Ewand (1865–1925). A German-born cabinet- and pattern-maker, he made several hundred mallard and pintail decoys that are the earliest documented birds on the Illinois River. His decoys were used farther upriver, by Peru, Illinois. They are solidly constructed with heavy bills, tack eyes, and fully rounded bodies. His paint

242

ABOVE: Pintail drake by Charles Walker; 1930s. Known as a "Skinner" decoy, this was made for Henry Gross, one of the first members of the Princeton Fish and Game Club. Walker decoys have a regal bearing, their heads held high to imitate puddle ducks swimming amid wild grass.

style was simple yet pleasing. Aside from a few decoys, nothing is left to tell the collector anything about August Ewand.

Probably the best-known carver from this stretch of the river was Hector Whittington (1907–81). Having migrated with his parents from Glouchestershire, England, he settled in Oglesby, Illinois, and remained there for the rest of his life. The need to help feed his family led Whittington to duck hunting and to the art of decoy making. He made his first decoys in 1924. Whittington was a perfectionist: he discarded decoy heads and bodies that did not meet his exact measurements. After sanding a block as smooth as possible, he would apply three coats of heavy white lead undercoats, sanding after each coat until he had a glasslike finish on which to paint. He used an elaborate paint pattern that utilized combing and an intricate feather design. Through correspondence with such noted East Coast carvers as Shang Wheeler, he improved his skills and assimilated their patterns, most notably the realistic sleeper with its head curved across its breast and back. He also incorporated their painting techniques, such as scratch painting the heads of his hens and black ducks. He made working mallards, pintail, teal, bluebill, and goose decoys. Whittington can be considered a transition carver who made working decoys and progressed to produce competition decoys for the contests that started during the 1940s in the East. While he was entering the contests, he made most species of waterfowl. His decorative swans were beautifully stylized. He produced these and other waterfowl in three-fourth, one-half, miniature, and full size.

One of Whittington's students was Chris Powers (1902–58) from Peru. Powers did not carve working decoys until the 1950s, when he became disenchanted with the poorly made factory decoys he and his son were hunting over. With his father's hundred-year-old violin-making tools, he crafted three dozen mallards for his own use. He went to Whittington for help and seems to have used some of the East Coast patterns

OPPOSITE TOP: Mallards by Charles Walker; 1948. Made for Cliff Jolley—and likely the last rig Walker made—these are probably Walker's most stylish and best-painted decoys. Note the elaborate patterns and pleasing lines, characteristic of Walker decoys.

LEFT: Pintail drake by August Haas. Little is known of Haas, and this decoy and two others are the only known examples of his work in original condition. He made several dozen mallards and pintails during the 1920s; his nephew repainted the mallards during the 1960s.

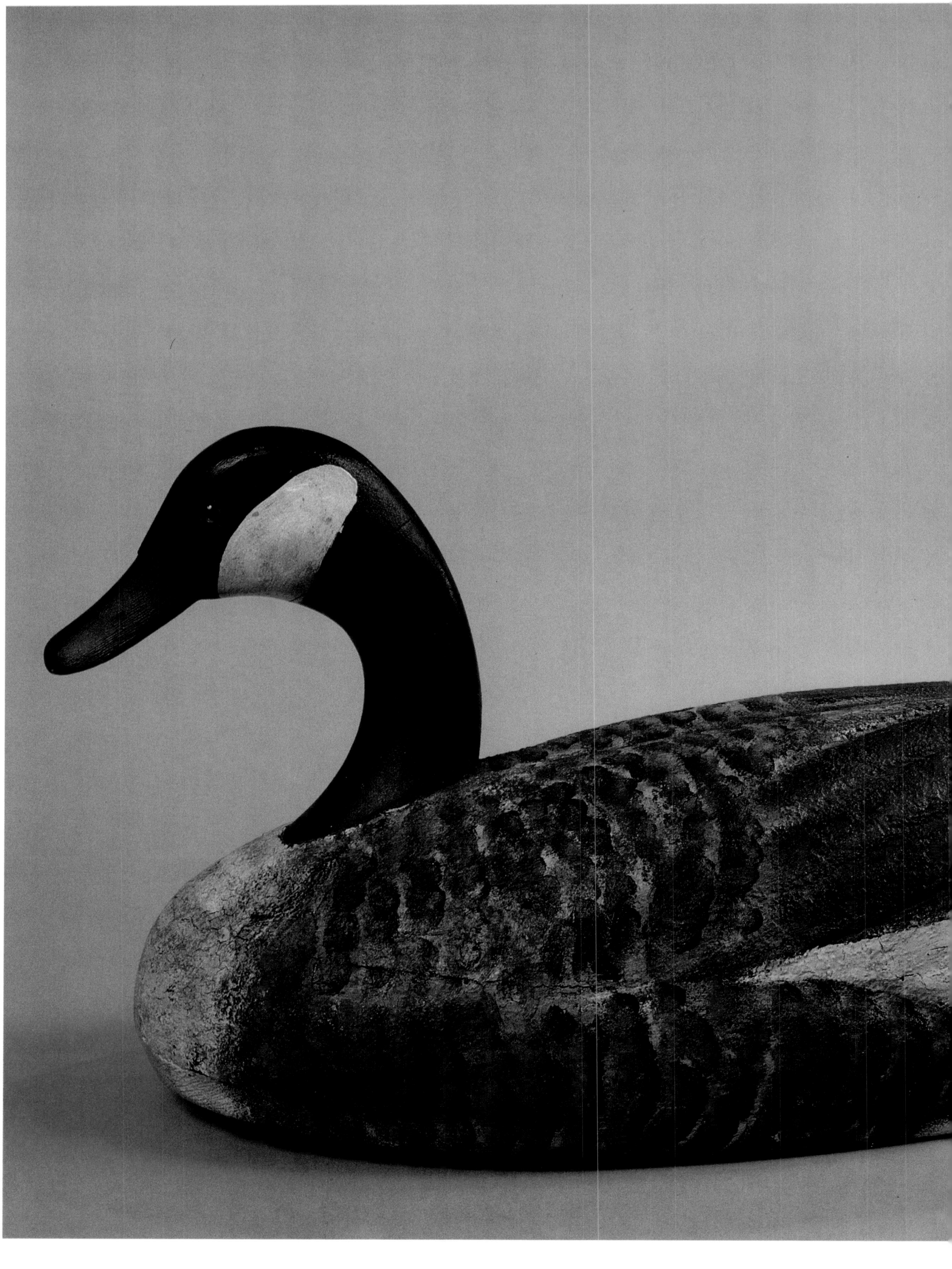

Goose decoy by Clair Hamburg. Like his other decoys, this goose was made with a cork body mounted to a wooden base with a wooden tail insert. The head is finely carved and detailed.

Whittington received through the mail. Powers's decoys were shallow and broad with a right angle cut beneath the tail area used to stabilize the decoy on the water. This feature was illustrated in Joel Barber's book *Wild Fowl Decoys.* His decoys are painted as intricately as Whittington's and even had metal tail curls on the drakes. Before he made his working decoys, Powers was well known locally for his miniature carvings and hunting scene dioramas, which he whittled and sold at his gas station in Peru.

August Haas (1893–1950) was a contemporary of Powers from his hometown. Although his pintail decoys are in the same class as Charles Walker's, he is virtually unknown. Listed simply by name, age, and residence in *Decoys and Decoy Carvers of Illinois,* he made only two dozen mallard decoys, all of which were repainted by his nephew during the 1960s, and three spectacular pintail drakes. These sprigs have a high-headed, regal bearing and a soft, feathery paint pattern.

A little-known commercial carver, Michael Vallero (1906–83) worked out of the basement of his Spring Valley home, shipping decoys to sporting-goods stores in Peoria and Chicago for sale. His decoys were used by local hunters, many of whom could not afford $36 a dozen for Perdew decoys—Vallero decoys sold for $1 each. They were quality birds none the less, with long, hollowed, and nicely rounded bodies and well-turned heads. Most of his decoys were painted by Edna Perdew or Henry Holmes during the 1920s and 1930s: since he could not paint well, he only primed them and sent them out to be painted before he sold them.

One of the true folk artists of the Illinois Valley was Walter "Tube" Dawson (1882–1955). As a young man, he hunted for the market and later worked as a "pusher" at Lake Senachwine hunting clubs near Putnam. (A pusher would push-pole the hunting boat out to the blind and serve as a guide for other hunters.) He started to carve decoys at 17, producing thousands of blocks during the following half century. He made basic mallards in two sizes as well as unusual folksy birds like high-headed mallards with six-inch necks that could be seen in tall marsh grasses. His sleepers were very stylized too, with an elongated head and neck that looked like a handle arched over the decoy as the bill touched one side of the back. He made mostly mallard and pintail decoys. A photograph of his workshop in *Decoys and Decoy Carvers of Illinois* illustrates drying racks, which held about two hundred decoys, loaded down with his decoys. He painted his own decoys with bright, glossy colors, using some combing on the backs and wet-on-wet brushing to feather them. A trademark was his practice of applying crescents of colors to suggest feathers on the wing area backward.

Perry Wilcoxen (1862–1954) of Liverpool, Illinois, made thousands of hunting decoys. All his birds have a strong folksy style that is easily recognized, but they vary extremely in dimensions because he whittled each decoy out of whatever size piece of wood was available. His heads are well carved with the eye area recessed but often without eyes. His paint pattern is also easily spotted by the small white dots he used to accent the back behind the head and the alternating black and white parallel lines that run down the back half of his decoy bodies. Wilcoxen produced large numbers of pintail, mallard, and canvasback as well as redhead, bluebill, green-winged teal, and ringneck decoys. An old photograph of Wilcoxen standing

246

with his decoys in *North American Decoys* shows a Canada goose and wood duck were among the birds he carved in miniature, so he may have carved working wood ducks too.

Many Illinois River hunters believed in using confidence decoys in their rigs. Such a decoy was supposed to convince the wary ducks that the decoys were actually live birds by creating a more natural setting. Most confidence decoys were coot or merganser, birds that were rarely hunted for the table. A striking pair of heron decoys was used on the Grand Isle Hunting Club near Bath, Illinois. The exact age and maker of these birds is unknown, but they are believed to have been made during the early 1900s. Their white paint is totally worn away: only traces remain in the crevices of the aged pine wood. The carving is exceptional. The head was mitered and detachable with a walnut bill inset. The bodies were well formed with walnut leg insets and copper tail feathers set among the carved tail feathers.

Not all of the decoys made in Illinois were used on the Illinois River. Many carvers lived on the Illinois side of the Mississippi River, and their decoys were used there. Pictured on the cover of *Decoys and Decoy Carvers of Illinois* was a pair of

shoveler decoys made by Frank Cassini (1899–1976). Cassini was a professional artist who worked in ceramics as well as taxidermy. He began carving decoys when he was living in Rock Island as a young man and continued to carve after he moved to Galesburg. Because of his artistic training, Cassini was able to produce very realistic decoys that often had their primaries and sometimes the entire wing area carved in relief. He was also an excellent painter, and his patterns were very accurate.

Before World War II, Cassini used white pine for his decoys, but war shortages forced him to construct his hunting birds with composition cork bodies and wooden heads. During this time he made his balsa decoys. They had wide, shallow bodies and a pine-wood head that was loosely attached with a long nut and bolt, so the head could swing freely around to more accurately imitate a live duck. These decoys were painted in oils with his realistic detailed pattern. Cassini was also known for his dove decoys. Carved of wood, these little gray doves were fashioned with clothespins glued to the birds so they could be hung or clipped among the tree branches while he enjoyed his dove shoot.

Although his decoys were used mostly on the Mississippi River, Verne Chessman (1897–1956) was strongly influenced by Charles Perdew, and many of his decoys were painted by Edna Perdew. His decoy patterns were very similar yet they have their own style and character. He made several hundred duck decoys as well as crow decoys during his forty-year carving career, including mallard, pintail, teal, canvasback, bluebill, and ringneck.

Entered in the International Decoy Makers Contest, February 1951, at New York, N. Y., in the Class 1, amateur "decoys made by exhibitors for their own use," was a pair of mallards made by Clair Hamburg (1906–66) of Rock Island, Illinois. If these mallards were anything like the cork decoys in collections today, they were fine birds, even though they did not win any ribbons. Hamburg worked as the bridge tender in Moline and whittled his decoy heads at work. His cork decoys were fine examples of workmanship. Cork can be difficult to work with, and his style was very refined. The cork body was mounted on a one-inch base board with a wooden tail insert. The head was carved of white pine. His decoys were naturally formed and very realistic. His painting style was very detailed and soft. His

geese were especially fine.

Jack Stiles (1908–1965) of Savanna, Illinois, made several hundred hunting blocks, including some unusual standing birds mounted on two wooden legs with an outstretched neck. When these birds were pushed into a sandbar they recreated an alluring feeding-style decoy. Stiles fashioned his decoys out of balsa with pine heads. Balsa is normally very soft, and he reinforced the wood by applying several coats of epoxy paint before painting them. Although color blind, Stiles was able to paint very realistically, with detailed and accurate paint patterns on his mallard, pintail, wood duck, green-winged teal, and blue-winged teal.

Many other carvers produced decoys used in Illinois. These men captured the waterfowl that they loved and hunted on the rivers and backwaters of this state. The birds they made were a tribute to a time when ducks and geese darkened the skies. Although wooden decoys are rarely used by hunters today, they often find a place of honor in the homes of sportsmen and art collectors. They are reminders of a time when waterfowling was a way of life and often a career that helped feed a growing nation.

CHAPTER 20:

WISCONSIN

by David Jon Spengler

To the Chippewa Indians who lived here, this land was *Wee-kon-san,* meaning "place of the gathering waters." The Winnebagoes spoke reverently of *Wis-koos-erah* to describe their precious "river of the flowering banks." Early French explorers took these names and fashioned them into *Ouisconsin,* and thus this land is today known as Wisconsin.

In 1634 Jean Nicolet, a French explorer, first set foot on the shores of shimmering Green Bay and thus opened to the white man the door to this magnificent, wild, and as yet untapped territory. From then until 1763 the French dominated; then, under the terms of the 1763 Treaty of Paris ending the French and Indian War, the British won control of the land. In 1836 Congress created the Wisconsin Territory, and twelve years later Wisconsin became the thirtieth state.

This is a land of tremendous resources. The soil is rich and productive. Water is abundant. Minerals abound. And vast stands of prime timber forests cover much of the land. More than 8,800 lakes in excess of 20 acres dot the countryside, created centuries ago by a series of glaciers that invaded most of the region. Fast-flowing rivers and meandering streams crisscross the state and have had a profound impact on the life here, including waterfowling. In addition to the rivers and lakes within its borders, Wisconsin is flanked on the west by the Mississippi River, on the east by 381 miles of shoreline on Lake Michigan, and an additional 291 miles of shoreline on Lake Superior form its northern boundary.

This place, this "gathering of waters," has historically served as a resting place and feeding ground for waterfowl

OPPOSITE: Coot by Gus Moak; ca. 1880. One of Wisconsin's premier carvers, Moak made only a few coot decoys, and coot decoys were used primarily as confidence decoys. Note the slightly turned head.

LEFT: Blue-winged teal drake (below) and redhead hen (above) by Dewitt Wakefield; ca. 1880. Wakefield was probably Wisconsin's first decoy carver.

during their annual spring and fall migrations. Thousands of ducks and geese are produced here each year. Wild rice, sago pondweed, celery, and a vast assortment of other natural feed supported large numbers of waterfowl in the past and to this day remain sufficient to maintain good levels. Waterfowl and waterfowling are important threads in the fabric of Wisconsin life. For this reason, the state has for over one hundred years been home to carvers and users of waterfowl decoys and more recently has become a cherished land for collectors.

Most scholars of Wisconsin waterfowl decoys would agree that Dewitt Wakefield (1849–1912) of Fremont was the first-known Wisconsin carver. He made his livelihood from carpentry, and the Wakefield decoys that remain are a testimony to his woodworking skill.

Fremont is a small but active community on the Wolf River, just upstream from Lake Poygan. On the western edge of town rests Partridge Lake, a shallow expanse once filled with natural feed for all forms of waterfowl. It was there that Wakefield hunted most. The Wolf flows peacefully down from the northwest, creating tiny Partridge Crop Lake. Onward it flows through the Templeton Bayou, Partridge Lake, and eventually into Lake Poygan. In the mid to late 1800s small steamboats

carried passengers and cargo from Oshkosh to Tustin and on to Fremont. I was told that Wakefield worked as a deckhand for a short time but found carpentry more to his liking.

Most of Wakefield's production was of bluebills. He did, however, make canvasback, teal, mallards, and a very few red-heads and wigeon. One report is that Wakefield made several loons as confidence decoys, but to my knowledge none has ever surfaced. Wakefield seems to have used whatever was available in making his decoys, and some appear with glass eyes and others with tiny old tacks. The variety of body sizes and shapes supports the theory that he did each by hand without use of patterns. This variation adds to the charm of each Wakefield decoy. He was an accomplished painter and must certainly have used quality paints, since many of his decoys retain their original colors after a long time and much heavy usage. His total production is presumed to have numbered far fewer than 1,000.

Because Wakefield passed away so early in the 20th century, few Fremontians remember him or can supply first-hand information on his life. Nonetheless we are told that he hunted for market as a way to augment his income from carpentry and to quench his thirst for hunting and the outdoors. To this day a small inlet on Partridge Lake is known as Wake-

*Pair of blue-winged teal by
William Hoberg and bufflehead
drake by Harold Hoberg. Rarely
have a father and son made such
good folk art.*

250

field Bay, though unfortunately it is rarely visited by the water-fowl flocks he so eagerly pursued. Changes in water levels and usage of the lake by motorboats have ended the extensive feed that once attracted rafts of ducks and geese.

Collectors fortunate enough to have Wakefield decoys prize them highly, not only for their special charm, but also for the role they play in Wisconsin waterfowl heritage. Decoys by Wakefield date to over one hundred years ago, and his work influenced the other Fremont carvers of waterfowl decoys who followed—such notables as Joseph Gigl, Clifford "Moody" Lind, and the Dorschners from nearby Zittau. To this day I can recall the bags of Wakefields Bill Springer had propped up behind his wood-burning stove in the corner of his shack on Mosquito Creek off Partridge Lake. These bits of history suffered the same fate as poor Bill when fire reduced the cabin to a pile of smoldering ashes. Wakefield clearly was the pioneer of the Fremont style of carving and perhaps of all Wisconsin carving as well.

August "Gus" Moak (1852–1942) of Tustin was a member of a family that emigrated from Germany in 1853. Like so many of their countrymen before them, the Moaks settled in Wisconsin. They choose the village of Tustin, located on the northwestern end of Lake Poygan and known from the mid 1800s until the turn of the century as the "Canvasback Capital of the World." Huge flocks of canvasback were joined by redheads and bluebills as they scurried across the lake in search of the day's tasty feast of wild celery. Thousands of coots congregated there on their migrations. Such were the numbers that waterfowlers from across the nation, and in fact royalty from across the seas, came to Poygan to hunt for sport. Poygan measures some nine miles east to west and three miles north to south, providing migrating ducks and geese a most comfortable place to feed and rest.

Moak learned carpentry skills from his father, "Root," and these proved useful in the making of decoys, boats, bog skis, and other tools of waterfowling. While it is uncertain when Moak first carved decoys, guesses place the date somewhere around 1870. In his article for *North American Decoys* (Fall, 1975) Bernard Crandell reported that Moak's grandson affirmed that Gus's most productive years would have been from about 1870 to 1900.

During the years of production Moak employed such a variety of painting techniques and body shapes that it is impossible to accurately state which were made when. Nonetheless, all of Moak's decoys reflect the skill and obvious love that went into their making. Moak decoys are usually finely hollowed, have convex board bottoms, and are superbly painted. The eyes of most are placed toward the top of the head, giving the impression that the rafted decoys were intent on watching their flying counterparts approach for landing.

Most of Moak's decoys were canvasbacks, priced at $55 per dozen, or bluebills priced at $50. A very few Canada geese and coots have made their way onto the shelves of collectors, and a pair of mallards has raised an interesting debate among collectors as to whose hands were responsible for them. Some say Moak all the way, yet others say the bodies are Moak canvasbacks with an excellent old mallard paint job by Joe Gigl, who lived just up the Wolf River in Fremont. Perhaps it is such little mysteries of decoying that hold our interest most. Moak

252

used babbitt found along nearby railroad tracks for keel weights as a substitute for higher-priced lead. Some of his decoys are restful, others are alert. Most have slightly longer tails than others carved in the area. But it was his painting that makes these decoys so very special. He used subtle little brush strokes to accent the excellence of his artistry. While overall paint patterns were somewhat simplistic, they were accurate and professional.

The region has produced a number of outstanding decoy carvers and painters, but Moak attained the pinnacle. He was known as an outdoorsman who judiciously harvested what he needed—be it fish, fowl, game, or the timber that supplied the wood used in creating his highly sought after decoys.

Like their neighbors, the Moaks, just down the road in tiny Tustin, the Sieger family left their beloved homeland of Germany for Wisconsin and life in America. They arrived at the time of the Civil War and bought a farm of some 100 tillable acres. They also acquired several parcels totalling perhaps another 500 acres of marshland bordering on the Wolf River and Lake Poygan. Alder Creek gently flows through the farm on its way to the lake.

Joseph Sieger (1871–1959) was born May 1, 1871, and he

LEFT: Pair of mallards by Enoch Reindahl; ca. 1938. This sleeping hen and lowhead drake show exceptional accuracy; Reindahl overlooked no details and painted the eyes rather than inserting glass ones.

253

lived his entire life on the farm. Being of German heritage, young Joseph learned early on the skills of knife and brush. He became an accomplished woodworker, making exceptional violins and some furniture. It was, therefore, not unexpected that he crafted some of Wisconsin's most classic decoys, which he used in the pursuit of waterfowl.

Although Joseph was twenty years younger than Gus Moak, the two often carved and painted decoys together in the Sieger toolshed, according to Mabel Sieger, Joe's daughter-in-law. Although there are some common traits, each of these premier carvers developed styles of his own. Sieger's use of brush was superb but differed from Moak's quite markedly. Sieger placed his eyes in a more traditional and lower position. Sieger's bottom board was flat, and X-rays have revealed that Sieger used screws to affix the bottom board to the body, while Moak nailed them. Again, X-rays show that Moak fastened the heads to the bodies by use of long, double-headed screws, while Sieger drilled down through the head, inserted a single-headed screw into place, and then filled the void created by the drill bit.

Though he cropped his fields, Sieger could best be known as a fur farmer. Mabel told me that he harvested the abundant muskrats, beaver, and other furry creatures that inhabited the marsh property. The family joined in the skinning and curing process as the valuable pelts were sold to furriers from Milwaukee or nearby Oshkosh and Berlin. Sieger made his own gunning boxes, bog skis, and canary-grass mats to conceal himself from waterfowl. Joseph also constructed several trim shallow-draft duck skiffs for himself and a few select hunting partners. These were double-pointed, unlike the pumpkinseed style Moak was noted for. Mabel recalled that Joe shaped his bog skis with the aid of a homemade steamer used to bend the wood, and that he carved paddles, push poles, and oars.

One can but dream of the thrill of being snuggered down in the skiff among tall cane that punctured the waters of Lake Poygan in an attempt to keep out of view of circling ducks until the precise moment of firing. Just to have witnessed a rig of Sieger canvasback decoys with their erect proud heads moving with the chop of Poygan's waves and the great wedges of speedy canvasbacks wheeling about to approach them are the thrills that waterfowlers dream of. Indeed, Sieger was a part of the glory years of waterfowling in Wisconsin—an important part of this state's gunning history.

William Hoberg (1882–1985) was born in Kaukauna, Wisconsin, which is situated on the banks of the Fox River. The Fox is one of the primary rivers in the state, both in terms of the historical importance of its trade and commerce and its role in waterfowling. The Fox flows north from Butte des Morts, where it is joined by the Wolf River, and travels on into Lake Winnebago and thence to Green Bay. All forms of waterfowl follow its course and offer hunters an opportunity for good shooting. William's father, John, moved the family to Green Bay in 1895, and though John was not himself a hunter, he encouraged William to hunt from the age of 15. The eastern shore of Green Bay drew rafts of diving ducks that fed on the abundant celery and "wabato" that covered the bay's bottom. It was up near Dykesville that William sought the majestic canvasbacks for sport and table. Most of his decoys were factory mades supplied by local sporting shops. However, he did carve and paint a rig of teal used mostly on the western shore of the bay near Duck Creek and Little Suamico, where expansive marshes, little bays and inlets, and a series of creeks attracted puddlers. When William had the urge to gun for teal, mallards, blacks, and wigeon, he would haul his Mannebach and Maes skiff to those waters for the day's shoot.

Harold Hoberg (b. 1914), William's son, generously shared stories of his father and also told me of his own interest in waterfowling. He said his father was a loner when it came to hunting, and while Harold and William often hunted the same areas at the same times, each would go his separate way as each had ideas of his own as how best to hunt. This separatism did not dampen Harold's enjoyment of hunting or diminish his respect for his father's skills and knowledge. It was an expression of the individualism that is so very common to waterfowlers.

In 1932 William Hoberg patented the Hoberg Decoy Safety Anchor, which an old advertisement describes as "adjustable, simple-acting, and kink-proof." No. 1 size was for large-headed decoys (3–3½ inches) and No. 2 size was for small (2–2½ inches). Harold Hoberg was also an accomplished decoy maker. He made several small rigs for his own use, including bluebills, canvasbacks, redheads, and buffleheads. All are superb examples of folk art. The Hoberg name will be remembered with others from the Green Bay region that have had an impact on waterfowling—such as Grosse, Danz, Paulson, Barkhausen, Frisque, Claflin, and Salvas.

Born in Fond du Lac on the southern shores of Lake Winnebago, Burton Kannenburg (b. 1910) spent most of his life in or near Milwaukee. His first job was that of a painter with the murals department of the Milwaukee Public Museum.

254

Pair of Canada geese by Enoch Reindahl.

255

While there, Burt learned to carve and paint decoys in the Milwaukee style from Owen Gromme and Gromme's co-workers in the taxidermy department, Warren Dettman and Walter Pelzer. These decoys typically were constructed of three to five 1–1½ inch boards laminated one on top of the other. They were nicely hollowed, very well painted, and most assumed content or resting postures. The finest oil paints were used as they were readily available at the museum.

Kannenburg began hunting about 1927. His one and only attempt at making decoys came in 1934 when he and two friends, Carl Boehm and Clarence Funk, joined forces to make exactly 150 decoys on an assembly-line basis. It had been agreed that upon completion straws would be drawn to determine the order of selection (the long straw to choose first, fourth, and so on). Each would receive 50 of the decoys for his personal rig. Gromme was considered the grand master carver, and he set the example. In addition to ringbills (marsh bluebills in Kannenburg's jargon), the trio made some teal and a handful of "woodies." Kannenburg made one Canada goose decoy in about 1935 or 1936, and he used it as a confidence decoy until his gunning days ended in 1968.

A relative of Boehm worked in a nearby lumberyard and was the source of the pine boards, each selected by hand so as to be knot free. Heads were made of cedar from end-cuts off larger blocks of wood. A few of the 150 received glass eyes, but most have tack eyes, as money for the fancier ones was needed for other more important uses back in the mid-1930s. According to Kannenburg, the tacks were painted at whim. They cut grooves in a couple of boards into which lead was poured for making keel weights. Once the boards were well scorched, the lead keels could easily be dislodged. Anchor weights were made by pouring molten lead into an old cupcake tin that rested on Boehm's workbench. Flat oils were used to paint the final colors applied over presealed and primed bodies and heads. Kannenburg acknowledged that they were more interested in making the decoys functional than beautiful.

It seems that Kannenburg had no special hunting grounds but rather moved from pothole to lake and creek to field as instinct dictated. His most productive waterfowling came at Lake Maria, a shallow pocket of water near Fox Lake in south central Wisconsin. It was there, however, that Burt suffered the ignominy of mistakenly shooting one of the group's two live ducks. Upon arriving at the museum the following Monday, Burt was greeted by a banner hanging in his office on which was painted a duck on its back with feet extended skyward and the immortal words "Once I was a live duck"! Burt was careful never again to point his trusty L.C. Smith 12 gauge at such a target.

Enoch Reindahl (b. 1904) was born on his family's farm in the township of Dunkirk just outside Stoughton. His Norwegian parents emigrated from Telemark, Norway, and joined relatives and friends who had settled in this region of Wisconsin. Enoch's early days were like those of the other boys of the time: hours spent in the small schoolhouse down the country lane, summer days working in the fields or relaxing at the swimming hole, skiing in the winter. Enoch certainly must have had strong inner feelings for nature, as they come boldly through in his carvings and paintings. This awareness of nature is also reflected in the hundreds of photographs Enoch took through the years, a

number of which have been published.

The Reindahls moved from the farm to the edge of Stoughton in 1915, though they kept the farm until the late 1940s. Enoch completed his formal education with graduation from Stoughton High School in 1921, and about then he began to hunt. With his father's help, he constructed his first duck-boat in the summer of 1921; it was the first of three he was to build. It was a double-pointed skiff in the style of the Dan Kidney's built at the time in DePere to the north. That year he carved his first rig of decoys—solid-bodied bluebills. These were proof that Enoch had an eye for waterfowl.

His favorite hunting was less than two miles to the north of his home in a place simply called Big Marsh. It was both spring-fed and received water from the Yahara River, which flowed through the marsh on the way to the Rock River. Two other spots drew Enoch because of the availability of waterfowl. On the shore of Lake Kegonas was a place called Snow Fence, where the divers could be taken, and to the east of Big Marsh lay Luten's Creek. Here, many springs kept the waters open late into the season, providing excellent shooting of mallards and blacks.

Most of Reindahl's production of decoys came in the 1930s and 1940s. In 1949 he sold an article, "How to Make Decoys," to *Field and Stream* magazine for $100. It was a step-by-step procedure complete with diagrams for carving and painting. Reindahl enjoys the position of being among the very finest carvers and painters of decoys. Some would say he was the best.

His knowledge of waterfowl, superb skill with knife and brush, and drive for perfection combined to yield truly magnificent decoys. He passed along his skills to several local friends, and the decoys of the Homme boys, brothers Ferd and Mandt, Gerrold Larson, and Russell "Raz" Berry attest to his sharing. Reindahl carved mallards, black ducks, pintails, canvasbacks, bluebills, and both Canada and snow geese. Most were nicely hollowed, enjoyed relaxed and natural attitudes, had crossed raised wingtips, and above all were skillfully painted in exacting detail. His carving and painting skills have been preserved

LEFT: Oversize canvasback "lead" decoy by an unknown maker from Lake Butte des Morts. Such decoys were used to lead low-flying ducks to the hunter's decoys; the use of lead decoys was uncommon.

BELOW: Works by unknown Wisconsin carvers. From left to right, a snow goose from the state's "thumb," ca. 1915; a tiny bufflehead, ca. 1860; an owl from Omro, ca. 1930.

for history as the result of his love of photography. He took photographs of each stage of production, from blocks of wood pictured on his workbench to hollowing, gluing, and sanding. There are photos of him priming and painting the completed decoys. In fact, he took photographs of himself in the marsh, paddling his duck skiff in toward shore, showing the decoys at rest at anchor.

Above all, Reindahl will always be remembered as both a naturalist and conservationist. Recently, he generously gave his beloved marsh property to the Wisconsin Department of Natural Resources to protect for the enjoyment of future generations.

Lost with the passage of time is information on other Wisconsin carvers, men who made only a few decoys for personal use and who have been long since forgotten. Because of the uncertainties, many have missed the opportunity to be included in books such as this.

In honor of all unknown Wisconsin carvers, the photograph above shows three outstanding examples of their work. The oversize canvasback drake measures 27 inches long and is a rare example of an authentic "lead" decoy. Shallow Wisconsin lakes such as Winnebago, Poygan, and Butte des Morts were often very rough, making standard-size decoys hard to see by low-flying diver ducks. Oversize decoys were used to draw the divers toward the hunter, until the standard size rig was seen. Few lead decoys remain.

In contrast to the canvasback is the little bufflehead drake rescued from the rafters of the Stillman boathouse on the shore of Partridge Crop Lake. The aging paint, old pack eyes, and overall primitiveness makes one believe it was around to witness the return of its owner from the Civil War to resume gunning of another sort.

Snow goose decoys are uncommon, and the one pictured came from a toolshed on a Door County farm. Late in the fall on crisp, clear days, small bands of snows and blues rest and feed in the rock-cleared fields holding droppings of the harvest. Certainly some ancient gunner used this decoy to lure unsuspecting snows into range. But when? And who?

CHAPTER 21:

MINNESOTA

JOHN TAX, THE LAST OF THE PRAIRIE CARVERS

by Joe Engers with John Lindgren

Nestle-headed black duck by John Tax. Tax varied the expressions within his rig; this example clearly displays an expression of contentment.

Minnesota is not well known for the number of its decoy makers, but one of the state's carvers deserves prominent mention in any book on decoys: John Tax. To decoy collectors nationwide, a Tax decoy is easily recognized by its bold, laminated construction and its full-bodied lifelike expression. During a decoy show in Milwaukee in 1969 at which a selection of Tax decoys was on display, a number of collectors came together to recognize John Tax as "the last of the prairie carvers."

Tax was born around the turn of the century in West Union, Minnesota, where he spent his entire life. A harness maker by trade, he managed a shoe-repair shop and harness shop in nearby Osakis. His true love was the outdoors, and he hunted and fished whenever time allowed. He once remarked to a friend who was a Catholic priest that he must have been baptized with slough water.

The decoys he made were as varied as his hunting methods and ranged from cork decoys to stuffed canvas-covered decoys to laminated hollow-bodied stickup decoys. His cork decoys were made with a wooden bottom board and wooden hand-carved heads. His canvas-covered birds were

stuffed with cedar shavings, and lead weights were sewn into the body for balance and helped them float upright when they were dropped into the water. Tax applied for a patent for his canvas-covered decoys, but the patent was never completed. The canvas-covered decoys were probably the earliest of Tax's decoys. He is believed to have made them in the early 1900s.

His field stake stickup decoys create the most interest among collectors. They were constructed of hollowed-out pine planks that were laminated together; even the necks and heads represented this unique craftsmanship. Tax attached leather carrying straps to each decoy, and heavy iron receptacles were inlaid into the bottom to receive the iron stakes that were used to stand up the decoys in the often frozen hunting grounds of Minnesota. Examples of his stickup decoys include Canada geese, snow geese, mallards, and one speckle-belly. A snow goose at a 1988 auction by the Richard Oliver Company of Kennebunk, Maine, sold for $26,000, and many others through private sales have brought high prices.

All of Tax's decoys portray a very lifelike impression of the original. He would make no two alike, alternating the ducks

ABOVE: *Snow goose by John Tax. The body is of laminated pine planks; with the inserted rod the decoy could be used as a stickup in fields.*

RIGHT: *Pair of mallards by John Tax. Tax often referred to Audubon lithographs to achieve lifelike paint patterns and realistic expressions.*

and geese with upright, preening, and feeding positions. When asked the reason for the variety of expressions among his rig, he once remarked, "Ever see all the ducks on a pond all look the same?" He was right. His painting style was also very lifelike and realistic. He owned an original set of lithograph Audubon prints and is assumed to have referred to the prints for both the painting and body styles of his decoys.

Besides the aforementioned species, Tax also carved full rigs of bluebills and teal, a few coots, and a wood duck. These represented the species of ducks generally found in the Plains states. Shortly before his death in 1967, Tax completed his last set of bluebills, and one of his last photographs pictures him presenting a few to astronaut Frank Borman.

Besides duck and goose decoys, Tax was known to have made a fine spear-fishing decoy, plaques, weathervanes, birdhouses, and hand-carved furniture. He also enjoyed doing taxidermy work.

It is estimated that Tax made about one hundred decoys during his lifetime; only about 85 are accounted for. Many collectors would be pleased to add a Tax decoy to their collection, but unfortunately only a few will have that pleasure.

CHAPTER 22:
THE WEST COAST

by Gerald M. Rosenthal

ABOVE: Canvasback drake by Charles Bergman. The hollow Bergman canvasbacks were much improved versions of the Mason Premier model; the design was ideal for the fast-flowing Columbia River.

Fantastic numbers of ducks and geese once wintered in the great valleys of California. Pintails, mallards, canvasbacks, teal, snow geese, Canada geese—there were millions of every species. Just follow a cow or a horse into a field and a single shot could fill a gunny sack. The ease of approaching the waterfowl, and the lack of people, held up the development of the western decoy until well into the 20th century.

There were only about 140 known decoy makers in California, maybe 30 in Oregon, and another 30 in Washington, all working before the end of World War II. There were 22 factories that made decoys; one, Johnson's Folding Decoys in Seattle, Washington, is still in business. The names of many other carvers are not known to us. We see examples of their work, but who they were and when they worked remain a question. They are called the unknowns. Out of all these West

OPPOSITE: Swan decoy by Charles Bergman. Bergman made a rig of swans for his own use sometime before 1918. They are his best-known and most desired decoys.

Coast decoy makers—somewhat over 200, including the unknowns—fewer than 20 are thought of as the creators of truly desirable decoys, and six are household names across the country.

In the Pacific Northwest, the best-known carvers were Charlie Bergman and Jerry Mastin. Bergman, from Astoria, Oregon, and Mastin, from Portland, were contemporaries, working in the twenties and thirties. Bergman's best was the swan rig that dates from the early teens; Mastin's tour de force was accomplished about 1937. Northern California's Humbolt Bay boasted two master carvers, William McLellan and Captain Olsen. Olsen, one of the earliest western decoy makers, and McLellan, a "depression" carver, are known and appreciated for their brant. The San Francisco Bay area held the most prolific of the Pacific Coast decoy makers. "Fresh Air Dick"

Janson, Hie Crandall, and Amiel Garibaldi all worked the northern part of the San Francisco Bay and the Sacramento River delta after 1920.

The river above Sacramento was home to the west's first decoy maker. Peter St. Clair worked around the Butte County, California, area in the 1860s, gathering ducks, geese, fish, and turtles. He made some decoys as well as building a market wagon that was used to hawk his game in the town of Sacramento. As a matter of fact, some of the decoys still exist. One or two are in collections, and his decendants still have four teal, two sprigs, and one wigeon that he made about the time of the Civil War. He was born in 1835 and died in Sacramento in 1910. His rough carved birds had no effect on any other makers, primarily because there were very few, if any, other decoy makers at that time.

Robert E. Smith, a former market hunter who lived in Tulare, California, shipped between 300 and 500 ducks each day to markets in Los Angeles and San Francisco. He did not recall seeing any decoys. "Just too many ducks. No need for decoys," Smith told his interviewer, Bill Mortland of Fresno, California. Smith was interviewed in 1976, one year before he passed away at the age of 98. Smith indicated that he used a 4-gauge swivel gun to kill the "mallards, sprigs, spoonies, and wigeons." His helpers, each using a 12-gauge double barrel to kill the cripples, picked up the birds after each shot. They gutted and sacked the ducks, but did not remove the feathers. They were aided by Smith's dog, a retriever on loan from a "fast woman" in Tulare. Smith was paid between $4 and $6 a dozen, depending on the variety, by the market men in the cities. In 1901, when the state imposed a bag limit of fifty birds a day, Smith retired. He could no longer afford to pay his two helpers, feed his dog, and maintain his horse and wagon. Just imagine: 300 to 500 ducks a day, each day, every day, and Tulare Lake was marginal. The greater concentrations of waterfowl were to the north, wintering in the lower San Joaquin Valley, the Sacra-

262

mento River valley, and the rivers and wetlands of Oregon and Washington.

At the turn of the century, when Smith was gunning, there were few population centers in the west. California had 865,000 people in 1880, and 1,485,000 in 1900. More than half, 745,000, were in and around the cities of San Francisco and Los Angeles. Washington and Oregon jumped from 250,000 to 662,000 during the same period. The hotels, markets, and restaurants in the urban areas had need for waterfowl to serve their trade. To fill the demand, men such as Smith worked on the great bays and estuaries along the Pacific Coast and inland in the river valleys.

The late George Ross Starr, Jr., writing in his *Decoys of the Atlantic Flyway* (1974), said, "It is axiomatic that the more ducks in any given area, the less need for decoys . . . the less need for decoys, the cruder they usually are." He could have continued by indicating that the fewer hunters and gunners, the less need for sophisticated decoys. Or any decoys.

The American Sportsman, a short-lived magazine, carried a story of waterfowling in California during the season of 1873.

263

OPPOSITE: Brant decoy by Captain Olsen. One of a rig of 36 hollow, redwood decoys that are considered the best California-made brant.

There was little or no mention of decoys, probably because none were used or needed. The paucity of western decoy makers born earlier than 1860 could indicate a very small fraternity of carvers working before 1880. As a matter of fact, one can find few decoys, other than those made by St. Clair, that date prior to 1890.

Despite the lack of an early decoy making, and using, tradition, there are many collectible waterfowl decoys in the West. The decoy makers were just late in getting here. William Lindsey (1840–1914), of Alameda, California, was working before the San Francisco earthquake. Tom Dailey, a San Francisco millwright, also made decoys at the turn of the century. He took orders from the "sports" and copied Mason Challenge-grade decoys on the lathe owned by his employers. It was the Mason factory that provided most of the decoys used on the West Coast early on.

Mason's demise in the early twenties might be blamed, in part, on the Migratory Bird Act of 1918. The act prohibited the sale or commercial use of all birds that crossed the border

ABOVE: Canada goose by Jerry Mastin. This is one of nine Mastin made for a "Mr. R. Eaton"; eight survive. Each of the stickup decoys had a different head position.

LEFT: "Muscle power" canvasback decoys by "Fresh Air Dick" Janson. This drake (below) and juvenile (above) show Janson's variety of styles.

BELOW: "Fresh Air Dick" Janson.

264

between the United States and Canada. As the waterfowl disappeared from the restaurants and markets, the demand for decoys used by the market gunners faded, and by 1924, Mason shut down and went to providing paint for Henry Ford's auto factory.

The best-known western carvers did not start their commercial careers until well after World War I and the closing of the largest of the factories. Charlie Bergman, along with other fishermen and boatbuilders from Astoria, Oregon, was working the Columbia River and selling ducks, geese, and swans in the Portland market by about 1890, but Charlie didn't carve for others until the late twenties.

Charles Bergman was born in Eknes, Finland, of Swedish ancestry, on August 1, 1856. After an adventuresome youth following the Norse tradition of going to sea, he decided that the lure of San Francisco was too great. Charlie jumped ship and became first an illegal alien then, later, a naturalized United States citizen.

For several years he worked for the U.S. Life Saving Service, later renamed the Coast Guard. Hearing of the great Scandinavian community located at the mouth of the Columbia River, Bergman moved to Astoria, Oregon, where he found work as a fisherman. In 1887, at the age of 31, tall, stern-looking Charlie married and moved across the Columbia River into Washington to take up farming. After a few unsuccessful years of that, he returned to Astoria and reentered the fishing industry, this time as a boatbuilder.

The Columbia River is joined, near Astoria, by five or six other rivers to form an estuary. Young's Bay, part of the delta, is the site of Fort Clatsop, the Lewis and Clark Expedition's home during the winter of 1805–6. It is also the winter home to great numbers of waterfowl. Even more birds stopped to rest during their southward migration. Charlie and others took advantage of the available birds. They hunted both for subsistence and the market.

Bergman's career as a full-time decoy maker did not start until he retired from the George and Baker Company boatyards about 1929. For more than ten years he finished a dozen of his western red-cedar decoys a week. Not working during the hunting season, that would mean a total production of

something better than 4,500 birds! His best-known, most desired, decoys are the two that remain of the twelve whistling swan decoys made for his own use. Bergman created the rig of swans several years earlier than 1918, the year that swan shooting became illegal. Stored away for many years, they became toys for Charlie's grandson, Chuck. After tripping over the swans once too often, Chuck's grandmother chopped all but two for kindling. The sophistication and style of these five-piece, hollow decoys make them as fine as any swans in the entire country. They are truly dramatic pieces of sculpture.

The hollow Bergman decoys, with the look of Mason's Premier models, but much improved, were carved as pintails, mallards, canvasbacks, baldpate, and green-winged teal. A small rig of scaup came from Charlie's hand in the early forties. Lost for many years, several of these bluebills have been found in the Seattle area. Bergman died in 1946, just short of his ninetieth year, but not before influencing several generations of Astoria decoy makers.

Frank Bay (1896–1980), whose canvasback decoys might

be the most refined to be found on the West Coast, showed more originality than some of the other Astorians. His bodies were less Bergmanish. Charles Pice was also a member of the Astoria group that drew much from Bergman. Pice, a joker, repainted several Bergman pintails in his own style. That has sure confused things! Pice passed away in 1945 after living 55 years. Oscar Hendrickson was another of the Astoria fisherman who, although a member of the Pice camp, owed his style to Bergman. Hendrickson died in 1953. Jim Titus, Sr., was a Bergman follower. Born in 1879, he also carved with Mason as a base, but was more of an abstractionist in his painting than old Charlie. Being closer in age, Bergman and Titus got on together.

Jerry Mastin lived up the Columbia River, in Portland, Oregon. Mastin, who was 79 when he passed on in 1959, is an enigma. Eight masterful, very hollow Canada geese, each with a different head position, survive from a rig of nine that he created for a Mr. R. Eaton. These decoys were stickups with removable head and neck. But where is the body of his work?

Pintail drake decoys by "Fresh Air Dick" Janson. High-neck decoys were used in the tall grass and pickleweed of California's Central Valley. Janson made more sprig—as the pintail is called in the West—than any other species.

266

ABOVE: The best of "Fresh Air Dick" Janson's decoys are the earlier birds, such as these bluebills, which were probably carved in the late 1920s.

No artist can be that sophisticated without having lots of practice. No piece of carving, other than the geese, is known or needs to be known. Mr. Eaton's geese assure Mastin's place as a master carver.

The Aberdeen area, on Grays Harbor, was the headquarters of the Washington market hunters and decoy makers. Charles Rayle is known to have been working in about 1911, making very hollow, oversized, very collectible mallards. Another early maker was Charles R. Pratsch. As he was born in 1857, it is likely that he carved earlier than World War I. Here again, the lack of people contributes to the dearth of early carvers. The entire population of both Oregon and Washington was well under 2 million during World War I. It was California that drew the growth.

During the last of the 19th century, Captain Olsen commanded the naptha-powered ship *Martha*, out of Eureka, California. He carried freight up the coast and in his spare time carved a wonderful rig of 36 brant. A hardwood bill was doweled into the head, the necks were dovetailed to the body, and he carved the outline of the wings. These hollow-carved redwood decoys are without a doubt the best California-made brant. Olsen passed away in 1900.

OPPOSITE: The rarest of the rare, a brant by "Fresh Air Dick" Janson. This is one of two known examples and is the only one in original paint. It was found on a shelf in an antiques store.

At the turn of the century, San Francisco was the ninth largest city in the United States. Tom Daley was replicating Masons on a copy lathe for the gunners at Hunter's Point, in San Francisco, and Alviso, at the southern end of the bay. After the earthquake, he moved to a house near the present-day Cow Palace. He was still active in 1921.

Joe Roesling arrived in Alameda, California, just after the earthquake, from Janesville, Wisconsin, at the age of 44. Influenced by Jasper Dodge, he used his carpenter's skills to produce between 300 and 500 comb-painted canvasback, sprig, and blackjack decoys. He even painted a few of his solid redwood decoys as juveniles for the early shooting. Very few of these early decoys survive.

There were problems with keeping California decoys. Before the irrigators arrived and built the dams, all of the river flooded into the wetlands almost every time it rained. Because the California hunters did not pick up their rigs after each shoot, the floodwaters carried away many of the decoys. Ed Snyder, a Rio Vista, California, carver and gunner, remembers fishing decoys out of the highwaters with a landing net. It was much easier than carving. The rising water freed the anchors, and away the stool went, down through the delta and into the

San Francisco Bay. The decoys eventually joined the logs and other flotsam to be lost in the Pacific outside the Golden Gate. Many of the decoys that Ed retrieved had been carved by California's most prolific carver, Richard Ludwig ("Fresh Air Dick") Janson.

Some called him "Dirty Dick," others "Fisher Dick," but most preferred his sailor name, "Fresh Air Dick," given to him because he slept on deck. Born in 1872 near Riga, Estonia, of Swedish parents, Janson worked as a ship's carpenter for Alaskan Packers. Between Alaskan fishing seasons, "Fresh Air Dick" lived on a barge tied up to the levee at the mouth of Sonoma Creek, California. He rented small boats to fishermen, fished and hunted for the market, and made decoys. "Fresh Air Dick" Janson didn't start carving for the trade until 1920 or so. His work did not seem to draw upon Eastern makers for style, but most of the carvers around the San Francisco Bay were greatly influenced by Janson.

The best of Dick's decoys are the earlier birds, from about 1920 through the middle thirties. They are truly handmade: he used only "muscle power" to create the pintail, mallard, canvasback, and bluebills that went into those rigs. In the thirties he added green-winged teal and at least one rig of brant to

268

ABOVE: Canvasback drake by Richard Allen. Allen was a pattern maker, and the minimal paint and simplified pattern of this decoy reflect his trade.

his inventory. Later, during World War II, with the help of "John Barleycorn," his work became heavier, and there was a sameness to the heads: they all looked like mallards. The paint lost its richness. It is not known how many thousands of decoys "Fresh Air Dick" sold to the local California duck clubs and individual hunters. Maybe he became weary, and, as he got older, allowed his standards to fall.

There are "Fresh Air Dick" decoys still in use in northern California. Several rigs have turned up in Oregon, but many were burned for firewood when the lighter plastic birds became available. While there are many collectible Janson decoys around, the collector must be wary. There were many replicators. Copiers and imitators might have been a solution for hunters who needed decoys, but they do not help the collector.

"Fresh Air Dick" Janson kept the faith. He drank and smoked to the point that one night his barge burned to the waterline. In 1951, without a place to live, he went to the "old folks home" as a indigent. He died, in bed, in another fire caused by another cigarette. He was 79.

While Janson was carving decoys that the less talented could copy, there were other "depression" makers who could also be called artists. William McLellan, a Eureka, California, brant hunter, made a very large rig of Pacific brant. Heavy, to withstand the wind and the chop of Humbolt Bay, they appear almost clunky. There is a story that someone lifted that first rig from his pickup at the end of the decoys' first season. What is

OPPOSITE: During World War II William McLellan made nine flying brant decoys to add to his rig of 65 floaters. This decoy's hinged wings are removable and adjustable.

270

known is that his first rig was made about 1933, and five years later he added another 25 decoys to raise the total to 65. All these decoys were built with heads and necks in various positions. During World War II, McLellan designed and constructed nine flying brant to add to the rig. These solid redwood bodies were winged aircraft fashion. A wooden frame, covered with cloth and paper was finished with "dope." The hinged wings were removable and adjustable. Bill, born in 1897, passed away in 1987. The McLellan flying brant fit the criterion of masterful decoys.

Richard John Allen was a pattern maker employed at the Mare Island Navy Shipyard. His simplified patterns and minimal paint reflected his trade. Born in Grass Valley, California, in 1891, Allen grew up in Berkeley. He moved to Vallejo when he went to work at the shipyard. He made a pattern for the lead ballast weights that he neatly inletted into the bottom of his several hundred pintail, canvasback, and mallard decoys. The weight also served as the anchor-line attachment. His sleeping cans are a "masterpiece of form."

During World War II, Allen did some "under the bench" production of a rig for the officers' mess. This rig of sprig and mallards contained some sleepers and is branded on the top "Com Mins." It has been called the "Commander Mins" rig, but the brand indicates ownership by the "Commissioned Officers Mess, Mare Island Navy Shipyard." The smooth, round forms of the Com Mins decoys do not resemble the simpler shapes of the Allen rig.

John W. Luedtke was the finest decoy maker to ever come out of Stockton, California. I don't know how many decoys he carved, but his sprig are without a doubt the most impressive of the "valley" decoys. A pair of Luedtke pintails belong in a discriminating collection. It is said that he also carved a few mallards.

To the north, in Sacramento, Amiel Garibaldi created refined decoys in the late thirties. He started carving decoys and hunting ducks in 1929, when he was 11. His rig contained close to 300 decoys of most species, sprig, cans, mallards, green-winged and cinnamon teal, redheads, and Canada geese. His long-neck sprig, especially the ones with the curved necks, carved for hunting in the pickleweed and grass, and his teal have that extra something needed to move them beyond tools. Now retired, the former pharmacist still hunts and, with his grandson, carves a few decoys.

OPPOSITE: *Green-winged teal by Horace (Hie) Crandall. These small, life-size masterpieces were displayed at the 1939 World's Fair in San Francisco.*

Horace L. (Hie) Crandall was born in Rhode Island. He was 36, living in Benicia, California, when he started to carve decoys. As a child, he was known to paint, both in oils and watercolors, and later studied taxidermy so that his early rig, some 200 decoys, was extremely lifelike. In 1934, he moved to Westwood, in the Sierra Nevada. There he continued to carve decoys and paint pictures. Several thousand Crandall decoys were sold through sporting-goods stores in San Francisco and the town of Chester. In 1939, Hie was asked to display his work at the World's Fair on Treasure Island in San Francisco Bay. The small, delicate, life-size masterpieces did not float well in rough water, but artistically had being. Crandall's work attracted several copyists, the ultimate form of respect. Hie moved to the Los Angeles area in 1942 to work for Douglas Aircraft. While there, he discontinued most of his production of decoys and turned his creativeness to paperweight decoys and full-bodied miniature birds. He continued to create decoys until he passed away in 1969.

Four years after Crandall's birth in 1892, Luigi Andreuccetti, the Sacramento stylist, was born in San Francisco. Employed by the Del Monte Corporation, Luigi carved and used

ABOVE: *John W. Luedtke's small rig of pintails is, without doubt, the most impressive of the valley decoys. This pair is the outstanding example of the Central Valley decoy.*

Amiel Garibaldi created refined decoys, and this long-necked pintail is one of his finest. The curved neck is rare in pickleweed decoys.

more species of waterfowl than any other California maker. His production started in 1914, but he did not get serious until about 1928. Over his lifetime—he died in 1978—Andreuccetti created more than 500 decoys, most of which carried his "LA" brand. He was a charming man who carved charming decoys.

There are few decoy makers who could produce the equal of the standing pintail decoys of the Suisun Marsh. An unknown carver made three of these lovely full-bodied carvings. They were found in the possession of an antiques dealer who was taking them to a stripper! One decoy had a little paint removed from its neck, but the others are mostly original. The decoys are branded with a "CO" that is thought to indicate that Carl Olsen might have been the owner. Most decoy experts doubt that Olsen was the carver. Who was this person who could give a common item a feeling of the sublime?

As the depression deepened in the thirties, more waterfowlers became decoy makers. They carved their own rigs and, if they were good enough, sold some to other hunters. These new makers could not fill the sporting hunters' demand for better decoys. The wealthy clubs had to look elsewhere. The Bolsa Chica Gun Club, near Huntington Beach, in southern California, the nearby Westminster Club, the north's Sacramento Outing Club, the White Mallard, and several other old California clubs ordered decoys from Robert Elliston, Charlie Perdew, and, later, from the Ward brothers. Some individuals purchased famous-maker decoys through dealers, and other hunters brought rigs of Crowells with them when they came west. When the United States Marine Corps took over the Bolsa Chica at the start of World War II, Oliver Schimmer, later of Los Banos, California, managed to get in and salvage some of

The maker of this lovely full-bodied carving is unknown. Few decoy carvers were capable of producing the equal of this standing pintail drake.

those old decoys. Schimmer loved to show off the Ellistons, the rare Masons, and the Perdews that he pulled out of the great pile of discards.

Examples of the decoy-makers' art are usually displayed, row upon row, with used brass shot shells, some old powder tins, and possibly a mounted trophy of a mallard or some other duck. If the exhibition is in a museum, the decoys are generally shown in the natural history department. They appear as historic or archaeological examples, not as folk art, primitive art, or even naive art. The form and grace, the drama, and the romance of these wooden renderings can be lost in a mass display.

There is little drama, or being, in most decoys. The majority of makers put little into their carvings, only enough for their purpose. But the Bergman swans, the anonymous maker's standing pintail, the Jerry Mastin Canada geese are among those that stand out, not because of their rarity, but because of the special qualities transferred to the wood by the artistic decoy carver. "Fresh Air Dick" added that unknown something to each of his thousands of decoys. McLellan's flyers and Captain Olsen's brant fall into this notable class, as does Pice, if only for his humor. Dick Allen's sleeping cans were copied by several makers, as were decoys made by Andreuccetti. Garibaldi's teal, both the green-winged and cinnamon, belong in collections as noble works.

Each of these Pacific Coast decoy makers had the attributes that moved their decoys from a hunter's tool to an appreciated art form. The knowledge, sophistication, and power shown in these western decoys certainly qualify their carvers as artists. They are true examples of individual expression.

CHAPTER 23:

CANADA

by Patricia Fleming

LEFT: Canada goose by Wilfred Beck, Vancouver. Beck's geese are unique. They were made for use on tidal waters with fully rounded bodies designed as floaters. However, when the tide went out they rested on large, flat feet, still in range of the hunters' guns.

OPPOSITE: Mergansers by Orran Hiltz (bottom); Otis Hatt, ca. 1930 (center); and Ned Mackay (top). Mergansers are the signature decoys of Nova Scotia, with their racy bodies, often raised wings and tails, and crests of leather, horsehair, tin, or wood.

THE ATLANTIC PROVINCES: NEWFOUNDLAND AND LABRADOR, PRINCE EDWARD ISLAND, NOVA SCOTIA, AND NEW BRUNSWICK

The Atlantic Provinces have unique hunting conditions, so the shape, design, and carving of decoys used in each province have developed differently. However, they have in common saltwater hunting and ocean coastlines, and they lie directly on the North Atlantic flyway for migrating waterfowl. The hunting of wildfowl here has always been superb—coastal fishermen, farmers, and boatbuilders shoot both for their own use and to supply the big-city markets. Sea ducks were an alternate source of meat to the usual diet of fish for coastal farmers. Inland, black duck were salted and packed in apple barrels for winter use. The sportsmen hunters came north year after year to their favorite camps or hunting areas.

Decoys must have been used on the Labrador and Newfoundland coasts, but only a scant few—including mergansers, eider, field geese, and a few loons—are known, and these are not enough to permit establishment of distinctive patterns for this area of the Atlantic coast or to identify any decoy makers.

Prince Edward Island is Canada's smallest and most densely populated province; yet it is more sparsely populated than thirty of the American states with a density about the same as Oregon/Washington states. The Micmac Indians gave the island the name *Abegeweita*, "home cradled in the waves." It lies in a great semicircular bay of the gulf of the St. Lawrence

River just north of New Brunswick. With its coastline of long inlets and large bays, rolling fields, and miles of sandy beaches with high cliffs, it is an ideal feeding and resting place for the annual southerly wildfowl migrations from the Arctic and the Labrador coast.

In the 1880s, brant and Canada geese and numerous species of shorebirds arrived in such numbers that they literally darkened the island skies. With such an abundance of waterfowl, the islanders, who were fishermen and farmers, turned to harvesting the birds to supplement not only their larders but their incomes. In 1870, curlews, which were salted and packed in barrels and shipped as far away as London and Montreal, were sold for five cents apiece.

Because the island is isolated, the hunters who made decoys developed their own styles not influenced by other areas. There is no other place in Canada where the brants and Canadas were made in such numbers and with such quality. John Ramsay (1858–1935) of Summerside is best known for his geese, considered to be the finest on the island. They are just numerous enough to be highly collectible. The brant are solidly made in many different positions and are usually carved from one block of wood. The Canadas are smoothly finished and hollow with tack eyes. The heads and necks are usually made from two pieces of wood.

John Brooks (1879–1962) and Henry Leslie (1851–1916), from Malpeque Bay, were obviously influenced by John Ramsay. Both men made hollow Canadas similar to those of Ramsay, but the heads and necks are of one piece of wood. Brooks branded his decoys "J.B." His floater and ice geese, floater and stickup brants, stickup black ducks, and plover have all been found.

Although rudimentary decoys are known from the early

1800s toward the end of the century, geese, plover, yellowlegs, and blacks were commonly made. Curlews, mergansers, and seagulls had very little use. Shorebirds were made as stickups that were placed in fields or sandy beaches. George Skerry (1916–65), a prolific carver, was a boatbuilder and fisherman by trade. His geese often have rootheads, unusual positions, with whittle marks clearly visible. The curlew and shorebirds have carved wing patterns.

Even before 1930, typical Prince Edward Island geese were found made as floaters or as full-bodied field geese resting on legs made from nails or spikes. Canada geese are almost the trademark of the decoys from Prince Edward Island, and they have been made in all natural positions—sleepers, preeners, feeders, or watchers—and are startlingly lifelike, gracefully and carefully made. Most of the decoys of Prince Edward Island have been taken off the island and are now spread throughout North America. They have lost their home base but not their identity and appeal.

Havelock Mills (1844–1900) of Malpeque Bay, is one of the earliest recorded decoy makers from the island. His family has identified geese, plover, and black duck that he made with crosshatching and knife marks showing and two-piece head construction. His plover are usually initialed on the underside. His hollow preening and feeding geese were destroyed in a fire, but they still may have been the inspiration for his nephew's decoys. W. Roy Mills (1901–65), Havelock's nephew, was a pro-

lific commercial decoy carver. Most of his well-rounded field geese are in feeding or alert positions and rest on three leg nails. Sometimes they have raised wingtips, and they are all carefully painted with muted colors. They are often initialed "W.R.M."

A British sportsman, John Rowan, traveled across Canada in 1870 and wrote a most appealing account of his shooting experiences on Prince Edward Island:

> *The plover shooter drives along in his wagon until he sees a flock of plover wheeling about in the air or feeding in the pastures. He ties his nag to a fence pole and sticks his decoys in a conspicuous place and hides himself within shot. The plover and curlews, when disturbed, fly about in all directions and sometimes give pretty good sport wheeling over the decoys.*
>
> *About August the 25th the golden plover makes its appearance closely followed by the Hudsonian and Eskimo curlews and great numbers of other plover, sandpipers, and godwits. After a Nor-easter, in early fall, great flocks of these birds can be found on the Island. And after them come the brant and Canada geese.*
>
> *However, the chief charm of this sport is the surroundings . . . with a fast trotting nag driving along the delightful country roads of the Island. In the evening there is generally some shooting of flight ducks and, if the*

276

weather suits, is wild and stormy, good shooting may be had at the geese as they come in from their feeding grounds on the salt water marshes to get their evening drink at the fresh water ponds.

As in other provinces, the styles of the decoys of Nova Scotia have been shaped by the hunting traditions of the different regions and by the occupations of the early settlers. On the bays and inlets close to shore, mergansers, whistlers, bluebills, and blacks were the common species shot. Offshore, large rigs of sturdy decoys of eiders, scoters, and oldsquaw were set. On the shorelines, shorebirds, yellowlegs, and plover, often with rootheads, were used.

On the eastern shore, typical of the ocean seaboard, the decoys of Harold Burke (1888–1970), a fisherman and keeper of the Drumhead Light, were used. He made several hundred eiders, scoters, and black ducks for himself and for sale. They are wide and flat bottomed with carved bills. William Rowlings (1891–1962) of Musquodoboit Harbour is known most especially for his roothead shorebirds. His duck decoys have high hump-backed bodies that slope off to a small jutting tail, and their heads are attached by a dowel driven through the top of the head. They are simply but realistically painted.

Lunenburg County on the Bay of Fundy on the west of Nova Scotia was settled by skilled boatbuilders of German descent. Found here are some of the most exciting decoys in

OPPOSITE: Brant goose by John Brooks, Prince Edward Island; ca. 1915. The area is known for its geese decoys in realistic poses. The chunky form of this sleeping brant shows its maker's skill and artistry.

BELOW: Eider hen by Jesse Obed, Nova Scotia. With its carefully inletted head, curved neck, and large smooth-surfaced body, this decoy is both serviceable—built for ocean shooting—and elegant.

Canada—the racy, slender, streamlined mergansers of Orrin Hiltz (1901–78), Otis Hatt (1871–1946), and Stan Sawler (1887–1966). The common characteristics of these decoys are the simple paint patterns, sometimes carved raised wings, prominent breasts, painted eyes, and tails raised up, often with unpainted bottoms. The mergansers of Hiltz have long scalloped crests, carved from the headpiece, whereas Sawler inserted leather crests. These are most coveted and collectible decoys.

The Levy name is identified with Little Tancook Island, lying close to the coast of Nova Scotia. The Levy's and others, fishermen, boatbuilders, and farmers, used great numbers of decoys for their ocean shooting. Offshore, as far as seven miles from land, 75 to 80 decoys were set, with the hunters concealed in gunning tubs or dories. The rigs of decoys were attached by lines to the boats. Lindsey Levy (1892–1980) made approximately four hundred decoys of all the common ocean species—eiders, scoters, mergansers, blacks, whistlers, and even a few loons. An identifying feature is that the heads were nailed to the bodies by a large spike driven through the top of the head. The different species were painted in clear, bold patterns on wide, flat-bottomed bodies that comfortably ride ocean waves.

The best of the eider decoys were made by Jesse Clayton Obed (1878–1932), the keeper of the Half-Moon lighthouse off the coast from Blandee, Shelburne County. These were both solid and hollowed, with inlet heads, carved bills, glass eyes, and elaborate painted detail. Obed paid much careful attention to making his stunning eider decoys.

Other well-known carvers are Willard Robertson (1884–1970), Edwin Backman (1872–1914), Frank Selig (1878–1943), and Ned Mackay (circa 1905–78).

Nova Scotia decoys, most especially the root- or branch-headed decoys, the boldly painted eider, and the elegant mergansers and other species, wide-bottomed and large in size, are perfectly suited for the rugged and difficult shooting conditions of this Maritime Province.

Along the north and northeast coast of New Brunswick down to the gulf of the St. Lawrence and Chaleur Bay (Baie de Chaleur) the land gently slopes into the ocean over sandy beaches and low, sandy barrier islands. Here the eel grass and marshes give food and protection for migrating birds. This was the home of the Micmac Indians and later was settled by French-speaking Acadians who adapted and developed their decoys from Indian methods.

Peter Ginnish (b. circa 1880), a Micmac from Neguac, a guide and a hunter, used the old methods. His brant and Canada geese decoy bodies were shaped with a hatchet from a wet cedar log section, then smoothed by using pieces of glass and then charred or burned over fire. Vienance Vienneau (b. 1919) from Shippegan learned these same techniques from his father and grandfather. The charred wood on the decoys was rubbed with burlap to give them a sheen. Paint was used for the lighter areas of the breast and undersides, and powdery clay was spread over the wet paint to give the decoys a dull grayish breast. The geese decoys of both men were made as stickups or could alternatively be used as floaters. Vienneau estimates he carved from five hundred to one thousand working decoys and decorative carvings.

The geese of Jim Gautreau (b. 1919) from Tracadie are easily identified. They are often in a swimming position with curved and outstretched necks. The bodies are narrow in the front, flat bottomed, and have large spadelike tails. Between 1930 and 1965 Gautreau made around 3,000 geese and black ducks.

The best-known New Brunswick decoy maker is Amateur "Mat" Savoie (1896–1983). A toolmaker and barber, his lifetime output of decoys is estimated in the 6,000 to 7,000 range. They are predominantly geese and black ducks, of which he made 200 to 300 per season between 1935 and 1970. He also made some 400 decoratives and half-models. He sold his decoys to American and Canadian hunters who shot in the Tabusintac area. His first decoy was made when he was nine years old on instructions from his grandfather Vitol Savoie (1820–1910), and his first carvings were done in the old Acadian tradition using an axe. In his later models, the axe marks were smoothed out and a feather stamp added. The very pleasing darkish-brown surface of many of the decoys, although in latter years produced by painting, harks back to the earlier charred-wood surfacing of the northeast Micmacs.

On the northeastern coast lies Tabusintac Bay, about twelve miles long by three miles wide, protected by a sand beach barrier. This is the only area in North America where shooting from a sinkbox is still legal. The sinkbox is waterproof, boxlike, about six-and-a-half feet by three-by-three feet, surrounded by wooden aprons that are often weighted down to water level by iron decoys. Floating decoys are set within shooting distance of the box. Archie Morrison (1912–80), as a guide, started his day at 3:00 A.M. By 5:00 A.M. a sinkbox and a hundred decoys were in place for a hunter. Shooting ended at 1:00 P.M. The pay was $2 for an eighteen- to twenty-hour day. Archie's personal sinkbox rig consisted of forty geese, twenty-five brant, and fifteen blacks.

The decoy makers of Tabusintac were also the guides for visiting sportsmen. The family of Ephriam Stymiest (b. 1919) settled here in 1810. Stymiest managed the Tabusintac Camp, which was started by Frank Loggie at the turn of the century. The decoy shed of the camp at one time had 350 Canada geese and brant and at least six sinkboxes and sand boxes. The geese Stymiest made are often forward-leaning, or as he says, "swimming against the tide or current."

James Callaghan (b. 1908) remembers hunting with his father as a boy and gathering dead marsh grass to make Indian decoys on the ice around the *gabion* ("blind"). For his geese—full-bodied stickups and floaters and some snow geese—he used heated roofing cement mixed with kerosene to make a flat charcoal color on the back.

Moving from Tabusintac south is the Saint John River in southern New Brunswick, which is a 100-mile navigable north-south waterway. It and its tributaries—the Tobique, Kennebacasis, and the Nerepis rivers—are laced with islands and marshlands—the Portobello Marshes, Grand Lake, Musquash Islands, Long Reach, and Belle Isle Bay.

In the late 1700s, when Americans from the New England states loyal to the British Crown came north to resettle, they brought with them the customs from New England. The decoys of the lower Saint John River were usually simply made, often from old cedar rail fences, sometimes with balsa heads, roughly shaped by axe, drawknife, and rasp. Although thousands of decoys were made here, they were more useful than beautiful. Geese, blacks, and whistlers were the most common species carved.

Ralph Howlett (1890–1985) of Saint John was the most prolific commercial carver. His total output is estimated to be in the 10,000 range. At one point in the period 1920 to 1975 he was selling 24 dozen decoys a season at $2 apiece. For open, rough-water use, Howlett's decoys had wide bulky bodies and large 2½-inch holes in the bottom that made the decoys lighter and more buoyant.

Murray Thomason (b. 1913) of Hampstead made 200 to 300 decoys, mostly for his own use. He carved the most exceptional and interesting decoys of the area, with detailed painting and many positions—feeders, sleepers, and preeners.

Grand Manan Island (population 2,600) lies 21 miles off the southeast tip of Nova Scotia in the Bay of Fundy. It is famous for its eiders, scoters, oldsquaw, and merganser decoys. It is the home of sea-duck hunting, and the decoys, in the tradition of New England, are called tollers.

Gerald Anderson, a fisherman, described how he hunted sea ducks from a dory with a string decoy lay-out. "We set off shore in a dory and put the oldsquaw decoys out. The ducks would decoy to us repeatedly even with us sitting in plain sight. We would attach a pair of decoys to the end of a narrow board or lathe about two-and-a-half-feet long and three to six pairs are floated in a string attached to the dory."

Two other Grand Manan carvers are important. The Harvey family has lived here since 1850. They have been keepers of the Machias Sea Island Light and the Gannet Rock Light. Lincoln Harvey is a gifted folk-art carver. His decoy output is not great in numbers, probably about a 100 blacks, eiders, and scoters—some hollowed, some with U-shaped bottoms. The paint is excellent and carefully applied. Jim Zwicker (1849–1933) made eiders that are spectacular, with simple, easily seen, stylized paint patterns and gracefully curved necks that slope into the body.

The decoys of the Maritime Provinces, for the most part with their origins in native Indian customs, are a pocket of historical culture that is wholly Canadian.

Black duck by Amateur Savoie, New Brunswick. Savoie made this sleeping black at the height of his career. He is said to have made about 400 of these, more decorative than useful as hunting tools.

QUEBEC

As the St. Lawrence River crosses the border from Ontario into Quebec it widens into shallow basins. The first of these, about ten miles wide by fifteen miles long, is Lac St. Francis, then comes Lac St. Louis to the southwest of the city of Montreal. Lac des Deux Montagnes, on the western shore of Montreal Island, is at the mouth of the Ottawa River and Lac St. Pierre lies between Montreal and Quebec City.

These large, shallow lakes with marshy shorelines dotted with weedy islands are perfect resting, feeding, and staging areas for migrating birds.

Hunters shoot from stationary blinds set on points of land with decoys laid out nearby or from concealed duck boats or floating blinds with a "two hundred yards from shore" regulation for decoy placement. On Lac St. Pierre and Lac St. Louis battery or sinkboxes are still used.

The battery box is a formidable affair with a 2000-pound platform surrounding a steel box that is cranked down to water level. Rigs of 70 to 300 decoys are commonly used as the hunter shoots from eye level to his decoys. Usually a team of three men work together—two men in the sinkbox and one working a pick-up boat.

About one hundred miles west of Montreal on the south shore of Lac St. Francis, Orel Le Boeuf (1886–1968) lived at St. Anicet for all of his 82 years. For many of those who collect early North American decoys, a deeply carved bluebill decoy, or perhaps a full-size decorative standing on two small wooden feet is considered a spectacular prize—a decoy made with originality, care, excellent paint, brushed feathering, and chiseled feathers. Le Boeuf's decoys could be called "small wooden sculptures" unlike those of any other maker.

For 65 years Le Boeuf made working decoys, first for himself and later for other hunters. He was a construction worker by trade, and at the end of the summer when work slowed down, the migrating waterfowl drew him to the marshes and islands near his home. He shot for the market. He took his hunting boat, guns, and equipment to one of the islands and stayed there until Christmas. Whenever he accumulated 200 to 300 ducks he took them to the Poulin Market at Lachine near Montreal and sold them at $15 for one hundred birds.

At $1 to $3 apiece, his decoys were ordered by hunters, but sometimes orders took two years to fill. They were carved from soft cedar blocks that were well cured. Le Boeuf used a penknife to incise the feathering and was extremely careful with his paints, comparing his mixed paints with the skins of the ducks killed. He added turpentine to the oil-based paints for a dull surface.

His earliest decoys were not so highly carved; in fact, an old working canvasback was almost smooth-surfaced, with only his trademark of three small white feathers on the wing.

After his wife's death he lived in a small house on a

280

neighbor's farm, an almost total recluse. His carving shed was tiny—four by five by six feet—lit and heated by a hanging oil lamp. The floor was knee-deep in shavings, and it is thought that he hid his best carvings in this ice fishing shed.

Three years before his death, when he was 79, his little house caught fire and burned to the ground. Under the ashes and shavings was his last decoy, singed by flames, its feathers painted with silvery paint. Its beauty wrenches the heart as much as the story of this man. He never carved again.

Some of Le Boeuf's neighbors from Valleyfield and St. Anicet were prolific carvers. His cousin Achille Hart made many simple decoys with a few feathers on the back. From Valleyfield there were five Laviolette brothers. One went to the Smiths Falls area and combined his Quebec patterns with what he learned in Smiths Falls.

Henri Laviolette (1878–1923) of Valleyfield carved beautiful canvasbacks that are very similar to those of Willie Leduc (1915–68). Another Valleyfield carver, Hormidas Thibert (1900–60) was a prolific carver who sold his decoys, which had deep wing carving, to other hunters.

Within sight of the skyscrapers of downtown Montreal, Verdun is a pocket suburb on the shore of the St. Lawrence. This small sheltered harbor, even today, has a hundred or more small huts and cabins, each with its dock and hunting boat. In

the autumn these boats are camouflaged with burlap and rush-covered sideboards that fold up or down in a variety of ingenious systems. Their owners, with decoys aboard, head out into the marsh areas surrounding Canada's second largest city and in a tradition that goes back hundreds of years shoot for themselves or for the markets of Montreal.

William Cooper (1885–1975) is the best-known of the Verdun carvers. His decoys have alert, upright, turned heads, nicely curved necks, wings that are relief-carved, and heavy tails with gouged ridges. Cooper's decoys seem literally to come alive. His skill and the beauty of his decoys quickly brought many customers for his work, which he sold at $15 a dozen. His total output reached around 6,000 decoys. Recently, one of Coopers black ducks sold at auction for over $2,000. Cooper's genius lies partly in the way he painted his decoys, using the best grade of oil house paint applied to unprimed wood, with the colors blended together while wet.

The Paquette family (Robert and Joseph) imitated Cooper's decoys nearly exactly. Robert Paquette made hundreds of decoys and drew decoy patterns for C.I.L. Industries Ltd. for commercial production.

Another Verdun carver, Jimmy Tomney (1885–1979)—taxidermist, hunter, and fisherman—made decoys that were greatly sought after. Beautifully carved and true to life, they

LEFT: Whistler hen by William Cooper, Quebec. The carved wings, broad, carved tail, and rasp work on the head indicate this decoy's Quebec origin.

BELOW: Merganser hen by Hormidas Thibert, Quebec. This chubby merganser has the bold paint patterns and simple form of good working decoys.

OPPOSITE: Hooded merganser by Orel Leboeuf, Quebec. A rare example of Leboeuf's later work, with careful and intricate feathering.

sold for $36 a dozen. He competed in New York in 1948 and took the second prizes to Ken Anger's firsts. He set a high standard with great competence.

Eastward from Montreal at Louisville on the north shore of Lac St. Pierre, Pierre Lacombe (b. 1914) has produced many, many hundreds of decoys—at one time, a thousand a year. He has had orders to fill from all over North America from his small workshed with his duplicating lathe. His trademark is a small arrowlike feather stamp. It is a great pleasure to stand in the shavings, smell the wood and paint, watch the dim sunlight filter through the windows illuminating hundreds of blank decoy bodies and heads, and talk to this generous and kindly carver whose sons now follow in his footsteps.

Quebec City, with its Citadel Fort high on the bluffs over-looking the St. Lawrence River, is steeped in centuries of history. Each autumn crowds of people collect just to the east of Quebec at Cap Tourmente to watch the spectacular gathering of geese when wave upon wave of Canadas, snows, and other species come into the muddy, marshy shorelines, wheel about, land, and feed and then continue on their journey. There are only a few places today when one can experience this massing of wildfowl, which was commonplace years ago.

A decoy of the Gulf of the St. Lawrence will be different from one from any other place in Canada. For instance, at

Quebec City, the Atlantic Ocean tides reach here through the Gulf of St. Lawrence, rising and falling as much as fifteen feet. Twice a day, shallow tidal shorelines change drastically. A hunter from east of Quebec City comments that he would set his decoys at the water's edge at low tide. Normally, the decoys float facing the wind; however, as soon as he sees the decoys' heads change direction, he knows that the tide has started to change. Then he quickly grabs the decoys and heads for shore—which might be as far as a quarter of a mile away—otherwise, he would have to wade through water and mud up to his knees. For these conditions, tough short-necked small decoys were made, decoys that would not break when thrown quickly into a gunny sack.

The ocean rigs of scoters, eiders and mergansers, are

282

often painted with shiny black or shiny brick-red paint. High-gloss paint is used so that the decoys can be more easily seen in this misty climate and on the ocean rollers. The heads are often secured to the body by strong spike nails hammered down through necks that have wide bases.

On the south shore at St. Jean-Port-Joli, near Rivière du Loup, wood carving has been a tradition for many of the townspeople for several centuries. From here a few beautiful geese are known to have been carved. Perhaps we will discover more excellent decoys from this area.

Inland, unlike the St. Lawrence River shore, the decoys are often rough-hewn and charred black over open fires in the native Indian custom. Near James Bay, geese bodies set on small legs are left in a good shooting area permanently. The hunter carries heads and necks with him and tacks them onto the bodies whenever he wants to hunt and takes them away when he goes home.

In all other areas of Canada are decoy carvers who are known to have produced literally thousands of decoys, but eastern Quebec decoy making meets the specific needs of an individual hunter, making the decoys of the gulf of St. Lawrence unique.

ONTARIO

If you found yourself 20,000 feet in the air headed south and needed food, water, and a good travel map, perhaps you, like thousands of geese and ducks, might look down and steer by the great waterways.

From the north to the south on the Mississippi River Valley, or southeast down Lake Huron, through the Georgian Bay to the St. Clair River, opening into quiet marshy Lake St. Clair—the paths are indicated by water. After a rest and feed, the birds proceed east on Lake Erie to Long Point over Hamilton Harbour to the sheltered Ashbridges Bay of Toronto Harbour. Pressing always eastward they cross Prince Edward County and at the east end of Lake Ontario are joined by migrants coming down the Rideau River system to Kingston and the Islands and then continue east along the St. Lawrence River to the Atlantic coast and south.

There have always been overlapping hunting traditions. The first and earliest was the settlers' need for food. This led to countless small rigs of decoys, homemade by almost every farmer and fisherman. From approximately 1860 onward there were sportsmen hunters, whose yearly expeditions to the places where they could get excellent hunting developed a whole new trade. Part of this trade involved excellent decoys made by competent guides and artisans and skilled woodworkers—decoys carefully crafted and painted with extra attention. Some of Canada's finest and most collectible decoys developed from this need.

From the west of Ontario, Lake St. Clair is a sort of heart-shaped shallow lake, about ten miles square, with a maze of channels and marshes. The shallow water allows the sunlight to filter through to the bottom, producing the wild rice or grass-roots upon which the waterfowl feed. This is the St. Clair Flats.

Here "King" Tom Chambers (1864–1950), a solitary, kind, and upright gentleman, reigned from the 1880s until 1943. Chambers was originally from Toronto, but in the 1880s

OPPOSITE: Wood-duck by Tom Chambers, Ontario. The stance and lift of the head of Chambers's decoys achieve a lifelike alertness.

BELOW: Canada geese by George Warin (top) and David Ward (bottom), Ontario; pre-1900. The two were cofounders of the St. Clair Flats Shooting Club.

BOTTOM: George Warin.

he was offered the job of managing the St. Annes Club. He moved from there to the St. Clair Flats Shooting Club, founded in 1874 by George Warin and David Ward of Toronto. Chambers managed the club from 1903 to 1943. For its members, Chambers carved large numbers of geese, redheads, canvasbacks, and blacks and a few rare species, teal and wood ducks. His decoys are both hollow and solid, using muted red and gray paint with fine scratched painting and feathering. Chambers's decoys—whether they are sleeping blacks, long- or short-bodied canvasbacks, those with slender upright heads or the more rounded heads—are desired by every serious collector. His style is "of Toronto," and he probably was friends with Warin, Ward, and Wells.

There are other clubs and special places around the perimeters of the lake: the Big Point Club, Mud Creek Club, St. Lukes Club, the Bradley Marshes, and Martins Island. Also there are countless numbers of good local carvers. Henry Catton (1854–1943) made canvasbacks with narrow snakelike heads and necks. The Dolsen family and its sons spanned the 1850s to the 1940s to the present. Their canvasbacks are best known, with sturdy necks, upright heads, and dusky soft coloring. Harry Martin (1870–1938) is well-known for his beautiful canvasbacks and other species made in countless numbers in his family's cottages on Martins Island.

Peter M. Pringle (1878–1953), known as Collyer, of Dunnville, a bachelor, was an engraver and a commercial artist by trade. He had his studio in Toronto but escaped whenever possible to Dunnville, a small community near London, Western Ontario, situated on the marshy banks of the Grand River, a few miles before it opens into Lake Erie.

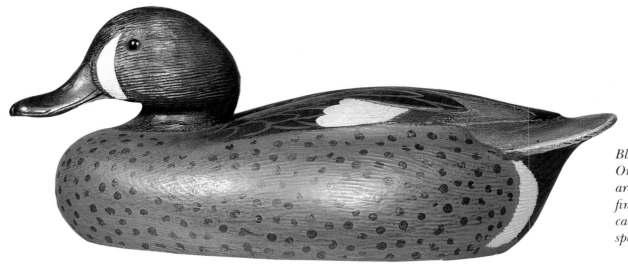

Blue-winged teal by Ken Anger, Ontario. Most of Anger's birds are large with a rough, rasped finish and wings outlined by a carved gouge. He made all species to fill hunting orders.

284

Pringle took great pride in his own personal rig of around one hundred decoys: "PMP" was deeply carved on the bottom of every decoy. The patterns of the blacks, redheads, and other species were true to life, carefully made, the wing and tail areas separated by carved patterns. He used a wood rasp to rough the surfaces.

A Pringle decoy is a prize to own, but since they are rare indeed, he will be best remembered through the impact his decoys had on a younger Dunnville carver, Ken Anger. Anger saw Pringle's decoys at Gull Island, offshore in Lake Erie at the mouth of the Grand. They had a higher profile than Anger's decoys and were more easily seen on the rough waters of Lake Erie. Anger consulted with Pringle, and from that chance meeting on all his decoys carry the trademarks of Pringle's work—substantial bodies, wing and tail areas relief-carved into the decoy, and rasped surfaces.

Ken Anger (1905–61) of Dunnville was a great outdoors-man and an avid birdwatcher with fine artistic ability. He started making his own decoys in the 1930s. With their textured, rasped finish and good paint, they were excellent and soon he found himself besieged with orders. In 1945 he exhibited five decoys in the International Decoy Makers Contest in New York City and won three firsts and two seconds. He was hooked. Having left his job, he now started carving decoys full-time and in the next twenty years produced from 3,000 to 5,000 decoys—hundreds of mallards, blacks, bluebills, canvasbacks, and redheads, some pintails, Canada geese, wigeons, wood ducks, and mergansers. When he was selling his decoys for $2 apiece, or to his friends for $1, it certainly never occurred to him that some day those decoys would sell for many hundreds or even thousands of dollars.

Anger's work has been described as more the work of an artist than a production carver. He took great pains with each decoy. Ninety percent were hollow and sensitively painted with

285

OPPOSITE BOTTOM: Pintail by Phineas Reeves, Ontario. The canvas covering of this pintail absorbed the sun and gave no reflection—the better to bring ducks in range.

ABOVE: Pair of canvasbacks by Ivor Fernlund, Ontario. Fernlund made just over 100 decoys, each with a balance and beauty rarely found in early Canadian decoys.

subtle color changes. He loved his work and is remembered by his friends and family not only for his great ability but as a modest and kindly man.

Long Point at the easterly end of Lake Erie is a thirty-mile crescent of sandy land and marshes that, narrow in width, catches migrating waterfowl like a magnet. It also, in 1866, caught the eye of American sportsmen from Boston and New York. They wanted their own restricted hunting ground, and the Long Point Company was formed with 100 shares at $500 each. The members, the majority American, considered the shooting good enough to travel from the East Coast to Long Point. They lived well, dined well, and were served well, and the ducks and geese did not let them down.

Their first manager and senior "punter" was Phineas Reeves (1833–92) of nearby Port Rowan. He and his brothers, sons, and grandsons were associated with the company for one hundred years. Their decoys are ancient, beautiful, and very desirable to collectors. Phineas designed the patterns for his hollow geese, pintails, canvasbacks, and teal and painted his decoys with his accomplished artist's hand. His son John (1861–96) definitely had his father's gift for graceful decoys and used the same patterns. Working at St. Clair Flats he may

have influenced some of the carvers of that area. Charles (1872–1941) was the most prolific carver. His canvasbacks have slender heads and bills, most are hollow, some are painted with fine gray feathering, and some are covered with canvas that is carefully tacked around the decoy to simulate the dull sheen of the feathers. Charlie's son Jack (1900–86) made both decoys and punts for the use of the company. His miniature punts— about eight inches long—are keepsakes for many members.

Although the Reeves story dominates the decoy making of Long Point and Port Rowan, there are many truly great old decoys here by unknown makers whose names are still to be discovered.

The other day I was driving south over the high Burlington Bridge by Hamilton. There was a misty drizzle and the hint of dim sunlight in the early evening. From the height of the bridge I looked west across the gray sheen of the waters of Burlington Bay, about two miles by two miles. The bay is surrounded by the tall chimneys of steel smelters, with Hamilton Mountain in the background. The small houses to the east that border the west end of Lake Ontario were the homes of many watermen, hunters, boatbuilders, and decoy carvers. The mist was conducive to dreaming a bit about other days.

This is where Ivor Gustav Fernlund (1881–1933) lived and hunted. If the time was 1916 Fernlund would have been in his screening boat built by Jack Morris of the Morris Boatworks— and doubtless he would have been also using his own superb rig of decoys. The Fernlund decoys are absolutely unique in Canada. Some consider Fernlund's work the finest of all collector's decoys. They are rare, only about a hundred and fifty in total, and were made for Fernlund's own use. He sought lifelike perfection, and no two decoys are alike. There are low- or high-

286

heads, turned heads, preeners. He used artist colors and the heavy oil paints that made it possible to texture bird plumage and to skillfully blend the colors. His family came from Sweden and emigrated to the United States. When he was 25 Fernlund came to Hamilton as a pattern maker for the Westinghouse Company, and he lived there for the rest of his life.

The hunters of this area all seem to have entirely different styles. Morris decoys are chubby and rounded; early Dalton classics are hollow; Shaw decoys are large, heavy, and hollow with rugged necks; Weir made well over 1,000 decoys; Jarvis made outstanding hollow blacks, all different. But Fernlund copied no one. Newly killed birds were the models for his entirely original handwork. He set about carving his decoys much as an artist approaches a new painting, each one a prize with long-lasting quality.

In 1789 Governor John Simcoe and his lady pitched their tents on the sheltered harbor fringed by islands that was to be Toronto. While the governor laid out the plans for the new city, Lady Simcoe sketched and rode her horse along the sandy shores. In her *Diary* she comments, "Beautiful . . . crystal waters . . . and flocks of wildfowl."

Compared to the huge shooting areas in the other parts of Canada, Toronto Harbour is like a pinpoint under a microscope. The microscope, however, captures such a great number of hunters, market gunners, guides, and sportsmen, and such an enormous number of decoys were used and made, that Toronto has become the epicenter of the famous and most treasured Canadian decoys.

The waterfowl were drawn by the marshlands of Ashbridges Bay to the east of Toronto Harbour, about five miles long by a mile wide. Protected by the sandy dunes of Fishermans Island, this was "the naturalist paradise" as described in 1870 by Ernest Thompson Seton. Seton sketched a map of the

bay in that year, and it and other contemporary outlines show the cottages and boathouses that dotted the shorelines and indicated the guidelines for the hunters in the marshes— "Knock'em Point," "Lily-Pad Pond," and "Catfish Joe's."

On Wards Island in 1830, the Wards and Warins, parents of David Ward and George Warin, made their homes. The Townsons and Southams had cottages on Fishermans Island in the 1880s. The hunting boathouses of Bill Loanes, market hunter, J.R. Wells, and Charlie Logan were on the edge of the marsh at the mouth of the Don River. The Burleigh brothers, the Humphrey and Dawson docks were on the Toronto water side. In Toronto Harbour itself, on the mainland, were the workshops and boatbuilding sheds used for the famous Warin rowing sculls. Nearby, the Ackroyd Boat Company was the headquarters for John Wells, the foreman for forty years. Harry Townson, boatbuilder and artisan, had a fine workshop and tooling equipment nearby.

As an example of this waterfront cooperation, George Warin invented a specialized racing seat for Ned Hanlan's scull. He took the plans to Townson, who built the seat. Later, with this seat, Hanlan won the World Rowing Championship. Warin also invented and patented a hollow oar and probably applied the same techniques to his hollowed geese and ducks. Another cooperative enterprise may have been filling an order of at least 300 decoys that Warin and Wells made and sent to Manitoba to coincide with the shooting for the Royal Family in 1901.

All the pieces were in place for the need for superb decoys: skilled woodworkers who were also knowledgeable hunters and sportsmen who could pay for and wanted extra-special decoys. Wealthy businessmen who wanted a quick afternoon shoot could be in the marsh in ten minutes—their guides, equipment, and decoys were on the doorstep.

The Queen's Hotel and the local markets could absorb all

LEFT AND BELOW: Scenes from the 1901 royal hunt on the Delta Marsh area of Lake Manitoba. Warin, with a missing left arm, is seen beside his canoe below. The man in the doorway of the lodge is the Duke of York, later George V of England.

OPPOSITE: Canvasback drake by John R. Wells, Ontario. Made for use in the royal shoots of the early 1900s, this is one of Canada's most important decoys.

the game the market gunners could provide. It is reported that Bill Loanes, known as "the greatest market hunter of them all," in 1878 brought in his skiff loaded with 106 blue-winged teal and in 1879 he shot 61 black-bellied plover in one day. In 1912, the year he died, David Ward killed 880 black-bellied plover.

Because the decoys of these early hunters—George Warin (1830–1905), James Warin (1832–84), and David Ward (1839–1912)—were so good, a lot of research has been done on their lives and work. Their decoys are famous. The few hollowed geese of George and James Warin represent the best of the decoy-maker's art. The Warins' redheads, canvasbacks, bluebills, and teal are identified by their long, slender, slightly turned-up bills, sometimes with high sterns, sometimes with the maker's stamp "G. & J. Warin, Toronto, Maker." They were always elegant. Of a slightly later period, J.R. Wells's (1861–1955) hollowed decoys, carefully painted and beautifully designed, are also much wanted.

These early carvings from the 1880s to 1900s led to a myriad of other excellent decoy makers. From Toronto Harbour every decoy man seemed to strive for excellence, even though many made and sold hundreds of decoys: Cliff Avanne (1891–1965)—10,000 decoys; the Burleigh Brothers (1900–70s)—well over 1,000; the Humphreys and Avis families made fewer but well-designed decoys; Tom Southam (1876–1929), Harry Townson (1858–1926), and Frank Patterson (1877–1951) all made decoys for their own use only, but they are superlative; Lawrence Davis (1909–82) supplied decoys for the T. Eaton Company and other private orders.

Recently, prowling around the east end of Toronto, I searched for and found the family of Tom Southam and with his son, Herb, investigated the exciting discovery of a rig of many Toronto Harbour shorebirds of nine species, including curlew, yellowlegs, knots, ruddy turnstones, black-bellied and golden plover, dunlins, semi-palmated plover, and sanderlings. Probably no other shooting rig of shorebirds was still together on this continent. Needless to say, these small birds, in excellent original paint and near to perfect condition, are rare Canadian treasures.

The trademark of all central Canadian shorebirds seems to be two wire legs and the wrapping of the thighs near the body. These shorebird decoys are by an unknown maker and may have came into the hands of the Southam family in return for some mechanical help or because in 1916 shorebird shooting was against the law and the decoys became superfluous, or they may simply have been picked up at a nearby dump—all these are suggestions of their present owners. In an advertisement of 1889 that appeared in a "Catalogue of Sporting Goods," shorebird decoys were offered: "Full-shaped yellowlegs and snipe decoys at $6 a dozen. Customers desiring decoys of any special style can have them in about 10 days by giving a little time for painting correctly."

Nowadays in Toronto the marshes are gone. A few birds still come by and are counted in the annual Christmas bird tally. The decoys that we know and enjoy from Toronto lead us back to a time when wildlife was abundant and remind us of the skill of the early hunters—they also lead to an awareness of the need to protect and care for the wildlife of today, which must have a fair chance to survive and increase.

En route to the eastern end of Lake Ontario are shoreline marshes. At Whitby, thirty miles east of Toronto, William Ellis (1865–1963) made hundreds of decoys for order and for himself. He took great care in the painting of his decoys. They are

*Black ducks by William Crysler
and Will Smith, Ontario. These
are typical of Prince Edward
County decoys: lightweight and
hollow to be easily carried
through marshes on a man's back.*

288

identified by their straight backs, low or extended heads, square tails, large and solid bodies. Ellis sold them for $3 apiece. His ad in *Rod & Gun* in the 1920s states, "High class. All hand made. All species."

The Peterborough Canoe Company of Peterborough, eighty miles to the north of Toronto, was Canada's most significant decoy factory. From 1892 to 1961 it made serviceable, well-painted decoys from two main patterns that were sold through the T. Eaton Company catalogues and the Hudson's Bay Company.

If you say "Prince Edward County" to decoy people, right away you will probably get back a quick assessment: "Desirable decoys, famous for black ducks, very, very lightweight, fine scratch feather painting on bodies and heads (underpaint yellow ochre, overpaint burnt umber, powders mixed with oil and turpentine), straight backs, hump under tail, and consistently fine quality from the earliest decoys to modern times." What's more, they are very collectible, often very old, and not yet fully evaluated for the public.

The number-one carver is probably C. W. Crysler (1880s–1930s) of Belleville. His lightweight, hollow black ducks with excellent painted scratched feathering on the heads and necks have three or four head positions and are large in size with oval weights. His bluebills, redheads, and mergansers all have diamond-shaped nostril holes and clearly incised mandible carving close to the head. They are often stamped "CWC" or "C" and his patterns were copied by his friends. For example, David Hitchon shot with him at Blairton Bay and Crowe Lake. Although Crysler came from Belleville he followed the path of the pre-1900 decoy makers from the county, which is a major peninsula jutting out into Lake Ontario and surrounded by marshes.

The black ducks of the Gorsline family, John Anderson, and Robert Jones are classic folk art, as are Nathaniel Branscombe's whistlers and geese. From the early 1900s the very lightweight decoys of George Aulthouse (1874–1977), Will Smith (1870s–1940s), and Dan Bartlett (1839–1936), made for their own use, are now eagerly sought.

In the surrounding area, Jesse Baker (1888–1961), the firechief of Trenton, made at least 1,000 useful working decoys. Harve Davern (1864–1958) of Brighton was a well-

known, genial, and competent hunter and guide. His decoys have a very original artlike form with small necks and chubby cheeks. Charles Duesberry (1896–1975) of Belleville made not only his own rig of black ducks but thirty-eight beautiful, full-bodied carvings of all species, standing on small legs. These early decorative carvings were bought by the Canadian Wildlife Service and are now in the Natural Science Museum in Ottawa.

In the 1920s and 1930s it was the custom for the keen shooters of Toronto, after the birds had begun to move south from that area, to follow the waterfowl to Prince Edward County. The Townson brothers—Harry and John—had a small log cabin and took parties of their friends from Toronto to shoot on nearby Weller's Bay. Their decoys and those of George Warin are still found in the county.

Even today, in the autumn, Prince Edward County is the place to be for geese and duck hunting. In these thirty square miles you are never far from water—East Lake, West Lake, Weller's Bay, Hay Bay, or Long Reach. Nicholsons Island on the west side of the county is a hunting club. Once a year a family sets out 300 old decoys and shoots over them from a low-to-the-water monitor boat as a salute to the past. There are still old Canada, brant, and snowgeese decoys from pre-1900 that were made by some unknown hand. In September 1615, explorer Samuel de Champlain wrote in his diary, as he paddled in the Bay of Quinte, "It is a rich and cheery country . . . abundant fish and waterfowl."

At the east end of Lake Ontario, the St. Lawrence River acts like a funnel for winds, flowing water, and waterfowl. At Kingston, the Rideau River system empties from the north, forming Kingston Harbour, which is protected by the large islands Wolfe, Simcoe, and Amherst.

If you put a compass point here, and drew a circle for sixty miles in all directions, you would take in the Bay of Quinte, the shallow marshes, bogs, and ponds around Smiths Falls, and the Thousand Islands of the St. Lawrence River toward the border of Quebec. The protective forts of early Canada are here. Doubtless the early settlers were grateful for the food from the skies, and the officers and soldiers from the forts probably practiced their shooting skills on the birds.

Some of the earliest decoys found in Canada are the small

Hooded mergansers by D. K. Nichol, Ontario; ca. 1900. This fine pair of mergansers shows the Nichol's family special style: smooth body, raised wings, careful paint.

mergansers and whistlers from the Rideau Lakes, thirty miles north of Kingston. Only a few of these entirely unique, small decoys (about 8½ inches long) exist. They are from the Hutchings family of Jones Falls. They are curved and deeply grooved on the bottom with chiseled wings and ancient crumbled paint. The charm of these small decoys lies in their originality of style and their age. They may go back to the mid-1800s. Certainly Sam Hutchings (b. 1892) has used the patterns for most of his working and hunting life. As he explains, "Very small decoys were fine in the small potholes of the rocky granite inland lakes—and they are easy to carry."

The greatest impact on eastern Ontario decoy making was made by the Nichol family of Smiths Falls. At least 3,000 decoys were made by D.W. (Davey) Nichol (1890–1977) of all common hunting species. Working in his small decoy workshop behind his house, he aimed at carving examples of every known species in the world. He had a clear style—smallish in size, well painted, raised wings, and a horseshoe stamp between the wings on the back. From time to time his decoy style varied slightly. Many of his contemporaries copied his decoys. Some said Davey's decoys were not strong enough. Reg Bloom (b. 1914) of Kingston made larger, heavier decoys that were also very popular and close look-alikes. Davey's cousin Bob May (1873–1950) carved decoys with some of the same characteristics. Davey's ability came from the incredibly stylish decoys of his uncles Addie Nichol (1864–1928) and D. K. Nichol (1859–1949).

On Wolfe Island, three miles south of Kingston in Lake Ontario, it seems that every farmer and fisherman was also a hunter and decoy maker. A great number of beautiful high-necked, sturdy canvasbacks were made by Robert Burke (1892–1962). Valty Bamford (1867–1960) made hundreds of very useful solid decoys with some characteristics borrowed from decoy makers of the nearby American shore of the St. Lawrence. Harry Norman (1899–1977) of Kingston had a style all of his own—deeply carved and heavily patterned wings. He made geese, mallards, and blacks.

In Gananoque, in the heart of the Thousand Islands—and the home of the St. Lawrence Rowing Skiffs of the early 1900s—the Andress family owned one of the few band saws. Ray Andress (1890–1955) took great care with the blacks and canvasbacks that he made for himself and for orders. Like those of the Nichol family of Smiths Falls, Andress decoys—small, portable, usually solid—became the model for many hunters who used his band saw and added their own particular touches.

Brockville, farther down the river where it narrows a bit, was the home of the Wilkinson brothers in the 1920s and 1930s. Their fine, hollowed decoys are distinguished by superb paintwork and a beveled bottom area. Here also Ferman Eyre (1882–1969) made blacks, whistlers, and bluebills that are all structurally solid and large in size and made to last for a long time of hard work.

Where the St. Lawrence River, en route to the province of Quebec, flows through the nearby farmlands to the east of Brockville, hundreds upon hundreds of settlers and farmers made their own small rigs of decoys. Documentation will eventually identify some of the great decoys found here, completing the decoy tradition of the province of Ontario.

290

ABOVE: Pair of canvasbacks by
Ray Andress, Ontario; ca. 1935.
The Andress family built
excellent boats, and the
careful woodworking of these
decoys parallels those
boatbuilding skills.

RIGHT: Canvasback by Duncan
Ducharme, Manitoba. This decoy
has all the earmarks of the
Delta Marsh style: prominent
chest, rounded stern ends, high
head set well back, simple
paint, and small wooden keel.

THE PRAIRIE PROVINCES: MANITOBA, SASKATCHEWAN, AND ALBERTA

In the central provinces of Canada, decoy-hunting customs differ considerably from those of the east or far west. The prairies were settled much later than eastern Canada. In 1870 there were only 12,000 people in central Canada and the west; by 1881, 66,000. Then came the silver rails of the transcontinental railway, and 900,000 people moved west between 1900 and 1911.

Statistics for 1900 indicate that 200 million wildfowl migrated annually. In the small lakes, potholes, sloughs, and marshy river systems of the prairies, two thirds of the waterfowl of the continent have their breeding and nesting grounds. The ducks and geese return each year to their ancestral areas, where the young are hatched early in the summer and the adults go through their annual molting period, during which they cannot fly. In the autumn, adults and immature young fly south to their winter quarters through the barrage of hunters.

On the way, in Alberta and Saskatchewan, the waterfowl drop down on the grain and corn fields to feed—not necessarily on the water of the ponds. For the settlers of these provinces the easiest and most common way of hunting was "pass," or field, shooting, with the hunter in a blind or wearing camouflaged clothing. Primitive geese stick decoys, perhaps with flapping wings, were sometimes used. They were easy to pack and carry. And sometimes all that was needed to bring the geese down were sticks jammed in the ground with white rags tied on them.

The topography of Alberta and Saskatchewan and the multitude of birds really did not require shooting over actual decoys. An experienced hunter commented that he had hunted waterfowl for forty years in Saskatchewan and had seen only five rigs of water decoys—three of them his own.

Old-timers tell stories of swan decoys used in the early days, and although no beautiful white-swan decoys have been found yet, this story is verified by the reports in 1900 of Edward Preble of the U.S. Biological Survey. He examined some old Hudson Bay Company papers that recorded 500 whistling swans traded annually at Ile-à-la-Crosse in northern Saskatchewan. Between 1853 and 1877 the company sold a total of 17,671 swan skins. The feathers were undoubtedly used to satisfy the vast feather trade for the fashionable ladies' hats of the later years of the 1800s.

Lake Winnipeg, with its interconnecting waterways and lakes, dominates the central part of Manitoba. Moose Lake, Swan Lake, Heron Lake, Lake Winnipegosis, Dauphin, Water Hen, Lake Manitoba, and many others were, and are, the staging areas where all species of duck collect and raft together before starting their southern journey in the autumn.

In contrast to the field shooting of the prairie lands, hunting with decoys in Manitoba with its acres of marshes and open water was the perfect method of bringing the ducks into range. The local settlers made their own decoys for their own use or, if they were guides, for visiting sportsmen. Ed Mayo (1883–1956), from Selkirk near the Netley-Liba marshes at the south end of Lake Winnipeg, was a special constable and guide. His family says he made hundreds of decoys. Jack Burr's decoys (1880s–1960s) from the same area were mallards, redheads, and bluebills that are distinguished by his way of indicating feather patterns by using a brace and bit. In 1895 Frank Beyette settled near Dauphin Lake, having moved from Brighton, Ontario. He

made and sold his canvasback decoys locally, but doubtless brought with him the style of decoys used near his former home of Prince Edward County on Lake Ontario.

The unusual "Manitoba" decoys originated because of the needs of the wealthy sportsmen who, with their friends, were drawn to the superb shooting of Manitoba. James Ford Bell from Minneapolis, just south of the border, was the founder of General Mills. He brought his private railway car north to the Delta marshes at the southern end of Lake Manitoba in the early 1900s. His head guide and caretaker enlisted the Ducharme family, local guides, to make decoys. Joe Ducharme made several hundred, but it was slow work.

His son Dunc Ducharme (1912–72) of St. Amroise was a prolific carver. His solid-made canvasbacks and bluebills are highly unusual and collectible. He used a penknife to carve the pine heads. Dunc was a well-known and competent guide. He and his uncles Dan and Dick, his father, Joe, his cousins Rod and Louis made the Ducharme family name synonymous with hunting in the Delta marshes. They are the subject of many colorful hunting stories.

Of great interest to decoy collectors is the number, at least 200, of superb Toronto decoys found in Manitoba. These include the geese, redheads, and bluebills of George Warin, the pintails, mallards, and shovelers of John R. Wells, and other fine canvasbacks by unknown makers. They are all in and around the Delta marshes.

James Ford Bell took a pattern, possibly from Heron Lake, south to Minneapolis and had several hundred bodies made. Local guides carved the heads for these canvasbacks. They had prominent breasts, small necks, and were bobtailed.

George Warin was a well-known Toronto sportsman and gentleman. In 1885, probably taking advantage of the recently opened railway, he and David Ward and a party of friends visited Manitoba. They are pictured in a Toronto paper with 3,200 ducks shot in eighteen days at Delta. In 1901, Warin was asked to equip and guide a shooting party for the Duke of York, later King George V. The duke was a superb shot and, by newspaper reports, enjoyed his few days in the Delta marshes. It is presumed that the Warin Toronto decoys were brought to Manitoba at this time. They were probably specially made for the royal shoot. Later, in 1919, the young Prince of Wales, Prince Edward, following in his father's footsteps, spent a few days in the marshes. Among the finest examples of Canadian decoys, the hollow, well-designed, elegantly painted decoys made by John R. Wells may have been brought to Manitoba at that time for the use of the prince.

In the 1920s a few of these Wells decoys changed hands and were sold for $10 each, then considered an extravagantly high price at a time when Mason decoys out of Detroit were $1.50 apiece.

The influx of sportsmen hunters led to the founding of the Oak Lake Club in 1907 by Winnipeg members. This club and others and some boarding lodges were the home bases for a constant stream of yearly hunters from the south and east. Mason decoys were commonly used, and when that decoy factory closed in 1923, the Manitoban's ordered Peterborough Canoe Company decoys from Ontario via the Eaton's catalogue. In Manitoba there was never any tradition, as in Ontario, of hunters making their own decoys.

Pintail by Percy Bicknell, British Columbia. The premier carver of British Columbia, Bicknell made 3,000 to 4,000 decoys, both hollow and solid, made of red cedar with high, raised tail areas.

At the southerly end of Lake Manitoba lies a 36,000-acre waterfowl nesting area—a marshland system of bays and pot-holes connected by narrow winding creeks—the Delta marshes. In 1923 James Ford Bell was one of the founding donors who created the Delta Waterfowl and Wetlands Research Station. Many of the careful assessments of the species and numbers of ducks and geese come from their scientific statistics. In the Delta in 1930 there were 250,000 ducks, now there are 25,000, one-tenth the number of fifty years ago. The 1955 statistics by species are equally ominous. In 1900 there were 62 million mallards; today 12 million. The natural lifespan of a duck is twenty to twenty-five years. In today's world, a duck will have four years only to nest and to increase a few times. The statistics themselves tell the story. The solutions, in spite of many generous projects and the insertion of millions of dollars, have yet to be found.

Manitoba, Alberta, and Saskatchewan are the heart of duck and geese migrations, and in the future the seed of the answers may also be found in the prairie provinces, perhaps coupled with severe shooting restrictions and even the elimination of duck shooting as it is known today.

BRITISH COLUMBIA

Brant, snow, or Canada geese, pintails, or mallards, or other species of duck heading south from the Aleutian Islands to pass the winter months in California swing down south along the mountains and coast of British Columbia on the great Pacific flyway. They pass over the jagged rocky inlets of the coast, the marshes and islands of the mouth of the Fraser River and Boundary Bay, south of Vancouver. They might pause to feed on the inland lakes and valleys of the interior of this spectacular province.

The variety of duck-shooting conditions in British Columbia is reflected in the kind of decoys made there. For the most part they are large, heavily weighted, and hollow: large to be more easily visible on the ocean rollers and weighted for stability. One brant goose decoy weighed in at 15 pounds. The decoys used were mainly mallards, pintails, wigeons, and teal and the saltwater feeding geese, brants and snows. There are fewer Canadas. In salt water, divers—whistlers, scoters, blue-bills, and mergansers—feed on clams and mussels, and their flesh takes on a fishy taste. They were not considered desirable eating. Blacks and canvasbacks are rarely seen west of the Rockies.

An experienced hunter commented that even today off the coast of Vancouver he has seen 20,000 brant rafted together when migrating. To entice the wary brant into a rig of decoys under severe winter conditions is still considered an art and a gamble. They will fly in to have a look at a rig of not fewer than forty to fifty decoys set near a shore blind, swing away, and perhaps, if the hunter is lucky, return to settle in with their wooden look-alikes.

In British Columbia, there is no known record that the native Indian peoples had any interest in capturing the waterfowl with decoys. The bounty of fish, mammals, roots, and berries was adequate. An Indian expression says, "When the tide goes out, the table is set."

However, when the emigrants began to pour into the Vancouver area in the 1880s to settle or to seek gold, they brought with them the shooting customs of the East. From that time on decoys became part of every waterfowler's equipment. Often the plentiful ducks and geese were the source of much-needed food for families, or, if sold in the markets of the fast-growing city, brought in a steady income.

The marshes at the delta of the Fraser River and the expanse of open water around Sea Island, Lulu, Westham, and continuing south to the shelter of Boundary Bay provided nearly perfect conditions for the water birds. Here they collected, resting and feeding. The hunters living at nearby Richmond or Ladner on the outskirts of Vancouver had only to step out of their cottages to have an evening meal.

Harold Percival Bicknell (1897–1959) grew up around these marshes. As a boy of 12, in 1909, with his brother, he mounted a gun on a punt boat. They sent their daily duck quotas into the markets of Vancouver with the postman.

Bicknell is acknowledged as the premier decoy carver of British Columbia. His son Gerald estimates that he must have made 3,000 to 4,000 decoys and, indeed, even in the year he died he made 350 birds. His unique style of carving his decoys was used as a pattern for his friends so that, like the influence that the Nichol family had on their area of Smiths Falls, or the Warin-Wells decoys from Toronto Harbour, Bicknell's decoys could almost be called the British Columbia decoy.

They are large, for the most part hollow, with a ³/₈-inch bottom board. Raised wings are carved in the bodies, which have a straight back and a high upswept tail, graceful forward-facing heads, and no eyes (except for a few dozen made for special order). They are built of red cedar with spruce heads. His decoys were mostly mallards and drake pintails and brants and snow geese, both solid and hollowed. His paint patterns are bold. Feathering is both painted in by brush and scratched into the wet paint. All his decoys are carved with care, in no way mass produced. He used them for market shooting until 1916. In 1929 they were sold for $10 to $12 a dozen. After 1916 he shot wildfowl for sport only. When he died, an obituary in the Vancouver paper commented, "Bicknell's shooting was a legend. He had great knowledge of waterfowl. If you could equal Percy at the duck hunting sport, then you were indeed a Master."

Harry Holloway (1895–1945) certainly used Bicknell's decoys as a prototype. But although hollowed, his heads had puffy cheeks. The wings were not carved in, and they were painted with a freer style, less precise than Bicknell's. He made about a 100 for his own use only.

The identity of the makers of many British Columbia decoys is still being discovered, and for the serious collector this is frustrating. Most hunters and sportsmen made or had made by others enough decoys for their own use: from 40 to 100 would perhaps be considered adequate. Among these Bill Gray (1854–1943) is one of the earliest. His hollow, primitive snow geese from 1890 are on record. William Lenfesty of the ammunition and sports company made wigeons in the 1920s. Bill MacDonald in 1918 made a set of brants. Jimmy Nimmo (1911–83) made carefully and skillfully painted decoys that included cork-bodied wigeons. Allan Mills, a friend of True Oliver, circa 1930, produced snow geese and brant. Walter

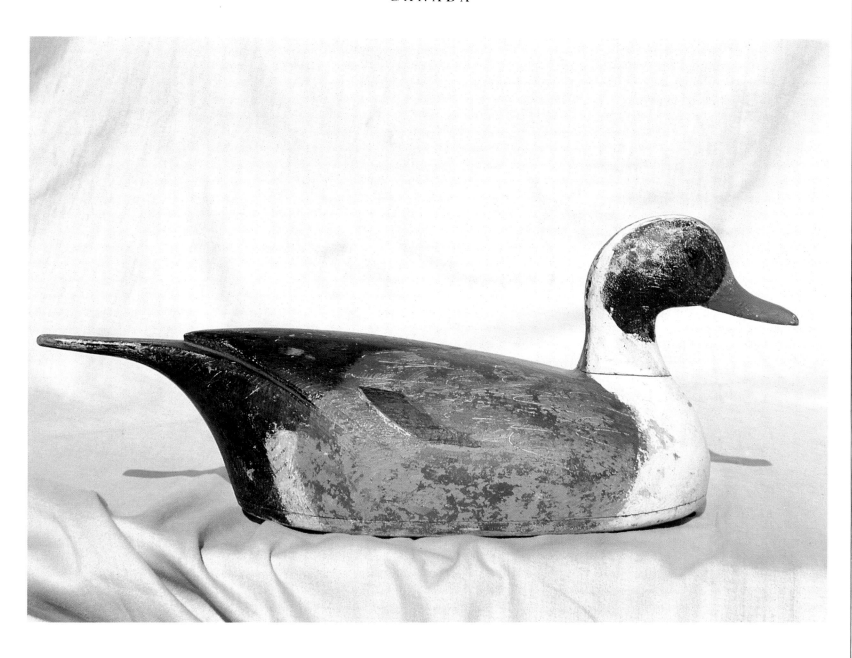

Stinson (b. 1913), still carves decoys. These are but a few of the many early carvers about whom little is known.

One day, following an ad seen in a Victoria paper—"Old 1923 decoys for sale, original paint"—I met the ferry in Vancouver. An erect older gentleman came off the ferry with some sacks on his back. In the late afternoon sunshine he laid out on a bench twenty mallard decoys that had belonged to the shooting rig of the former lieutenant governor of British Columbia from 1923. The present owner had been the gamekeeper, and these ancient battered decoys had come into his hands and had now reached the end of their working life. These decoys were typical of the small rigs of beautiful decoys of British Columbia made by unknown carvers. I have an excellent hollowed feeding or reaching mallard drake, and since that time I have seen tip-up bodies and other mallards by the same hand. This unsolved mystery may unravel bit by bit.

On the inland lakes of British Columbia decoys were not always used. "Pass" or "jump" shooting with the hunter concealed in a blind on a point of land was all that the hunter needed.

Wilfred Beck (1902–72), an executive of the Canadian Pacific Railway and a devoted sportsman and fisherman, made for himself and his friends decoy rigs of most duck species. He sometimes shot at Pitt Lake, northeast of Vancouver, or on the North Vancouver Flats. His few Canada geese are beautiful and original. These fully round-bodied geese are in many positions: feeding, resting, preening. They are carefully painted and designed as floaters. However, as the tide went out the geese were left standing on large, flat feet, still within shooting distance of the hunter's blind.

True Haviland Oliver (1880s–1950s) lived at Ladner. Like Bicknell, Oliver made a lot of decoys, probably about 1,000. Brants, Canadas, snows, and mallards were his most common species. They are hollow, straight-bodied, with sturdy broad-neck bases and with "T.H.O." carved on the bottom board. Old-timers remember him riding to his duck blind on a bicycle loaded with his decoys and equipment to Beach Grove Spit on Boundary Bay. These are most desirable collectors' decoys.

The Maeda family of Ladner built top-quality duck punts with cedar planks. Pole punting in the marshes is a rare style of hunting. Combined with their springer spaniels and their decoys, the Maedas were respected and dedicated duck hunters. Rokosuke Maeda (1889–1970) came to Canada in 1903. He and his sons made careful and skillfully carved decoys of red cedar that were hollow, extremely lightweight, and oversize. Most are mallards and pintail drakes. Rokosuke painted all the decoys in oil, outlining the feathers and species colors with his innate skill. His grandson Warren sums up his family story with an account of a day's shooting:

> *It is an exciting sight to see a great flock of birds suddenly catch sight of your decoys, set their wings in a downward position as the whole formation banks and wheels toward you, getting closer and closer until the hissing sound of the glide can be plainly heard. The sport offered us a great amount of enjoyment and memories which will last forever . . . of the sheer joy of life in such unspoilt environment and the rapport we had with the wild creatures and the regard we had for their wily ways.*

CHAPTER 24:

EUROPE

by Horst Fuhrmann

LEFT: Title page of one of the oldest German books about fowling, which mentions the use of wooden carved ducks.

THE LOW COUNTRIES

Although the art of wildfowl decoys originated in North America, the word *decoy* comes from Europe. More precisely, it comes from two old Dutch words—*de kooi*—that mean "the cage." European duck hunters used live birds to lure their prey within the reach of cages or nets.

The earliest known hunting method used in the Netherlands involved domesticated ducks used to lure wild ducks into nets or cages. The hunter then killed the captured birds by cracking their neck bones. This method of hunting reached perfection in the Netherlands during the 14th and 15th centuries. Owing to the geographical location of the Low Countries—on the coast of the North Sea and English Channel along the migration routes of ducks—the hunting was good, but only later were wooden carved decoys used, and always to a lesser extent than live birds.

Duck hunting literature from the 17th and 18th centuries does not mention the use of decoys, and there are no known descriptions of hunting methods employing decoys. Of course, decoys may well have been used during those centuries: they may have been so common that no one thought it necessary to write about them. The earliest mention of the use of decoys in Holland is in a small hunting manual printed in 1838 that describes the use of wooden ducks for wintertime hunting. The manual presents this as a quite normal activity, and nothing in the text suggests that the author intended to describe something novel to his readers. From this we can conclude that wooden decoys were sometimes used alongside live ducks as decoys.

Today, decoys are used in duck hunting in all parts of Holland. There are no legal restrictions, as there are, for in-

BELOW: Mallard drake with triangular cross-section from the area of the Zuidersea; 1950s.

stance, in the Lake Constance district of Germany. The majority of these decoys are made of wood, some of cork. Many duck or bird hunters make their own decoys, following traditional shapes and manufacturing methods. Although many decoys are used, no factories for their manufacture are known to exist or to have existed.

Until the end of the 1950s, a specially shaped decoy was used in the southeast corner of the former Zuider Zee. This decoy has a triangular cross-section. It has a flat, very broad bottom and a very narrow back. This construction does not require a weight at the bottom. Duck hunting in this area came to an end when construction of the Eastern Flevoland polder was completed and the land was drained.

FRANCE

The duck-hunting methods used in the Low Countries did not appeal to the French. In general, hunting in France was considered primarily a sport and only in a secondary sense a way of making a living. Indeed, running duck decoys corresponds more closely to the Dutch and German mentality than the French. Thus, although passionate duck hunters, early Frenchmen disdained the unsportsmanlike wringing of duck necks, preferring pass shooting—waiting for ducks from behind duck blinds and then firing at them as they flew by. To attract the flying ducks to the blind, both live duck and wooden carved decoys were used.

A hunting method described in 1826 for the marshlands of the Somme River near the town of Peronne in Picardy in northern France involved the use of live trained ducks to lure their fellow species members. This was done with the hunters inside a kind of hut. The method is still practiced in that area today.

H. C. Folkard, an Englishman, published a book on duck hunting in France in 1875 in which mention is made of hunters who placed stuffed birds among their live ones when they faced a shortage of trained ducks. An 1880 source refers to the use of wooden decoys on sticks being placed in front of the huts. Such references suggest that the live birds, tied by a cord, were often killed accidentally by busy hunters, thus creating the need for artificial birds. This need opened the way for the manufacturing of wooden decoys, and in fact the use of wooden decoys increased around the turn of the century. During the first decade of this century the demand for factory-made decoys increased rapidly, and small shops and factories for their production were established. By the end of the 1920s, factory-made decoys were in frequent use in France.

At the beginning of the 1930s, factory-made decoys rivaled the numbers of handmade decoys in the area of southern Brittany. However, it appears that only handmade decoys were used in La Camargue on the Mediterranean coast and in Picardy on the Channel coast. The situation was different from that usually found in the United States, however: the carving and painting of the factory decoys were usually superior to that of the handmade examples. Even so, the quality of the decoys as handicraft was comparable to that of the working decoys in North America. A movement toward decoratives did not take place in France, and the decoys remained purely workaday tools.

This solid-colored carving probably represents a curlew and was carved in Brittany, France, by an unknown hunter; late 1930s.

European pochard in original paint made by the Briere factory; 1930. This example shows the beauty, shape, and character that distinguish these French decoys.

295

Three decoy manufacturers in Brittany are worthy of emphasis. All three were in operation until the early 1960s, when plastic decoys replaced the wooden ones.

The most productive factory in Brittany was that of Briere. It enjoyed great popularity among hunters. Of high quality, the decoys were made of aged pine, were hollow carved to reduce weight, and were carefully painted, with emphasis on a naturalistic representation of the plumage.

Only three types of diving ducks are known from this factory: European pochard, red-crested pochard, and tufted duck. The roundish body is hollowed from the bottom. The joint between the bottom plate and the body does not contain any special packing material, although it always lies underwater. Instead, both parts were made completely plain so that after nailing the plate to the body the join was watertight. Iron nails were used and were countersunk, the holes filled with putty. If the hunter used care and dried his decoys after each use, the joints remained tight for many years.

The small factory producing the Briere decoys was owned by Jean Jagu and was located in the small village of La Chapelle-des-Marais, a few miles north of Saint Nazaire at the mouth of the Loire River. The production numbers of the factory are unknown, but many thousands are believed to have been made.

Decoys made by the Vilaine factory follow the pattern of those of Briere but were made entirely of cork: only the bill is made of wood. Such decoys weighed less than the wooden Briere examples. The smoothed cork surface was primed by a mixture of linseed oil and chalk, and the painting was done over it according to the desired species.

The decoys made by the Oust factory were, again, diving ducks, but these were always in a resting position, and the manner in which these decoys were carved was unique: body, head, and bill were carved from a single piece of wood. Doing so required that the head be lower to the body, thus creating the resting position. The body of these decoys was hollowed in a way found nowhere else in Europe. A hole, about five centimeters in diameter, was drilled from the back near the tail through the body into the chest. Using a knife, the carver enlarged this hole from within without enlarging the opening at the surface. The opening was then closed with a cork stopper. The Oust factory operated at Saint-Philbert, south of the city of Nantes.

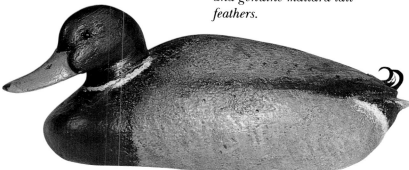

Lowhead mallard drake by Emil Ribi of Lake Constance; dated 1954. This decoy has an inletted head, carved wingtips, and genuine mallard tail feathers.

GERMANY

The first mention in German hunting literature of the use of wooden decoys is in a book by Johann Conrad Aitinger. In 1653, he published a comprehensive work discussing all the methods of hunting and trapping birds then used in Germany. In the chapter on the hunting of wild ducks, he writes that several hunters used to carve and paint "images" of ducks or used duck skins stuffed with straw and placed these within net traps alongside live ducks. Whether using only live ducks or live ducks together with the decoys, the effect, Aitinger reported, was the same: "The wild ducks see a crowd of decoys and are attracted." This work includes a copper engraving Aitinger made himself in which are shown stickup decoys placed inside an arrangement of movable nets to form a trap. In most cases, decoys were used alongside live birds.

German hunting literature of the 18th and 19th centuries makes frequent reference to "luring" ducks, but in those cases the authors are referring to live ducks specially selected and trained to serve as decoys. Only in certain very rare exceptions did hunters learn that carved wooden decoys were equally capable of performing that task. Thus, with the exception of the area of Lake Constance, decoys were used in Germany only rarely.

The southwestern finger of Lake Constance (its German name is Untersee, which means "lower lake") was, at the beginning of this century, a large and important region for waterfowl hunting. Indeed, it had been so for a very long time: according to records of the Benedictine monastery on the island of Reichenau, founded in 724, fowling was practiced along with fishing and provided an important contribution to the food of the inhabitants of that region. Today—more than one thousand years later—we know very little of the details in which waterfowl were hunted by these people. A contract from 1534 defined the laws for jointly executed hunting of waterfowl on the Untersee by German and Swiss communities. But there is no hint that nets or other traps were used. Documents from the 18th and 19th centuries, a period during which net traps were used with great success in other parts of Europe, make reference only to "gunning."

Actually, how long decoys have been used in Germany cannot be determined. Nor is it known whether decoys were invented independently in Europe or were, like so many things, inspired by news from the New World. None of the hunting regulations for the Untersee area make explicit mention of waterfowl hunting with decoys. According to a document entitled "Fishing Regulations," dated 1861, the use of

Mallard drake by the Reichenau hunters and carvers G. Deggelmann and A. Huber; 1950s.

"bird blinds" on the lake was permitted. These were platforms mounted on four poles directly over the surface of the water. One or two hunters sat inside the structure, hidden behind branches and leaves. The use of such a structure, of course, presupposed something employed to entice the waterfowl within range of the hunters' guns. Thus, we can conclude that at least since the middle of the 19th century wooden decoys have been used in the area of Lake Constance, and their use probably dates back even earlier.

The German and Swiss hunters shot mallards, tufted ducks, coots, and European pochards, and they used decoys. Each hunter usually made his own decoys or did so in cooperation with a fellow hunter. The absence of factory-made decoys is explained by the low demand and the limited number of hunters. In April 1985 a contract was signed between the Swiss canton of Thurgau and the German state of Baden-Württemberg forbidding fowling on the lake.

Two types of decoys are used in the city of Constance. Both were made by the locksmith Ernst Blum. The decoy type usually referred to as "Untersee" is a bit undersize and is carved with straight lines to profile the body and head: nothing is done to make recognizable eye and cheek areas. During the 1930s, such decoys were painted in bright colors. Those colors have grown darker over the years and today have a very appealing patina. These decoys, signed on the bottom by a branded letter "B," are excellent examples of folk art, hunting tools made with an artistic touch, with simplified shapes and well composed colors.

These Untersee decoys are carved from beech and are therefore too heavy to float. However, they were made to serve a special purpose for which they were not required to float. In many areas of the Untersee, the water was so shallow that the ducks were used as stickup decoys. Each has a hole on the bottom but no weights. The shape of the so-called Rhine type is derived from the Untersee but is less stylized and stiff and well imitates the roundness of a duck's body. Some have a threaded sword keel instead of balancing weights along with a hole for the stickup pole. These are the only decoys in Europe with a sword keel.

During the 1950s, Gerhard Deggelmann and Arnfried Huber, from the island of Reichenau in the Untersee, carved a decoy type with a lowhead, resting position.

On the Swiss side of the Untersee, Emil Ribi created what is recognized as the high point of the decoy-carving tradition of that hunting area. He made his decoys for his own hunting rig only and was actively carving between 1954 and 1961. His careful observation of live ducks during all seasons over a period of many years and his intrinsic love for detail were the foundations for his perfect sculptures with lowered heads in resting positions. The work of this skillful carver exceeds in terms of quality and aesthetics all other working decoys used around Lake Constance.

296

DENMARK

This country occupies both geographically and historically an intermediate position in terms of duck hunting between the Netherlands and the Scandinavian countries. As in the Netherlands, Danish duck hunters made large use of live ducks as decoys, but at the same time they also used the kind of air nets widely used in Sweden and Finland for the capture of birds. During the 18th century a shift took place from the use of live birds and air nets to the use of wooden decoys, but the older hunting methods have never been completely abandoned.

Hollow red-breasted merganser drake carved by Martin Christensen of Denmark; 1940s.

Both live-bird decoys and air nets were still in use at the end of the 1950s. Hunting with decoys has never been forbidden in Denmark.

Martin Christensen (1897–1974) is one of Denmark's best-known decoy carvers. Having worked at the professions of watchmaker, instrument maker, and gunsmith, he finally settled during the 1920s in the small city of Rudkøbing on the island of Langeland. He took up the carving of working decoys and soon enjoyed a growing reputation for his work. He carved a large number of decoys, some of which are now on display in Danish museums.

FINLAND

In the strip of coastline and islands that runs from the southern Swedish island of Öland past Stockholm to the southern Finnish archipelago near Helsinki, the predominant bird-hunting method involved the use of so-called air nets. These are large nets (about eight meters high and 60 to 200 meters wide) spread out between two tall poles across an air space frequented by birds, such as the narrow passage between two islands or the route taken by wild ducks when flying from sleeping grounds to feeding areas. Such nets, when extended, did not touch the surface of the water. The suspension was not rigid and was controlled by a hunter using cords. The hidden hunter would wait until, at dawn or dusk, the first birds of a flock struck the net; he would then suddenly make the net fall, catching most of the birds beneath it. Using this technique, a hunter could catch up to one hundred ducks in a morning's hunt. The use of these falling nets in Finland can be traced back to 1548. A Swedish document from 1555 describes the use in that country of a net that was probably very similar.

The use of air nets was abandoned in Finland during the 19th century; in Sweden their use came to an end during the 18th century. The decline in air nets was a result of the availability of firearms, which favored the employment of wooden carved decoys.

This hollow red-breasted merganser hen was made by an unknown carver on the Finnish island of Turku; ca. 1940. The large bottom board stabilizes the decoy, which thus requires no balancing weight.

Finnish decoys often display a unique feature: a flat bottom board that is larger than the body of the decoy itself. The bodies of these decoys are a bit undersize, particularly when compared to the Swedish decoys that were used in very similar environmental situations. The enlarged bottom board improved the decoy's ability to float and eliminated to a certain degree the need of a balancing weight.

SWEDEN

Duck hunting in Sweden followed the course taken in Finland. As in Finland, live ducks were not usually used to lure birds, and air nets were the preferred tool. The advent of firearms at the end of the 18th and beginning of the 19th centuries changed the hunting methods, particularly along the eastern coast of Sweden, which offers favorable conditions for the breeding of migrating ducks and birds. The decline in the use of air nets led to the use of carved wooden decoys.

Swedish decoys have their own characteristic style. They are broad and flat, hollowed carefully from the bottom with emphasis on thin walls to make them very light. A thin board is nailed or screwed on from underneath. Being broad and lightweight, they ride high in the water, and only the part of the body that is above the surface is carved. These decoys do not need a weight for balancing and rarely capsize.

Eider male made by an unknown carver on the Swedish island of Ingaro; ca. 1940. Hollow carved, this is very light and very broad.

NORWAY

In Norway, too, the preferred duck-hunting method involved the use of air nets. But in this country, the transition from air nets to guns and decoys was not as marked as in Sweden and Finland. Although carved wooden decoys are known in Norway, their use for hunting did not become general practice until recently. Even so, a small number of decoys is on display in two museums.

GREAT BRITAIN

The use of live ducks and nets and cages that evolved in Holland in the 15th century was being employed also in England as early as the first half of the 17th century. In the last quarter of the 19th century, English sportsmen began to adapt the French method of the *chasse à la hutte* ("decoying to the gun") and introduced wooden decoys. The use of decoys did not become widespread, however, because most hunters thought it too laborious to haul five to ten decoys overland to their favorite hunting sites. Thus, J. C. M. Nichols reported in 1926 that "in all parts of England wooden decoys are used only to a little extent." Even so, several works relate that before 1911 many hunters were interested in the use of decoys and that efforts were made to reduce the weight of the decoys, so that they could be carried for longer distances.

Only after 1945 did decoys in England achieve the desired lightness, and sportsmen began to employ them to a greater extent. In his 1953 book, Michael Shephard devotes an entire chapter to the use of decoys and relates his own hunting experiences using them. He himself used decoys of canvas over wire frames and silhouettes. He was also familiar with expensive, carved-and-painted examples.

In the first part of this century, decoys were known and used by hunters in the Solway Firth in Scotland, on small ponds and marshlands in Cumberland, in Lincolnshire, in the North Sea bay known as The Wash that forms the south border of Lincolnshire, in the Fens east of Peterborough, on the southwest coast of the Bristol Channel, and on the western coast of Ireland. There is a certain similarity between the roundish body of a working decoy used in the Solway Firth and a Mason Standard Grade decoy.

This beetle-headed English mallard drake has an extended breast and several interior, puttied iron weights. This was made near the city of Carlisle during the early 1920s.

The decoys manufactured in the neighborhood of the city of Carlisle have what is known as an interior weight, a feature that does not appear anywhere else in Europe. The weights are not only countersunk but are puttied over as well. Three or four holes about two centimeters in diameter were drilled in the center of the bottom, and iron bolts were inserted into them so that they rested five to eight millimeters beneath the surface. The remaining space was then puttied in carefully. The head of the Carlisle type has an unusual shape. Its back is pointed and drawn out, its forehead and the area toward the bill are so flat that the bill points downward. The heads in general are very small.

ITALY

Italy has been the classic home of fowling since the Middle Ages. The methods employed in Italy presumably hark back to ancient practices. Songbirds, in particular, were caught in nets, a practice that has recently brought heavy protests from animal protection groups.

The main areas in which duck lures were used are the Venetian lagoon, the marshlands along the Po River, and, to a lesser extent, the hunting regions of Tuscany. Exactly when the use of decoys became general practice is not known. A report on duck hunting from 1910 says that the decoys were "very old." Their widespread use during the second half of the 19th century is certain. In view of the Italy's ancient fowling tradition and its absorption of hunting methods from throughout the Mediterranean area, the use of decoys can be assumed to be quite old.

Mallard drake with raised wingtips by Giovanni Simoncin of northern Italy; early 1960s. The body is of cork; the head is wood.

One widespread decoy form used especially for coots has a body made of reed and the head of wood. This decoy is very lightweight and is easy to make, requiring no special carving skill. Since coots have a uniform black plumage, little skill is called for in the painting of such decoys. However, because the reeds are elastic, the paint cracks quickly in use, and repainting may be necessary during a hunting season. After a short time water penetrates into the body and settles in the spongy pulp of the stalks, destroying the decoy in a short time. Thus, these decoys must be carefully dried after each used. Also used for the making of decoys is cork, another material that renders decoys lightweight. There are reports of decoys made from wooden blocks in use in southern Italy.

298

SPAIN

A Mediterranean country located along the migration flyways of northern European birds, Spain has old hunting traditions similar to those of Italy. Two different hunting methods have apparently been used in Spain, the two being practiced in different regions or provinces. Each method called for a different form of decoy, and these are called ground ducks and floating ducks.

The floating ducks are made to float and are equipped with a balance weight and anchor. These floating ducks thus resemble the normal decoy as used in most other hunting regions. These are carved from a block of pine and have a feature that is unique among European decoys: the bill is detachable for easy repair. Also, the head and neck are carved to form a movable plug that is inserted into the body and fixed in place with a wedge. Thus the direction of the head can be changed, and the entire head can be removed for repair. Most of these were made and used in Andalusia, and some of the oldest date to about 1880.

Ground ducks were carved from heavy fruit wood and thus cannot float. They have no weight, no anchor, and no hole for a stickup pole. Such decoys were used on stubbly fields, on marshes barely able to support the weight of a hunter, and on other kinds of damp soil. These decoys are remarkable for their coloring, which is unnatural, making it often impossible to determine a specific species; what's more, they are often of a fantastic shape, with bodies and heads that are in no way related to a specific family or species. Of course, considering the wet and muddy environments in which these decoys were used, the colors had to be brighter than natural because these decoys got very dirty as soon as positioned.

These ground ducks were made around Albufera, a lagoon located south of Valencia, and on the delta of the Ebro River, about one hundred miles north of Valencia.

The west coast of Spain has long been an important tourist area, and since the 1970s large quantities of ground ducks have been carved and artificially aged for sale to tourists as souvenirs. In this way, the shape and painting of the original decoys was with time exaggerated, resulting in even more unnatural bodies, heads, and colors.

Ground duck carved in the shape of a merganser but painted in a fantastic pattern. Used in the Albufera region south of Valencia, Spain. This decoy was made by an unknown carver following a traditional shape; ca. 1970.

DECOYS IN EUROPE

With the exception of southern Germany, hunting with decoys is legal throughout Europe, and decoys have a long tradition in Europe. Even so, since the 1970s the use of decoys in Europe has been undergoing a change from hunting tools to mantelpieces, from working implements to decorative objects.

This new interest in decoys can be traced to several sources. Many European collectors became knowledgeable about American decoys before investigating European examples. In the United States, of course, the shift from working decoys to decorative collectibles had already taken place and dated back to the 1920s, after market hunting was outlawed. European collectors, following the lead of their American counterparts, began to extend their collections to include European examples and began collecting them systematically. Other Europeans, ignorant of the decoy tradition in other countries, discovered decoys as a result of the increasing interest in culture and folk art.

A folk art exhibition held in the French city of Rheims in 1977 included the first display of decoys. Ten years later an exhibition dedicated to decoys as folk art was held in Munich, Germany. This show put together participants from eleven European countries and included a total of 230 examples, by far the most important such show yet held in Europe.

This new interest in decoys has had to face several setbacks. A significant factor in the movement toward an appreciation of folk art was the so-called plastic invasion, the widespread use of plastics in all areas of everyday life that occurred during the early 1960s. Plastic even made its way into the duck-hunter's rig, and many European hunters put aside their heavy wooden decoys in favor of the lighter plastic examples. At that time, decoys were not yet avidly sought as folk art—neither the public at large nor the hunters recognized them as collectible and valuable artifacts—and many old decoys were burnt or left to rot. During that period a large number of invaluable old decoys was lost, and the number of old, hand-carved decoys available to European collectors is, sadly, enormously smaller than that in North America.

CHAPTER 25:

COLLECTING DECOYS

by Robert Shaw

ABOVE: *Joel David Barber, the father of decoy collecting, exhibiting part of his flock in New York in the 1930s.*

OPPOSITE TOP: *One of Barber's many watercolor studies of historic decoys. As an architect and carver, Barber delighted in analyzing construction methods.*

OPPOSITE BOTTOM: *The first decoy in Joel Barber's collection.*

Ten years ago, when I first began working at the Shelburne Museum, I knew nothing about decoys, but, having always loved wild birds, I found myself immediately fascinated by Shelburne's extraordinary collection of some 1,000 old working decoys and decorative and miniature bird carvings. I spent hours at home with my Peterson bird guide trying, often without much success, to connect Roger Tory Peterson's drawings of the various ducks and shorebirds with the wooden decoys I worked with during the day. I also began to recognize the distinctive touch of certain master carvers—the impressionistic "wet on wet" paint of Elmer Crowell's brush, the strong flowing lines of the Dudley brothers' canvasbacks and ruddy ducks, the hollow bodies and turned heads of Albert Laing's and Shang Wheeler's decoys.

As I learned about the many regions where decoys have been made, I again became a student of geography. Assawaman, Virginia; Long Point, Ontario; Barnegat, New Jersey; Havre de Grace, Maryland; Bureau, Illinois; Monhegan Island, Maine; and Knotts Island, North Carolina, all had to be located on my Rand-McNally. North America came alive in my imagination as I connected makers and styles with towns, rivers, lakes, and bays all over the nation.

As curator of the Shelburne collection, I was required to research its history; to find out, wherever it was still possible to do so, how the various carvings had come to the museum and who had originally collected them. I soon discovered that the most important figure in the formation of the Shelburne collection was a man named Joel Barber, whose collection was acquired by the museum after his death in 1952. It has been on

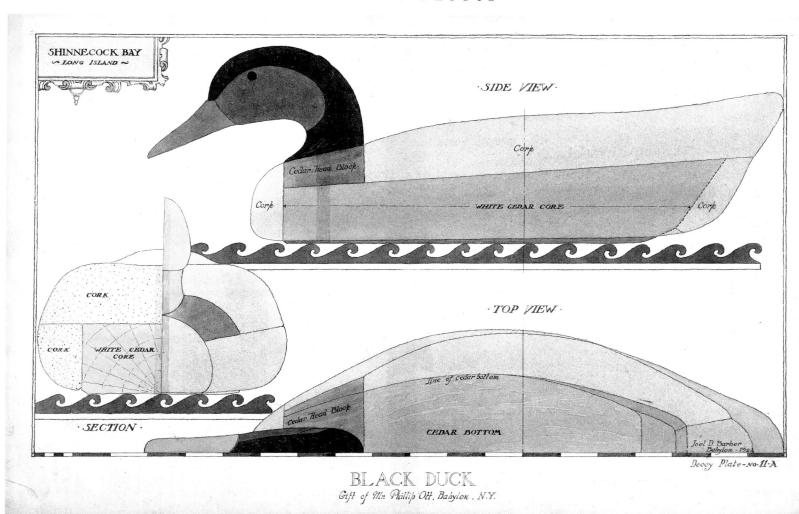

SHINNECOCK BAY
~ LONG ISLAND ~

· SIDE VIEW ·

Cork

Cedar Head Block

Cork
WHITE CEDAR CORE
Cork

· TOP VIEW ·

CORK

CORK
WHITE CEDAR
CORE

· SECTION ·

Line of cedar bottom

Cedar Head Block
CEDAR BOTTOM

Joel D Barber
Babylon - 1924

Decoy Plate - No 11·A

BLACK DUCK
Gift of Mr. Phillip Ott, Babylon, N.Y.

public exhibition at the museum ever since. Joel Barber turned out to be the seminal figure in both the history of decoy collecting and the recognition of the decoy as an American art form.

The first decoy collectors were undoubtedly carvers and hunters who put aside a particularly well made bird or two to be admired during the off season. None of these men would have considered himself a collector, however, nor did any of them approach the subject in an organized or comprehensive manner. Joel David Barber was the first true decoy collector and is recognized today as the father of decoy collecting. In 1918 Barber, an unassuming New York City architect, was living in Babylon, Long Island, an area then still largely undeveloped. One day that year Barber found an old decoy in an abandoned sailing loft. The decoy was a female red-breasted merganser. She was weathered by hard use in salt water over the years but remained sound and attractive. Although Barber never identified the carver, we know now that the decoy was actually a "married" piece: the body was carved by William Southard of Bellmore and the head was a replacement of Southard's original made by Frank Kellum of Babylon. Undoubtedly, a local hunter had put the two pieces together while gunning over the decoy. In any case, the wooden bird intrigued Barber, so he brought it home and placed it on his mantel.

Barber was a gregarious man, and his curiosity about the old decoy soon led him to friendships with many of the baymen who fished and hunted Long Island Sound and the Great South Bay of the island. Through these men Barber began to learn about decoys. Many of the old-timers were storytellers, and Barber listened with fascination to their tales of the days of market gunning and guiding the "sports" who came from New York to gun on the sound and the bay. Barber also learned about the old carvings and the men who crafted them, about how and where they were used, and how they were made. Decoys soon became his hobby and his cause. Barber freely admitted his obsession, declaring, "Of all the birds subject to

attraction by decoys, I am, perhaps, the most susceptible bird of all." He became convinced that the decoy was an art form unique to North America (he called it "the only floating sculpture") and that it represented something important about our national history. Discovering no one else particularly interested in collecting and documenting the old birds, and realizing that their era was passing before his eyes, Barber set out to capture what he could of the American decoy before it was gone. Throughout the 1920s he traveled up and down the Eastern seaboard, from Maine to the Carolinas, in search of decoys and decoy makers and brought back dozens of birds and stories to New York, where he filled his home with decoys, painted documentary watercolors of outstanding examples, and wrote down what he had learned in his travels. In 1934 he published a compendium of his tales and drawings called *Wild Fowl Decoys*. The book, published in a deluxe leatherbound edition of but 55 copies by Eugene Connett's Derrydale Press and a trade hardcover by Windward House, hardly set the world on fire. It remained the only book available on the subject until the 1960s.

Decoys on display in the Dorset House of the Shelburne Museum.

Wild Fowl Decoys is still in print today and has served to introduce several generations of collectors to the field. Despite the dozens of titles that have supplemented it over the past twenty-five years, it remains my favorite decoy book. Barber, who considered his talent to be art, claimed that writing came hard to him. Perhaps so, but to my mind no one has ever written so evocatively of the decoy or explained so well its appeal. As collectors and students of the decoy, we are all deeply in Joel Barber's debt.

After devouring *Wild Fowl Decoys,* I moved to the works of two other important early decoy collectors and historians, William Mackey's *American Bird Decoys* and Adele Earnest's *The Art of the Decoy.* Both books were first published in 1965, and both deserve the attention of every serious collector and student of the decoy. Mackey, who was a formidable competitor, amassed some 2,000 decoys during his lifetime; his was arguably the greatest and most comprehensive private collection ever assembled. His book is similarly comprehensive in its scope, covering the work of hundreds of regional decoy makers. It remains the bible of many collectors today for its mix of solid information, good storytelling, and many photographs of superb examples. Mackey's collection was sold at auction in 1973 and 1974 by the Richard A. Bourne Company of Hyannis, Massachusetts. While the prices paid for many of his decoys seem like bargains by today's standards, the Mackey sales astonished the decoy-collecting world of the time and marked the beginning of a growth in interest and investment in the wooden bird that continues undiminished to this day.

In contrast to Mr. Mackey's work, the emphasis of Mrs. Earnest's book is, as its title indicates, on the decoy's artistic merits. Mrs. Earnest, an important early dealer in American folk art and a sophisticated student of sculptural art, was able to bring broad artistic knowledge to bear on her approach to the decoy. Her insightful writing on form, construction, painting techniques, and regional variations has influenced all subsequent collectors. Mr. Mackey paid her perhaps the greatest of all compliments by adding a chapter on the art of the decoy to his own book at the last minute.

Another important and influential early collector and author was Dr. George Ross Starr of Duxbury, Massachusetts, whose book *Decoys of the Atlantic Flyway* was the first of the dozens of useful regional studies that have appeared in the 1970s and 1980s. As a beginning collector, Dr. Starr was befriended by Joel Barber, and their writings share a sense of camaraderie and fun that gets to the heart of what decoy collecting is, or at least should be, all about. Like Barber, "Doc" Starr was a born storyteller, and his delightful book should not be missed by anyone who wants to know what the "good old days" of decoy collecting were like. George Starr died in 1985, and his collection was dispersed at auction in March 1986 by the Bourne firm. As was the case with the Mackey auctions held a dozen years earlier, the results amazed many collectors and marked a standard against which other sales and collections are measured.

As this book amply demonstrates, decoys offer a wide range of aesthetic choices to the collector. Because the marketplace is equally complex, the aspiring collector would be well advised to seek counsel, as he enters the field, from someone whose judgment, integrity, and knowledge are well established. He will enter alone at his own peril. It is all too easy today for an inexperienced collector to make costly mistakes.

Books can be very important tools for learning about decoys. They are, however, no substitute for contact with the

artifacts themselves. My real learning has been "hands-on," examining decoys first hand at the Shelburne and other museums, at auctions, and in dealers' showrooms and collectors' homes. There is no better way to learn. A collector should take advantage of every opportunity to see and examine birds he is unfamiliar with. Only in this way will he learn to trust his own eyes. When one goes back to the books after first-hand observation, one is invariably reminded that photographs can deceive as often as they reveal. Only by spending a great deal of time studying books and examining birds in person can one come to recognize quality when one encounters it. It is necessary to have a broad knowledge of the material in order to make informed decisions about what is truly outstanding and what is average.

It has been my privilege to travel widely and study many of the finest private collections in the United States and Canada. I have found collectors almost uniformly gracious and willing to share their knowledge with fellow enthusiasts. Anyone just entering the field would be well advised to get to know some other collectors and to view existing collections before attempting to form one of his own. There are a number of collectors' organizations around the country that always welcome new members and offer an excellent opportunity to meet people with a shared interest in the decoy. Although decoy collecting remains largely a private passion, several museums do exhibit outstanding collections of decoys. These institutions, which, in addition to the Shelburne, include the Ward Foundation in Salisbury, Maryland, the Museum of American

Folk Art in New York, the Museums at Stony Brook on Long Island, the Noyes Museum in New Jersey, and the Abby Aldrich Folk Art Center at Colonial Williamsburg in Virginia, also are excellent places to study and compare decoys. Remember, however, that museums are hardly infallible. The fact that a bird is owned and exhibited by a museum should not render it immune from careful analysis and criticism.

How should one look at a decoy? Whenever I encounter a decoy for the first time, my approach is threefold. First, I react to the bird on a gut level. Either I like it immediately or I don't; either it "speaks to me" or it doesn't. This first impression is very important and should always be heeded. But it should never be left unquestioned. Second, I analyze the bird. My first reaction to a decoy might be "Wow! This *appears* to be some-

304

LEFT: Dr. George Ross Starr—author, collector, and raconteur—with part of his collection.

BELOW: The great collector William Mackey holding the prize of his enormous collection, a curlew by Bill Bowman.

OPPOSITE: Many museums have added new decoys to their collections. This Long Island herring gull was purchased by the Museums at Stony Brook on Long Island in 1987.

thing pretty great." I then have to force back my excitement and turn my mind to a careful examination of the piece. This is the time when one's accumulated knowledge comes into play. Can I prove the bird wrong in any way? Is the decoy indeed what it appears to be? Is there anything that doesn't seem quite right about it, that doesn't conform to what I know about similar decoys? Is it too good to be true? If so, it probably isn't true. I scrutinize every detail of the bird's construction and painted surface, looking for evidence of restoration, repair, or repaint. Then, I follow the advice of the great collector William Mackey and hold the bird with my eyes closed to make sure it "feels right," a sense experienced collectors develop after handling hundreds of old decoys. Decoys are tactile objects. They were made to be held and used. Finally, after I have thoroughly examined the bird and discovered as many of its faults as I possibly can, I can allow my initial excitement to join with my analytical study of the piece for a third and final judgment. When the two opposite approaches of immediate emotional reaction and careful intellectual examination combine in a complementary way, I know I've come across an object that will provide lasting pleasure and satisfaction. Neither approach will stand the test of time by itself.

Let me offer a few generalities about criteria for judging decoys. The most important element of a decoy is its form. Decoys were made to manipulate, not to imitate, wild birds. They were made as tools and had to be functional objects first and foremost. Like weathervanes, most decoys were made primarily to be seen from a distance, as forms floating on the

water or silhouetted against the sky. A good decoy therefore captures something essential—perhaps a sense of watchfulness, repose, or weariness—about the bird it was carved to deceive. The form of a decoy should convey at a quick glance from several feet away a strong impression of the species it is meant to represent. When I enter a museum, auction gallery, or collector's home, I always study the decoys on exhibit from across the room before examining them close-up for details of their paint, construction, and condition.

Paint is the second important element of a decoy. All decoys were painted, both to protect the wood and to enhance their ability to lure. Paint styles varied tremendously from region to region and maker to maker, depending on how the birds were to be used and the skills of the craftsman with a brush. Ideally, a decoy should retain enough of its original paint surface to document its history and use. Particularly in coastal regions where birds were subjected to hard use in salt water, decoys were frequently repainted "in-use." So long as the paint surface on such a bird is old and worn to a pleasing and varied patina, this lack of original paint is perfectly acceptable. It also is natural and indeed desirable for a decoy to show such signs of use as shot and rope marks and small chips and rubs to the wood. While some collectors prefer examples with surfaces as close to pristine as possible, I feel strongly that the condition of a decoy's paint has been overemphasized in recent years. To my mind, paint is not primary. If a decoy's original paint pattern is clearly defined by what remains and if what remains is old and attractive, aesthetic decisions should then revert to

considerations of form. I heartily subscribe to the dictum that one should take a decoy out of the gunning rig, not right out of the carver's shop.

Structural condition is another important consideration. Because they were used as tools, most decoys show some wear. Major cracks, chips or checks in the wood, or broken or missing parts that detract from the visual integrity of the object can be serious detriments. Bills and tails deserve especially careful scrutiny as these are a decoy's weakest and therefore most commonly repaired points. An in-use repair effected by the maker or gunner is often acceptable and can sometimes add to the bird's historical appeal. However, *any* type of restoration or reconstruction should be made known to a prospective buyer. A great deal can be discerned with the naked eye under strong natural light. Look for any changes in the surface and explain them to your own satisfaction. If you have lingering suspicions that all is not as it should be, the use of a black light can often reveal changes in the painted surface that escape normal vision and mask structural repairs. In extreme cases an x-ray by a friendly radiologist will dissect the decoy's structure and tell many secrets about the bird's construction and history. Re-heads, repairs, and fills will show clearly.

There is no substitute for experience. Knowledgeable collectors develop a sixth sense that tells them whether a bird is "right" or whether it has been mucked with. This sense comes only from looking at and handling many, many decoys. In so doing, one develops a mental inventory of makers' styles and methods; significant deviations will raise questions and require

further investigation. Trust your instincts and trust your knowledge, but be realistic about both. In other words, know what you don't know and be willing to admit it, at least to yourself.

The fourth important consideration in evaluating a decoy is provenance—the history of the bird's ownership. If this line can be clearly traced, it can answer a host of questions. Provenance is all important when dealing with major paintings and pieces of furniture; it is becoming increasingly important with decoys, as well it should. My caveat about museums holds here as well: don't overvalue the association of an object with a particular owner, no matter how distinguished. Approach provenance as an informational tool, not as an endorsement. Rarity can be an important factor too. Be aware, however, that rarity, like provenance, is a documentary quality; it has no aesthetic value. It also can be very expensive.

How does one decide what to collect? Unless you are extremely wealthy, you will have to limit your scope in one way or another. Many collectors today focus on decoys from a particular gunning region and seek only decoys used on the St. Clair Flats, the Connecticut shore, or the Delaware River, for example. Others limit themselves to representations of a favorite species, collecting only teal or redheads by a variety of different makers. Still others concentrate on a particular maker's handiwork and search for birds by, say, the Mason Factory or Elmer Crowell. Most difficult and perhaps most rewarding of all might be a collection that mixes makers, regions, and species and still makes a coherent statement. Whatever your decision, you should set goals and stick to them without compromise. A clear objective is absolutely essential to any collector.

Let me also offer some general guidelines on how to care for and preserve decoys. Collectors and museums are only custodians of the decoys they own. Ownership of these objects is a privilege and a responsibility. We must hope that our decoys will outlive us to be enjoyed by future generations and should treat them accordingly.

The most important thing a collector can provide for his decoys is a stable environment with fairly constant humidity and temperature. Be aware that sunlight and fluorescent light produce ultraviolet rays that damage paint. Changes in humidity are the worst enemy of painted wooden objects. Wood expands and contracts as humidity levels change; paint does not. Flaking paint is the all too common and potentially disastrous result of wide fluctuations in humidity. Humidity in a normal house ranges from 20 percent in the winter to 80 percent in the summer. You can try to maintain humidity in the safer 40 to 60 percent range by using a humidifier in the winter and a dehumidifier in the summer. Extreme, abrupt change is the real enemy. It is better to maintain 30 percent year round than to have 30 percent at one time and 70 percent at another.

307

Mallard hens by Robert Elliston, of Bureau, Illinois, ca. 1890 (above) and Judge Glen Cameron of Chillicothe, Illinois, ca. 1925 (below).

308

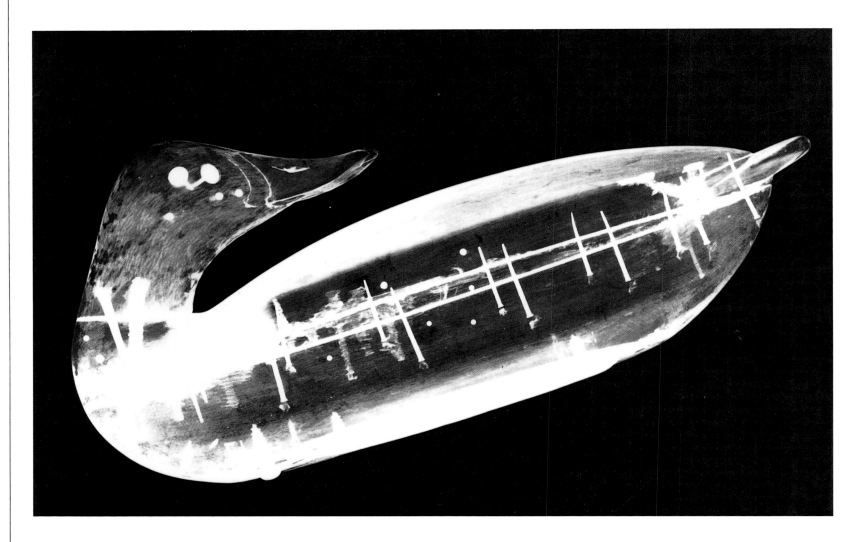

I strongly recommend against treating the surface of decoys with any type of oil. The standard museum text on object care offers the following sage advice on this subject:

> *Avoid the erroneous notion that wood or its finishes require "feeding" regularly. That term—"feeding"—derives from certain traditional treatments utilizing tung oil, lemon oil or linseed oil. . . . The oil used in the highly touted "feeding" solutions is usually slow to dry and so attracts dust to its cell walls, so there is no additional protection against environmental conditions. Although the "feeding" oil may spruce up the appearance of the wood for awhile, it darkens with age and also, finally, penetrates the wood, making later removal difficult and often damaging the original surface. For light, protective layers over finished wooden surfaces, you may use good commercial paste waxes made of beeswax, carnuba or candellilla wax. . . . Do not use liquid self-polishing waxes . . . many of them contain silicones which may penetrate the wood. . . . Waxing may be done once or twice a year but it should not be a weekly practice, or a gummy, sticky surface may be the result. Dusting with a clean rag is the best regular care for wood.*

When I first began to acquire decoys for the Shelburne Museum collection, I set some collecting rules for myself which I have never regretted abiding by. These are:

1) Set clear objectives.
2) Aim as high as possible. Set your sights beyond your means. Reach.
3) Be patient. Wait for what you want; don't settle for less.
4) Don't be distracted by things that don't further your objectives, no matter how appealing they seem.
5) Don't look for bargains.
6) Make up your own mind. Don't collect someone else's taste or opinions.

ABOVE: X-ray of a decoy showing its interior construction. X-rays are extremely useful in detecting structural repairs and changed heads.

OPPOSITE: Black-bellied plover attributed to "John Dilley" of Quogue, Long Island; ca. 1880.

A number of years ago I made up a short list of priorities for addition to the Shelburne Museum decoy collection. I have been following that list ever since, taking great satisfaction in deleting key decoys from it as I am able to add first-rate examples to the Shelburne collection. As the museum's ambitious goal is to represent the best work of important makers from every gunning area of North America, I organized the list by region. The most glaring omission was birds from the Illinois River area; at the time I made up the list, the museum lacked representative works by all the masters of the region, including such important carvers as Robert Elliston, Charles Perdew, Charles Walker, Charles Schoenheider, Glen Cameron, Fred Allen, Mr. X, and G. Bert Graves. Filling in this gaping hole in the collection thus became my initial area of concentration. I am proud to say that none of those names remains on the Shelburne Museum's want list today.

A close look at a couple of the birds I acquired for the museum from this region may be helpful. To my mind, the most important Illinois River carver was Robert Elliston of Bureau. Elliston (1849–1915) was, according to the best information available to us, the region's stylesetter, an originator whose work exerted a profound influence on succeeding generations of local carvers. A prime example of his work was therefore at the top of my list. The next question was what species to choose? After studying Elliston's work in books and in collections, I decided that my preference was for his hen mallards.

All of Elliston's decoys were painted by his wife, Catherine; I found the tight scratched half circles of her feather painting on hen mallards an ideal complement to Robert Elliston's carving. My opportunity came when a very fine Elliston hen mallard came to auction in the spring of 1986. Catherine Elliston's paint was applied quite thinly and often has flaked badly over the years. This bird was in very good condition; she had some flaking to bare wood on her left side, but the right was almost completely intact. My judgment of the bird's quality was confirmed by several long-time collectors of Illinois River decoys who felt this was one of the best Elliston mallard hens they had seen. She is now a part of the Shelburne Museum's permanent collection.

Another superb Illinois River mallard hen the museum acquired from a private collector makes an interesting comparison with the Elliston. Carved by Judge Glen Cameron of Chillicothe a generation later than the Elliston, the bird's body is thicker and rounder with a more pronounced and rounded breast and a longer, more pointed tail. Its head is flatter and more gently curved than the Elliston's, which rises in a nearly straight line from the tip of the bill to the crown before curving to the bird's flat back. Viewed head on, the shape of the Cameron's head is basically triangular while the Elliston's is oval. The Cameron's paint is looser in style than the Elliston's, with light browns daubed on in short, unblended strokes. While I prefer the subtlety of the Elliston, these are both fine Illinois decoys.

My list also included a number of shorebirds. Two makers whose work I was particularly anxious to represent in the museum's collection were the mysterious "John Dilley" and New

*Black-bellied plover (above)
and yellowlegs (below) by
George Boyd of Seabrook, New
Hampshire; both ca. 1910.*

310

Two ruddy ducks by Lee Dudley of Knotts Island, North Carolina; both ca. 1890. This photograph was taken not long after the two decoys were collected from Mr. Dudley by Joel Barber.

Hampshire's George Boyd. Both men rank among the finest of shorebird makers, along with such masters as Bill Bowman, Elmer Crowell, and Obediah Verity.

Dilley was perhaps the most skilled painter of all decoy craftsmen. His meticulously detailed brushwork is immediately identifiable, and his work is particularly interesting because he painted every conceivable plumage phase—summer, winter, breeding, and so on—of the major shorebird species. One year, while attending the annual Mid-West Decoy Collectors' Association meeting outside Chicago, I learned that a fortunate person had discovered a previously unknown group of Dilley shorebirds. I was lucky enough to be among the first to see the birds, which were extraordinary. Some years later I was able to acquire a black-bellied plover from this group. The decoy is among the finest Dilley plovers I have ever seen, with a plump body, raised wing carving, and beautifully executed and preserved paint, laid on in intricate patterns with an extremely fine brush. Dilley's complex paint lends a soft pliant feathery feel to the decoy's surface. Dilley excelled at creating texture through paint; one's eye is drawn to the surface of his decoys rather than their form.

George Boyd's work, on the other hand, is hard edged and direct. In contrast to Dilley, Boyd carved only two shorebird species: black-bellied plover and yellowlegs. Both are stylized and distinctive, with simple linear forms that convey the species at a glance and split-tail carving typical of New England makers. Boyd's plovers are compact and bold, his yellowlegs more elongated and delicate. Both have squared-off heads with shoe-button eyes. (Like Joe Lincoln, Boyd worked as a shoemaker.) Boyd's detailed paint was put on in very short strokes with a stiff brush; in contrast to Dilley, his palette was extremely limited. The wing on a Boyd shorebird is described by a boldly drawn black line that repeats and emphasizes the shape of the bird's breast and belly, while the tail feathers are

black Vs that echo the shape of the tail and, in reverse, the tail notch. Because Boyd did not use patterns, each of his decoys is slightly different. A rig of Boyd shorebirds, like nature itself, would have presented a host of slight variations on a common theme. In 1988 I acquired one of each Boyd shorebird species for the museum, a plover at auction and a yellowlegs some months later privately. I was particularly pleased that the refined-looking yellowlegs had received better treatment over the years than the plover, thus further accentuating the subtle differences between them. They make a delightful pair.

Let me close with a look at a bird that has it all: a ruddy duck made circa 1890 by Lee Dudley of Knott's Island, North Carolina, and originally collected by Joel Barber (see pages 172–73). Dudley is recognized by collectors as a master craftsman with a unique and instantly recognizable style. The bird is fabulously rare—ruddy-duck decoys are uncommon, and the number of legitimate Dudley ruddies extant can be easily counted on one hand. The decoy's history has been carefully recounted by Barber in *Wild Fowl Decoys*. This bird and a mate, both now in the Shelburne Museum collection, were collected directly from Mr. Dudley himself in the 1920s. Both were well used, so Barber asked Dudley to repaint one of them for him. The decoy's structure is sound and unblemished by significant chips or other losses. The paint is original, and although worn to bare wood in most areas, the patina created by age and wear is, as an examination of the repainted example makes clear, far more appealing than a "better preserved" surface would be.

The little bird is truly a piece of floating sculpture. The decoy's lines are exquisite, moving in an unbroken flow from bill to tail. The straight line originated by the tail bisects the body at its midpoint, creating a feeling of stasis around which the curved lines of the body move. The fat cheeks and flattened crown of the erect head are echoed in the wide curves of the plump body, while the elegantly curved forward thrust of the

311

Group of expert collectors scrutinizing black-duck decoys at the Shelburne Museum during a survey of the collection in April 1981.

breast is balanced by the broad, flat tail. The tail and bill are separated from the body by sharply carved triangular indentations; in the case of the bill these appear both above and below. The nostrils are also carved. Enough paint remains to clearly delineate the original pattern: white over black on the cheeks and belly, pure black on the bill and eyes, black over white lead primer elsewhere. The paint has worn with the natural grooves of the cedar it was laid on, the cracked, swirling circles adding yet another dimension to the bird's already pleasing surface. Finally, the carver's brand "L.D." is burned deeply into the base adjacent to the original lead weight, and the decoy retains remnants of its leather lead-line thong as well as Barber's round brass collecting tag. No one could ask for more.

Over the course of the past twenty-five years, decoy collecting has grown from the pursuit of a small community of hunters and folk-art enthusiasts to a multimillion-dollar-a-year business dominated by auction houses and professional dealers. Prices for rare and choice decoys, which when new sold for a few dollars apiece at most, now often range well into five or even six figures. Because old gunning decoys have come to be perceived as valuable American antiques, the days when fine examples could be discovered in local boat and club houses are largely over. Collecting is still an extremely rewarding activity, but it requires patience, research, knowledge, care, and discipline, particularly because of the sizable investment of time or money now required for the acquisition of outstanding decoys.

My involvement with American bird decoys has brought me great satisfaction and pleasure over the past decade and many wonderful and enduring friendships. Never in my wildest dreams could I have imagined how wooden birds would inform and enrich my life. I hope that every collector's experience will be as fulfilling.

PUBLIC COLLECTIONS OF DECOYS

Abby Aldrich Rockefeller Folk Art Center
P.O. Box C
Williamsburg, Virginia 23187
(804) 220–7670

The Abby Aldrich Rockefeller Folk Art Center has over 60 decoys in its collections. The birds represented include 32 species. The majority of decoys are ducks and shorebirds, but there are outstanding decoys in the other areas as well. Fourteen states are represented, but the major collections are from Michigan, Illinois, Maryland, and New Jersey. The Abby Aldrich Rockefeller Folk Art Center is currently closed for renovations and will reopen in 1991.

The Canadian Museum of Civilization
Canadian Center for Folk Culture Studies
1100 Laurier Street
P.O. Box 3100, Station B
Hull, Quebec G8X 4H2
(613) 776–7000

Over 1,000 rare early Canadian decoys are part of this excellent permanent collection.

The Delta Museum
4858 Delta Street
Ladnor, British Columbia V4K 2T8
(604) 946–9322

Representative early decoys from British Columbia are in this selective collection.

Havre De Grace Decoy Museum
R. Madison Mitchel Place
Havre De Grace, Maryland 21078
(301) 939–3739

The Havre De Grace Museum houses a fine collection of Upper Chesapeake Bay decoys. Along with its display of old masters, the museum features complete collections from many of the contemporary makers who still frequent the area. Wax figures of some of the legendary upper bay makers are a highlight of the display.

Museum of American Folk Art
2 Lincoln Square
New York, New York 10023
(212) 977–7298

The Museum of American Folk Art has a fine collection of decoys. The collection was given national prominence through a cooperative effort with Jeff Waingrow that resulted in a book featuring decoys from the museum's collection.

The Museums at Stony Brook
1208 Route 25A
Stony Brook, New York 11790
(516) 751–0066

The Museums at Stony Brook owns a fine collection of decoys representing choice examples of Long Island's most well-known makers, including Bowman, Verity, Southard, and Gelston. The collection also includes decoys from other regions.

The Noyes Museum
Lily Lake Road
Oceanville, New Jersey 08231
(609) 652–8848

The Noyes Museum collection features mainly examples from New Jersey and the Delaware River. The museum offers changing exhibits that feature decoys from prominent collections as well as carvings by contemporary makers.

Peabody Museum of Salem
E. India Square
Salem, Massachusetts 01970
(508) 745–9500

The Peabody Museum of Salem has an outstanding collection of Massachusetts decoys, featuring choice examples by Crowell, Lincoln, and Chadwick along with a fine presentation of miniature decoys.

Refuge Waterfowl Museum
P.O. Box 272
Chincoteague, Virginia 23336
(804) 336–5800

The Refuge Waterfowl Museum is dedicated to the native carvers of Chincoteague, a small barrier island on the eastern shore of Virginia, and features choice examples from the region's most famous carvers—Miles Hancock, Ira Hudson, and Dave "Umbrella" Watson—along with other fine working and contemporary decoys.

The Shelburne Museum
Route 7
Shelburne, Vermont 05482
(802) 985–3346

In 1952 the Shelburne Museum acquired the complete collection of Joel Barber. Since then, the collection has grown steadily through donations of individual birds and small private collections and selective purchases. Today, Shelburne's collection includes some 850 working decoys and 200 miniature and decorative carvings.

Upper Bay Museum
119 Walnut Street
North East, Maryland 21901
(301) 287–2675

The Upper Bay Museum, along with its fine collection of Upper Chesapeake Bay decoys, features outstanding examples of hunting artifacts from the 1800s, including sinkboxes, put guns, bushwack boats, and sculling cars.

Virginia Beach Marine Science Museum
717 General Booth Blvd.
Virginia Beach, Virginia 23451
(804) 425–3476

The Virginia Beach Marine Science Museum features a changing exhibition of both old and contemporary decoys. Previous displays have included decoys by the Ward brothers as well as decoys from the eastern shore of Virginia and the Delaware River.

Ward Foundation Wildfowl Art Museum
655 S. Salisbury Boulevard
Salisbury, Maryland 21801
(301) 742–4988

The Ward Foundation Wildfowl Art Museum is dedicated to the memory of the Ward brothers, Lem and Steve, legendary decoy makers from nearby Crisfield, Maryland. The museum features a fine collection of their carvings along with other choice examples from Maryland and the eastern shore of Virginia.

Wendell Gilley Museum
P.O. Box 254
Southwest Harbor, Maine 04679
(207) 244–7555

The Wendell Gilley Museum houses a small collection of decoys, all from the Wendell Gilley collection. The decoys include black ducks, scoter ducks, and common eiders. The museum holds demonstrations on decoy making and occasional exhibits on decoys.

313

RECORD DECOY PRICES AT AUCTION

1. Elmer Crowell preening pintail..... *July 1986*.... $319,000
2. Joseph Lincoln wood duck .... *May 1986*.... 205,000
3. Elmer Crowell hissing Canada goose .... *July 1986*.... 165,000
4. Nathan Cobb, Sr. hissing Canada goose........................... *July 1989*.... 99,000
5. Gus Wilson pair red-breasted mergansers..................... *May 1986*.... 95,000
6. Lothrop Holmes pair red-breasted mergansers .... *October 1985*.... 93,500
7. Joseph Lincoln hissing Canada goose .... *April 1986*.... 90,200
8. Elmer Crowell preening wigeon .... *November 1986*.... 88,000
9. Elmer Crowell preening black duck........................... *April 1986*.... 70,400
10. Lothrop Holmes ruddy turnstone .... *March 1986*.... 67,000
11. Sam Barnes/"Daddy" Holly swan........................... *July 1987*.... 66,000
11. Charles Schoenheider standing Canada goose.................... *July 1988*.... 66,000
13. Gus Wilson pair red-breasted mergansers .... *November 1985*.... 61,600
14. Elmer Crowell feeding black-bellied plover .... *July 1986*.... 57,750
15. Albert Laing/"Shang" Wheeler surf scoter .... *November 1986*.... 57,200
16. Elmer Crowell redhead...... *September 1986*.... 55,000
16. Elmer Crowell ruddy duck .... *July 1986*.... 55,000
16. Elmer Crowell pair canvasbacks .... *July 1986*.... 55,000
16. Charles Birch swan............... *July 1987*.... 55,000
20. William Bowman golden plover....................... *February 1985*.... 50,000
21. Bailey's Island, Maine eider with mussel .... *May 1986*.... 50,000
21. Joseph Lincoln oldsquaw .... *July 1986*.... 50,000
23. Albert Laing sleeping surf scoter........................ *October 1989*.... 48,950
24. Joseph Lincoln oldsquaw .... *July 1986*.... 49,500
24. Elmer Crowell green-winged teal hen .... *July 1986*.... 49,500

24. Elmer Crowell black-bellied plover......................... *April 1987*.... 49,500
24. Elmer Crowell preening goldeneye .... *July 1987*.... 49,500
28. Elmer Crowell sleeping Canada goose .... *October 1983*.... 48,400
29. Albert Laing sleeping bluebill..... *July 1989*.... 46,750
30. Joseph Lincoln American merganser...................... *July 1986*.... 45,000
30. Lothrop Holmes/Clinton Keith pair red-breasted mergansers...... *May 1986*.... 45,000
30. Ward brothers pair pintails ..... *August 1986*.... 45,000
30. Elmer Crowell pair wigeon .... *May 1986*.... 40,000
34. Elmer Crowell black-bellied plover .... *December 1985*.... 39,000
35. Elmer Crowell blue-winged teal .... *July 1986*.... 38,500
35. Caines brothers oversized mallard .... *February 1988*.... 38,500
35. Charles "Shang" Wheeler black duck.................... *February 1988*.... 38,500
35. Charles "Shang" Wheeler black duck........................... *July 1988*.... 38,500
35. Albert Laing "Shang" Wheeler sleeping black duck .... *April 1989*.... 38,500
35. George Boyd hissing canvas-covered Canada goose........ *November 1988*.... 38,500
41. Ward brothers black duck .... *July 1985*.... 38,000
42. Lothrop Holmes black-bellied plover......................... *July 1986*.... 37,400
43. Obediah Verity pair of bluebills *October 1989*.... 37,300
44. Frank Kellum seagull............. *May 1986*.... 36,000
45. Elmer Crowell oversized golden plover......................... *April 1986*.... 35,750
45. Elmer Crowell canvasback .... *September 1986*.... 35,750
45. Elmer Crowell bufflehead .... *September 1988*.... 35,750
48. Joseph Lincoln wigeon........ *December 1985*.... 35,000
48. Elmer Crowell yellowlegs.......... *May 1986*.... 35,000
50. Sam Soper swimming Canada goose .... *April 1987*.... 34,100
51. Nathan Cobb Canada goose..... *August 1986*.... 34,000
52. Cape Cod running curlew .... *September 1987*.... 33,550
53. Albert Laing/"Shang" Wheeler preening black duck.......... *December 1985*.... 33,000

NORTH AMERICAN WATERFOWL FLYWAYS

Most migratory birds travel within broad north-south air routes known as flyways. There are four major flyways in North America: the Atlantic, Mississippi, central, and Pacific. These flyways begin in the cooler climates of northern Canada and extend into Mexico, the Caribbean Sea, and South America, with each route determined by the availability of feeding and nesting grounds. Some bird species migrate south along one flyway and return north along another.

Duck hunting prospered along these flyways until the Migratory Bird Act of 1918, regulated by the governments of the United States and Canada, brought an end to market gunning. The cooperation of the two governments was essential since most of the breeding grounds of North American waterfowl are in Canada. This is also why much of the money raised by such groups as Ducks Unlimited is spent on cultivating new feeding and breeding grounds in both Canada and the continental United States.

The great migrations of birds along the flyways were responsible for the creation of today's collectible decoys.

ATLANTIC FLYWAY

The Atlantic flyway begins in northeastern Canada, high above the Maritime Provinces, and follows the U.S. Atlantic coastline south to Bermuda, the Caribbean, and South America. Much of the travel takes place off the coast, but the birds move overland to feed or when forced by inclement weather. The flyway touches the shores of Maine, New Hampshire, Massachusetts, Rhode Island, Connecticut, New York, New Jersey, Delaware, Maryland, Virginia, and North and South Carolina.

The Atlantic flyway is rich in natural feeding grounds. The many rivers, bays, inlets, and marshlands of the east-coast tidewater regions provide shelter for many species of ducks and geese as well as shorebirds. The Atlantic flyway is rich in Canada geese, brant, and both puddle and diving ducks and has the largest concentration of shorebirds in the United States. The flyway is also known for the large number of sea ducks—eiders, scoters, and mergansers—that travel the coastline. Sea ducks are relatively rare in other parts of the country.

MISSISSIPPI FLYWAY

Originating in north-central Canada and converging on the Mississippi River valley from both sides of the Great Lakes, the Mississippi flyway is the largest and most heavily used of the North American flyways. The lush vegetation along the many waterways that feed the great Mississippi provides feeding grounds for the birds. The flyway travels south along the river valley, leaves the North American continent at the Louisiana delta, and continues into the Caribbean and South America. Many species that travel south along the Atlantic flyway use the Mississippi flyway for the return flight north.

This flyway influenced hunting in Michigan, Illinois, Indiana, Ohio, Wisconsin, Minnesota, Iowa, Missouri, Tennessee, Kentucky, Arkansas, Alabama, Mississippi, and Louisiana. The majority of the species that traveled the flyway were puddle ducks—mallards, black duck, pintail, and teal—although divers, such as canvasback, redhead, and bluebill, were hunted along its route, particularly in the more northern areas along the cold, choppy waters of the Great Lakes. Although the numbers of all waterfowl species have dwindled during the 20th century, migration patterns and numbers can be determined by the decoys left behind.

CENTRAL FLYWAY

The central flyway begins in Canada's Manitoba and Saskatchewan and follows prairie potholes and lush cornfields through Minnesota, the Dakotas, Nebraska, Kansas, Oklahoma, and Texas and then moves across the Gulf of Mexico into the interior of Mexico. The northern part of this route—Canada, Minnesota, and the Dakotas—is rich in Canada and snow geese, but the majority of the species that follow it are puddle ducks—mallards, pintail, teal, gadwall, and wigeon.

PACIFIC FLYWAY

The Pacific flyway begins in the far northwestern reaches of Canada and Alaska, travels through Canada's British Columbia, follows the Pacific coastline of Washington, Oregon, and California, and then continues into Mexico and Central and South America. The more northerly areas of the flyway are rich in geese, particularly Pacific black brant. Perhaps the richest feeding grounds in the United States during the 19th and early 20th centuries were the lush natural marshlands of Central California, particularly the Sacramento and San Joaquin river valleys. The concentration of such puddle ducks as pintail was so great that decoy production in this area was extremely limited until well into the 20th century: quite simply, hunters had no need for them.

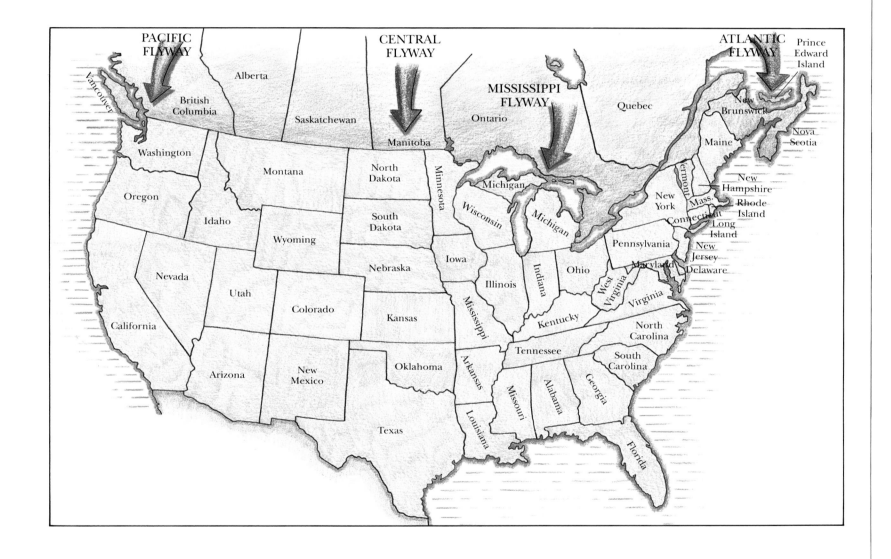

BIBLIOGRAPHY

Barber, Joel. *Wild Fowl Decoys.* New York: Windward House, 1934. Reprinted by Dover Publications, 1954

Berkey, Barry and Velma. *Chincoteague Carvers and Their Decoys.* Herff Jones University Press, 1983

Brisco, R. Paul. *Waterfowl Decoys of Southwestern Ontario.* Erin, Ontario: Boston Mills Press, 1986

Cheever, Byron. *L. T. Ward & Bro.* Heber City, Utah: Hillcrest Publications

————. *Mason Decoys.* Spanish Fork, Utah: Hillcrest Publications, 1974

————. *North American Decoys Magazine.* Spanish Fork, Utah: Hillcrest Publications, 1967–79

Chitwood, Henry C. *Connecticut Decoys.* West Chester, Pa.: Schiffer Publishing, 1987

Clark, Malcolm. "The Perry Wilcoxen Story, 1862–1954," in *North American Decoys,* Autumn 1971

Colio, Quintina. *American Decoys.* Science Press, 1972

Connett, Eugene V., ed. *Duck Shooting Along the Atlantic Tidewater.* Bonanza Books, 1947

Conoley, William Neal, Jr. *Waterfowl Heritage: North Carolina Decoys and Gunning Lore.* Wendell, N. C.: Webbfoot, 1982

Crandell, Bernard W. *Decoying: St. Clair to the St. Lawrence.* Erin, Ontario: Boston Mills Press, 1988

Delph, John and Shirley. *Factory Decoys of Mason, Stevens, Dodge and Peterson.* Exton, Pa.: Schiffer Publishing, 1980

————. *New England Decoys.* Exton, Pa.: Schiffer Publishing, 1981

Doughty, Robin W. *Feather Fashions and Bird Preservation.* Los Angeles: University of California Press, 1975

Earnest, Adele. *The Art of the Decoy: American Bird Carvings.* New York: Bramhall House, 1965

Engers, Joseph, and Williams, Jeff. *Decoy Magazine,* 1979–90. Ocean City, Md.: *Decoy Magazine*

Fleckenstein, Henry A., Jr. *American Factory Decoys.* Exton, Pa.: Schiffer Publishing, 1981

————. *Decoys of the Mid-Atlantic Region.* Exton, Pa.: Schiffer Publishing, 1980

————. *New Jersey Decoys.* Exton, Pa.: Schiffer Publishing, 1980

————. *Shorebird Decoys.* Exton, Pa.: Schiffer Publishing, 1980

————. *Southern Decoys of Virginia and the Carolinas.* Exton, Pa.: Schiffer Publishing, 1983

Fleming, Patricia, ed. *Traditions in Wood: A History of Wildfowl Decoys in Canada.* Camden East, Ontario: Camden House Publishing, 1987

Frank, Charles W., Jr. *Louisiana Duck Decoys.* New Orleans, 1975

————. *Wetland Heritage: The Louisiana Duck Decoy.* Gretna, La.: Pelican Publishing, 1985

French, Joseph B. "Mr. X., Mr. Y. & Mr. Z.," in *Decoy Collector's Guide,* 1969

Fuhrmann, Horst. *Europaische Lockenten* (European Decoys). Stuttgart, Germany, 1987

Gard, Ronald J., and McGrath, Brian J. *The Ward Brothers Decoys.* Plano, Tex.: Thomas B. Reel, 1989

Gates, Bernie. *Ontario Decoys, Some Carvers and Regional Styles.* Ontario: The Upper Canadian, 1982

————. *Ontario Decoys II.* Ontario: The Upper Canadian, 1986

Gosner, Kenneth L. *Working Decoys of the Jersey Coast and Delaware Valley.* Philadelphia: The Art Alliance Press, 1985

Guyette, Dale and Gary. *Decoys of Maritime Canada.* Exton, Pa.: Schiffer Publishing, 1983

Haid, Alan G. *Decoys of the Mississippi Flyway.* Exton, Pa.: Schiffer Publishing, 1981

Harrel, Loy S. *Decoys of Lake Champlain.* West Chester, Pa.: Schiffer Publishing, 1986

Huster, H. Harrison, and Knight, Doug. *Floating Sculpture: Decoys of the Delaware River.* Spanish Fork, Utah: Hillcrest Publications, 1982

Johnsgard, Paul A., ed. *The Bird Decoy.* Lincoln, Nebr.: University of Nebraska Press, 1976

Kangas, Gene and Linda. *Decoys: A North American Survey.* Spanish Fork, Utah: Hillcrest Publications, 1983

Koch, Ronald M. *Decoys of the Winnebago Lakes.* Amherst, Wis.: Palmer Publications, 1988

Lewis, Elisha J. *The American Sportsman.* Philadelphia: Lippencott, Grambo and Co., 1855

Mackey, William J., Jr. *American Bird Decoys.* New York: E. P. Dutton, 1965

Matthieson. *Wildlife in America.* New York: Viking Penguin, 1959, 1987

Merkt, Dixon MacD. *Shang: A Biography of Charles E. Wheeler.* Spanish Fork, Utah: Hillcrest Publications, 1984

Murphy, Stanley. *Martha's Vineyard Decoys.* Boston: David R. Godine Press, 1978

Parker, Jackson. "New England's Gold," in *Wildfowl Carving and Collecting,* Winter, 1986

Parmalee, Paul W., and Loomis, Forrest D. *Decoys and Decoy Carvers of Illinois.* DeKalb, Ill.: Northern Illinois University Press, 1969

Rice, C. G. *History of the Massachusetts Waterfowl Stamps and Prints.* Salem: Peabody Museum, 1981

Richardson, R. H., ed. *Chesapeake Bay Decoys.* Cambridge, Md.: Crow Haven Publishers, 1973

Sorenson, Harold D. *Decoy Collector's Guide, 1963–77.* Burlington, Iowa: Harold D. Sorenson

Starr, George Ross, Jr. *Decoys of the Atlantic Flyway.* New York: Winchester Press, 1974

Townsend, E. Jane. *Gunners' Paradise.* New York: The Museums at Stony Brook, 1979

Waingrow, Jeff. *American Wildfowl Decoys.* New York: E. P. Dutton, 1985

Walsh, Clune Jr., and Jackson, Lowell G., eds. *Waterfowl Decoys of Michigan and the Lake St. Clair Region.* Detroit: Gale Graphics, 1983

Walsh, Harry M. *The Outlaw Gunner.* Centreville, Md.: Tidewater Publishers, 1971

Webster, David S., and Kehoe, William. *Decoys at Shelburne Museum.* Shelburne, Vt.: Shelburne Museum, 1961. Revised edition 1971

PHOTO CREDITS

INDEX

Numbers in *italics* refer to pages with illustrations